GW01339074

August '82
To Brian - Vera
to meeting again
and happy days
John - Eileen

THE STORY OF VOLVO CARS

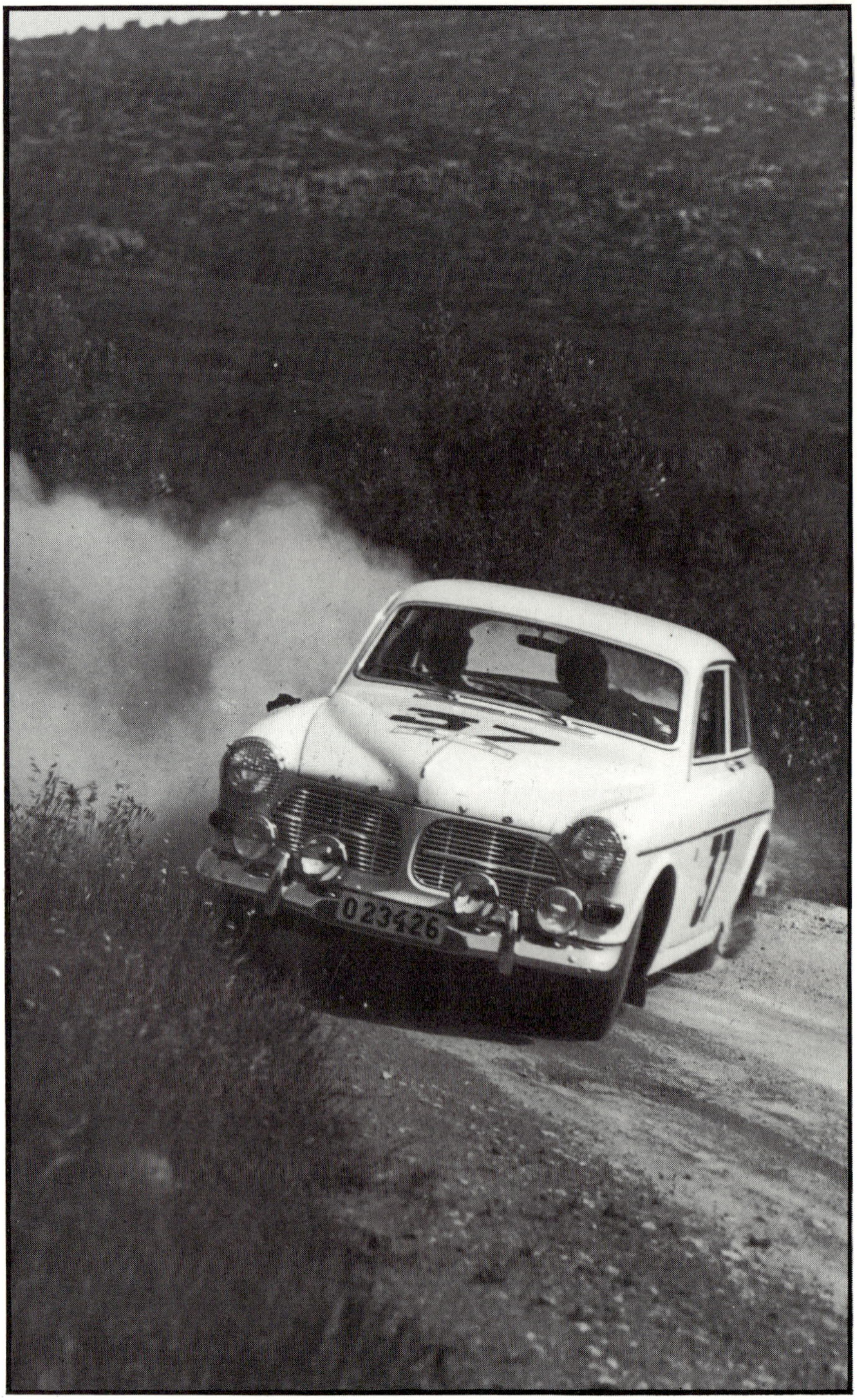
37
O23426

THE STORY OF VOLVO CARS

GRAHAM ROBSON

FOREWORD BY HAKAN FRISINGER
PRESIDENT, VOLVO CAR CORPORATION

PSL Patrick Stephens, Cambridge

© Graham Robson 1983

All rights reserved. No part of this publication may be reproduced, stored in a retrieval system or transmitted, in any form or by any means, electronic, mechanical, photocopying, recording or otherwise, without prior permission in writing from Patrick Stephens Limited.

First published in 1983

British Library Cataloguing in Publication Data

Robson, Graham
   The story of Volvo cars.
   1. Volvo automobile
   I. Title
   629.2'222   TL215.V/

ISBN 0-85059-591-X

Frontispiece *The way to drive an Amazon really fast on a rally was to get it sideways—and to have Tom Trana driving it. Here he tackles a dusty special stage in the 1965 Acropolis Rally. Carl-Magnus Skogh won the event in a similar team car.*

Photoset in 10 on 11 pt Plantin
by Manuset Limited, Baldock, Herts.
Printed in Great Britain on 115 gsm Fineblade coated cartridge by St Edmundsbury Press, Bury St Edmunds, Suffolk, and bound by Leighton Straker Limited, London NW10, for the publishers, Patrick Stephens Limited, Bar Hill, Cambridge, CB3 8EL, England.

Contents

	Foreword by Hakan Frisinger President, Volvo Car Corporation	7
	Introduction	8
Chapter 1	**'Jakob' and the SKF connection** The birth of Volvo	10
Chapter 2	**Six cylinders in the 1930s** The second generation	23
Chapter 3	**PV444—a 'world' car from Sweden**	35
Chapter 4	**The mighty Amazon**	53
Chapter 5	**Sports cars and coupés** P1900 and P1800	70
Chapter 6	**Safety fast!** The factory in competitions	93
Chapter 7	**140s, 240s and safety** Leading the world into the 1970s	106
Chapter 8	**Expansion overseas** New factories, DAF and Renault	141
Chapter 9	**Volvo for the 1980s** New styles, new engines, new partners	158
Appendix A	**Volvo cars since 1927** A technical summary	178
Appendix B	**Important company milestones** Who, what, when and where?	183
Appendix C	**The rise, and rise, of Volvo car production** 1927 to 1981	185
Appendix D	**Prototypes and specials—*not* for sale**	187
Appendix E	**Trucks, buses, tractors, aero and marine engines** The other faces of Volvo	207
	Index	214

6

Foreword by Hakan Frisinger
(President, Volvo Car Corporation)

To write the history of a company is to describe the soul and spirit of a company. The soul of Volvo Car Corporation has the spirit of a small ambitious specialist car maker with one goal, which is to retain a place in the customers' hearts based on personality, quality, driving pleasure and safety. I am happy to see the company's soul so well described by a specialist in motor history.

Graham Robson has reminded us of the obligations we have towards our customers in the light of a successful past and indicates our expectations and obligations for the future.

More new models will follow which are demanded from a company, which in spite of the difficult economic climate affecting all car manufacturers, has shown a dynamic will of life. Volvo Car Corporation is determined to continue with enthusiasm to strengthen the virtues the Volvo customers have appreciated. We are aware of the customer's expectations of us and are thus stimulated to improve further our work in styling, engineering, development, comfort, quality and safety. This determination is illustrated by the new model Volvo 760 GLE.

I have personally taken great pleasure in reading the presentation Graham Robson (with sound professional experience from automotive industry and journalism) gives to Volvo and its history—an exciting and thrilling story for all Volvo friends.

Left *Hakan Frisinger, President, Volvo Car Corporation.*

Introduction

The complete story of Volvo cars has never been told before, and I am still not sure that I know the reason why. I simply do not understand how such an important marque can have been ignored by other historians for so long. I am therefore very happy to offer this book, which should fill in one of the remaining gaps in the history of modern motoring—to put the history of the Volvo car on display for the very first time.

Before starting this project—a major one, by any standards—I expected to find all manner of difficulties, problems which might explain why other authors have looked at Volvo, dabbled with the idea of writing a book, and shied away in dismay. But once I got involved, I found that there were none. It was really quite amazing—for the factory archive is comprehensive, well-kept and regularly updated, while there is substantial material available which Volvo's publicity departments have prepared for previous anniversaries.

So, why has the Volvo car history not been tackled before? After all, there is a fascinating story to be told. Volvo is a company which has now been in existence for more than 50 years, continues to expand, and is still proudly and securely independent. The cars themselves have been world leaders in matters of safety and longevity for many years. The Volvo group, which is by no means solely concerned with private cars, is the largest industrial concern in Scandinavia, by a very large margin.

One reason, I am sure, is that Volvo people are not, and have not been, addicted to orgies of heritage worship. At any time, Volvo have been far too busy looking forward—to the next new model, to the next piece of expansion, to the next technical, industrial or economic challenge—to spend much time consulting their past. Volvo people, for sure, never need to excuse present failings by reminding the world how great they were in bygone days.

There is another reason. It has never been easy for motoring enthusiasts—car buffs, if you like—to get excited about Volvo cars. Very few of the five million Volvo cars so far built have set out to be flashy, very few have been searingly fast and none could be classed as 'follies' or corporate indulgences. It means that the people who get fired up by the performance of a Ferrari, the styling of a Jaguar, or the sight and sound of a Lamborghini, find it difficult to get excited about a Volvo.

All of which made this a wonderful challenge to me, as a professional motoring historian. It wasn't just that I had been irritated on numerous occasions by the lack of a source for Volvo reference material. It wasn't just that I have always been a fan of cars like the P1800 coupés. It wasn't just that I was impressed by the rallying

Introduction 9

performance of the rugged Volvos of the 1950s and 1960s. Above all, it was because the Volvo seems to have acquired so many devotees, in so many countries. There was, and is, a mystique that had to be identified, a character that had to be exposed.

Two instances, personal experiences if you like, made the writing of this book almost inevitable. One of my dearest friends bought his first Volvo estate car at the end of the 1960s and, at the time of writing, is on his third, in the updated style; every time I quizzed him as to his choice of car, he merely looked at me as if I was a half-wit, and defied me to suggest something more suitable. The other case was of a fellow journalist telling me why he was proposing to move away from one particular part of southern England: 'I can't stand it any longer,' he said, 'it's all too suburbia, all green Wellies and Volvo estate cars!'

Clearly, there is a lot more to Volvo ownership than meets the eye. Those 'Volvo Virtues' which were quoted at me by a company executive must mean something to a lot of people. It was a story which had to be told, and I am delighted to be able to tell it.

GRAHAM ROBSON
January 1983

Acknowledgements

Many people helped me to assemble the material for this book, and I would like to thank them all for making my job easier. Kevin Gover of Volvo Concessionaires, in Great Britain, made the whole thing possible in the first place, and DFDS (UK) Ltd (the shipping line linking the UK with Sweden) helped me a lot to get to and from Gothenburg in the summer of 1982.

I would like to thank the Volvo Car Corporation for all the illustrations used in this book, particularly the prototype photographs, some of which have been released from Volvo files for the first time.

Many people in the Volvo Car Corporation made themselves available for lengthy interviews. I start with Hakan Frisinger (because he is, after all, the President of the Corporation!), and also mention Gunnar Andersson, Bengt Berntsson, Lennart Franson, Bror Grandinsson, Uno Gunnelid, Erland Gustafsson, Rune Gustafsson, Carl Eric Haggstrom, Johan Hallenborg, Olof Peterson, Stig Weiertz, Dan Werbin, and Jan Wilsgaard.

None of this would have been possible without the efforts of Svante Mannervik and Mats Kling of the Public Relations division, and their colleagues, Lars Andersson, Goran Ekstedt, Britt Fennvik, Lotta Hultberg, Bengt Kjellberg, Karl Kohler, Per Lojdquist, Christer Olsson and Inge Westerlund.

In addition, there were many occasions when friends and colleagues in the motoring business provided advice and assistance, so to Ray Hutton (*Autocar*'s distinguished Editor), Lionel Burrell (of *Thoroughbred & Classic Cars*), Bryan Kennedy (of *Connoisseur Carbooks*), and Richard Langworth (in the United States) I also acknowledge that they made the task easier.

Chapter 1

'Jakob' and the SKF connection
The birth of Volvo

Although the world's first motor car took to the roads in 1885, and there was a motor industry of sorts in the 1890s, it took a long time for the habit to spread to Scandinavia. Sweden in particular was a large country with a small population, terrible roads and an unfriendly climate. Even by the mid-1920s there were only 100,000 cars in the country, and new-car sales were only a few thousand cars a year. It was no wonder that the Swedish motor industry, as such, was almost invisible.

Two companies—Scania-Vabis of Sodertalje, the Thulin of Landskrona—built cars in the 1910s and early 1920s, but neither sold in significant numbers, and the Swedish market was completely dominated by cars imported from North America. It was in this situation that two forward-thinking individuals and one big engineering concern came to change the face of the business. The two people were Assar Gabrielsson and Gustaf Larson, the company was Svenska Kullagerfabriken, better known as SKF. Their first links with cars—other company's cars—came before the First World War, and their first thoughts of a new car to be built in Sweden began to crystallise in the early 1920s, but it was not until 1927 that the public heard anything about this. The new car, when it came, was called a Volvo, and a great Swedish tradition had just been founded.

Before delving into the conception and birth of the Volvo car, therefore, I ought to set down a little more about SKF, and the two resourceful people who did so much to turn their crazy idea into a real machine which people would buy. Svenska Kullagerfabriken—and I really think I must now shorten this to SKF for all further references—was a company founded by Sven Wingquist in 1907, with offices and factory premises in Gothenburg, in order to make a particularly advanced type of self-aligning ball bearing. By the time the World War (later, unhappily, to be renamed the *First* World War) broke out in Europe, SKF had expanded considerably, and had set up factories in other countries as well. By the early 1920s it was one of the largest industrial concerns in Sweden, its products known and respected throughout the world.

Assar Gabrielsson, born in Korsberga in 1891, moved to Stockholm with his family in 1900, and eventually graduated as a specialist in economics. For four years he worked as an administrator in the Chancellery of the Lower House of the Swedish Parliament, but in 1916 he joined SKF on the commercial side of the business. By 1920 he had become managing director of the French branch of SKF and, three years later, he returned to SKF as sales manager of the entire group. It was in France, more than anywhere else, that he came so closely into contact with

The joint founders of Volvo in the 1920s—Assar Gabrielsson and Gustaf Larson.

the bustling new world of motor cars, and once back in Sweden he not only knew that SKF bearings were better than anything on offer from the opposition, but that they could be supplied at extremely competitive prices to many countries.

Gustaf Larson, on the other hand, was born in Vintrosa, near Orebro, in 1887, and always showed an interest in technical things and in machines. After leaving a technical school in Orebro, where he decided that a life in engineering, particularly motor car engineering, was for him, the 24-year old Larson sailed off to England, to work for the engine manufacturers of White & Poppe, in Coventry.

Right away, therefore, an early connection with Coventry, the spiritual centre of Britain's burgeoning motor industry, was established. We know of no detailed reason why Larson went to work for White & Poppe, but there is a direct Scandinavian link. The 'Poppe' half of the company's title, was Peter Poppe, a gifted engineer who had once worked for Steyr in Austria, whose nationality was Norwegian. Although Larson had little responsibility at this stage of his career, quite clearly he took to this sort of work like a duck takes to water. Before he came back home to Sweden, in 1913, not only did he become peripherally involved with the W & P contract to supply engines to a new car company in Oxford, to be called Morris Motors, but he also met the company's future chief designer, Hans Landstadt, who at the time was chief draughtsman of White & Poppe.

Gustaf Larson studied the internal combustion engine when he returned, at the Royal Institute of Technology in Stockholm, joined SKF in 1917, then in 1920 became technical manager for AB Galco in Stockholm.

Gabrielsson and Larson, therefore, had met and got to know each other in the years when both were working for SKF in Gothenburg, but there was something of

By 1926, the early prototypes had been built (with non-standard wheels).

a gap before they got together again in 1924. It was in this year, so the story goes, that they began to talk about building cars in Sweden and it is here, also, that the legends and the handed-down stories begin to proliferate.

It was in the summer of 1924 that the two bumped into each other, just as Larson was rushing off for a holiday, and it was not until August that they could get together for a sensible discussion. At the first meeting, all that Gabrielsson had time to suggest was that as Larson now 'knew all about cars', they should meet to discuss future prospects. Gabrielsson, it seems, with his wider knowledge of the world of motoring, the cars it was making, and of the Swedish market, was the one who thought he should have a slice of the rapidly expanding cake—and Larson was the man he thought he needed to design a car for him.

At the time, in 1924, the market for new cars in Sweden was running at about 15,000 cars a year (only about ten per cent of the number of cars being sold in Great Britain at the time, by the way, and less than one per cent of the number of Model T Fords being made in that year *alone*), and about 95 per cent of this demand was being satisfied by American machines. Yet, for all that, the American cars were by no means ideal for Swedish conditions—for one thing their rather soft suspensions were not suited to the unmade, sometimes rough, Swedish highways, and for another they were certainly not very durable. In spite of the fact that Thulin, Scania-Vabis and Tidaholm had all half-heartedly tried to build cars for their own domestic market, without success, Gabrielsson thought he could do the job successfully.

According to the legend, Gabrielsson and Larson met up again at a crayfish party in a Swedish restaurant, and that on this occasion they had plenty of time to chat. The crayfish in Sweden are at their best in August, and food-loving Swedes make time to feast on these delicacies. Even if it was not at this festive occasion that the new car was born, it still led to a tradition in later years, that senior Volvo men would get together at a crayfish supper once a year.

The very first Volvo OV4 production car taking shape in the Lundby factory in 1927.

No matter. The two settled down to discuss the future of the car market in Sweden as they saw it, surveyed the cars which were on offer at the time, and decided that something could be done about this. They had to decide if a new type of car could be sold, if it could be designed and put on sale at the right place, and they had to discuss, at least, if not decide, where it could be built, and how the finance to set up a production factory could be raised.

Dreams, however, are cheap, and at first the two were only interested in the 'why' and the 'what', rather than the 'where' and the 'how'. They readily agreed that if a car was to be put on sale, it should be properly tooled up for series production, rather than for built-to-order manufacture like the latter day Scanias and Thulins. It also had to be sold at an attractive price (there were not yet all that many people in Sweden who could afford to spend a small fortune on their motoring), and above all it would have to be simple to maintain, and very rugged, so that it could withstand harsh Swedish winters, and the battering of the primitive road network.

It would be a huge decision today, and it must have been a serious decision even then, but the two visionaries decided that this was a project they could tackle. At first, however, it was a very informal business. Gabrielsson and Larson agreed that Larson, the engineer, should start designing a new car, while Gabrielsson should start looking round for financial backing and for some way of building the cars when they were ready for production. Even at this early stage, incidentally, they took the important decision to buy as much as possible of their new car from specialist suppliers—a policy which still exists, in modified form, in Volvo today. Getting the car ready for production, finding a factory in which to do it, and paying assembly workers, would be quite difficult enough for the time being—there was no way, for instance, that they wanted to get involved in tooling up for engines, transmissions, or body shells.

As with so many other famous products, work on this car started on a part-time basis. Gabrielsson and Larson kept their regular jobs at SKF and Galco respectively, but for two evenings every week, using a kitchen table as a drawing board, Larson's home in Stockholm became a design studio. It was a slow and ponderous way of getting the project under way, but with the help of a bright young engineer called Henry Westerberg, recruited by Larson on the 'friend of a friend' basis, the design of the new car began to take shape. At this point, I ought to emphasise, it still had no name, and there was still no guarantee that even the first car would ever be made, let alone a series of cars be sold to the public.

Larson the engineer, however, seems to have had faith in Gabrielsson the businessman, and never seems to have doubted the outcome. By June 1925, therefore, all the chassis, engine and transmission drawings for the new car were complete, though no thought had been given to a body at that stage. Larson had hedged his bets at first, by making sure that the original design could also be used as the basis of a light truck.

There was now an inevitable delay, of several months, as Gabrielsson tried to raise financial backing for the project. He had not approached bankers and businessmen before this time, for he had nothing at all to show them. Even now, he only had an impressive set of blueprints to back his eloquence, but he also had his marketing and manufacturing philosophy worked out in advance.

It was greatly to Gabrielsson's credit that he planned his strategy in this way. Far too many other motor car projects, before or since, have been launched hastily on a wave of optimism, and the car itself rushed into production without proper backing. Gabrielsson, who was a businessman and a realist in all his dealings, and not at all a starry-eyed visionary, moved ahead with the caution which was to become a Volvo hallmark in future years.

The problem, however, was that financial backing was impossible to find; not

The original Volvo engine was 1,944 cc, had four cylinders and side valves, and there was a transmission brake behind the gearbox. All engines of the 1920s and 1930s evolved from this layout.

even SKF, who respected Gabrielsson's abilities, would commit themselves at first. The bankers, to be fair, had no previous experience on which to base their judgements. They could only take the view that, as there was no quantity-production of cars in Sweden at this time, this might mean that there was no demand, or no potential, for any in the future.

Gabrielsson and Larson, therefore, found themselves in a very difficult situation, one familiar to many aspiring business tycoons. Without money, it seemed, they could not build any cars, but without making at least a few prototypes, they could not really convince anyone to put up money for future quantity production. Larson had no money of his own to spare and Gabrielsson had very little.

Assar Gabrielsson then took one of the few really hair-raising gambles of his long and ultimately distinguished business career. But now quite convinced that *this* car could succeed, he told Larson and his small band of helpers to go ahead and build a series of ten experimental cars, and that he, personally, would put up the money to make this possible. Nine of the cars were to have open tourer bodies, and a single one was to have a four-door saloon style.

Accordingly, he then set out to find specialist manufacturers to build the major components, and used all his business experience, and the Swedish 'Old Boy' network, to locate the best suppliers. The most important item of all was the engine, which was a simple three-bearing four-cylinder unit with side valves—very American in its simplicity and its rugged layout—and in October 1925 the contract for ten units was placed with Pentaverken of Skovde.

The most famous Swedish coachbuilding concern of the day was Freyschuss of Stockholm, so Larson naturally turned to them for his bodies. Erik Carlberg and Karl Sagvall were both engaged in the design, but Larson also took the bold step of consulting Helmer Mas-Olle, a Swedish landscape and portrait painter, on matters of detail styling.

Settling the design for the bodies, getting the components together, and assembling the prototypes, with very limited hours of working, and few people to do the job, took a long time, and it was not until June 1926 that the very first running prototype, one of the open tourers, was ready for trial in Stockholm.

The name of 'Jakob' now joins in to our story, and it is here that I hope I can shed a new light on a very murky subject. Without exception, every other journalist, author, or even Volvo archivist has skated rapidly over the reason for such a name being chosen, and most of them apply the name, quite wrongly, to all the prototypes, or even to the first production car of 1927.

The truth, as suggested to me by Olof Peterson, sales manager of Volvo for so many years, is more interesting, and even more particular. Karl Ludvigsen, writing in *Car Classics* of August 1977, says that: 'One of the last of the ten chassis was given a somewhat different open body. Instead of wrapping closely around the front wheels, its fenders [wings] arced much higher, in a more sporty French line, back to shorter running boards . . . Thus singled out as an individual among the first ten test cars, this one was given the nickname of Jakob.'

Even Karl, however, does not suggest where the name came from. Olof Peterson, however, makes the simple point that this car, being built towards the end of the sequence of ten cars, was completed and took to the road for the first time on July 25 1926—and July 25 is a day named in all Swedish diaries as 'Jakob' day!

(Other Swedish companies think the same way. When work began on the brand new Saab 99 in the early 1960s, the car was given the project name of 'Gudmund',

Above *There was nothing advanced about the body skeleton of the first OV4 Tourers as this photograph shows.*

Below *The famous desk, across which Messrs Gabrielsson and Larson faced each other for so many years at Lundby.*

The straightforward 'vintage' styling of the 1927 OV4.

for approval for work to begin was given on that particular Swedish 'name' day, which is April 2.)

The cost of building the ten prototypes had been a massive 150,000 SKr, all provided by Assar Gabrielsson himself, so it was with some care, and a number of pioneering adventures, that all ten were eventually ferried over atrocious roads from Stockholm to Gothenburg, by October 1926. One convoy, comprising three cars, all open tourers, was particularly important to the enterprise. Not only were Gabrielsson and his wife in the first car, Larson in the second, with Henry Westerberg and Erik Carlberg in the third, but all the drawings, costings and other design documents were packed in alongside the occupants. It was a 500 km (300 mile) journey which took the best part of three days—a journey made no easier by the fact that daylight hours are very restricted in Sweden in October, and that only the lead car, driven by Mr Gabrielsson himself, was equipped with headlamps. It was, however, a journey made in high spirits, for financial backing for the project had now been assured.

Having seen the first car completed in June 1926, and driven safely down to Gothenburg, where Assar Gabrielsson still had his home, he lost no time in demonstrating it to the SKF board of directors. This time, with an actual car to look at, rather than just a sheaf of pretty drawings on which to make their judgement, the SKF executives decided to back their employee's scheme.

It was the sort of deal which Gabrielsson had always dreamed about, but one which he could never have expected entirely to pull off. Not only were SKF prepared to put up launch capital, but they would also provide the framework of a company for the new venture, and they would help locate manufacturing premises as well.

On August 10 1926, the SKF board agreed to invest 200,000 SKr in Gabrielsson's scheme, and they also decided to reactivate a company called AB Volvo to manufacture the cars. AB Volvo was a dormant patent company registered by SKF in

1915, but never used. Volvo, of course, means 'I roll' in Latin, which was a very appropriate way of summarising the properties of ball bearings, for which SKF was world famous.

Space for AB Volvo was found in an empty factory building once used by Nordiska Kullagerfabriken AB, a ball-bearing competitor to SKF. Although it was conveniently close to the centre of Gothenburg, in the suburb of Lundby, on the north side of the river, and had a large area of undeveloped land all around it which the new company hastened to secure, it was by no means ideal for motor car manufacture. It looks for all the world like a Victorian mill building, with five storeys, and was long, tall and narrow.

The deal was that Gabrielsson and Larson would leave their existing jobs, take over at AB Volvo, and start preparation for manufacture as soon as possible. In the beginning, it was agreed that a series of 1,000 chassis should be laid down, 500 to be fitted with open tourer bodies, 500 with closed shells. It was understood that months must elapse before the flow of components could be assured, and a workforce built up, but SKF wanted to see the first cars ready for sale in the spring of 1927. Assar Gabrielsson, whose own money had assured the building of the first cars, was installed as AB Volvo's first managing director, with Gustaf Larson as his deputy. In truth, however, the two always acted as equal partners and throughout their long working partnership they not only shared the same office, but indeed worked opposite each other, at a large desk.

In October 1926, Volvo's founders moved into the gloomy shell of a building, where they eventually settled in a very large open office on the top floor. For years, it seems, one or other of the partners answered every telephone call which was made to the factory (for a rudimentary exchange was set up in their office), and the business of transferring a caller from one to the other was simply made by tossing the telephone receiver from one side of the table to the other.

Olof Peterson also recalls how they used to operate an 'open door' policy in later years: 'If we needed to go speak to them, we would simply go up to the open door, knock and wait, until we were signalled in. But the door was never closed, never. One day, however, I actually did find it closed, and worried that some awful thing was going on in secret. But it wasn't as serious as that—there had been a draught which caused the door to slam!'

A drawing of the factory cross-section (not, I am afraid, of a quality which can be reproduced here) shows how inconvenient the five-storey layout actually was. Canteens and offices were on the top floor; design and the manufacture of minor trim parts on the floor below that. Body manufacture took place on the second floor (which, confusingly, my American friends would call the third floor), while painting and some body trimming took place one floor below that. The ground floor, of course, was reserved for final assembly, and primitive hoists were used to lower the completed body shells, or other components, from the floors above.

Even so, the winter of 1926/27 was the time when dreams were feverishly turned into reality. Much work still had to be done to develop and finalise the design of the chassis, and arrangements also had to be made for AB Volvo to make their own body shells. Personally, I have never understood why a decision was made to build all the open tourer bodies first, especially as most of the imported cars with which Volvo would have to compete were closed saloons, and especially because the Swedish climate was hardly one in which open cars could be enjoyed for more than a few months in the year.

'Jakob' and the SKF connection

Above *The original Volvo factory at Lundby is an ex-SKF building. Final assembly took place on the ground floor. This complex is still used by Volvo (truck division) for offices.*

Below *The first derivative of OV4 was the PV4 (Personvagn) which featured a closed fabric-skinned four-door saloon car style.*

Work on the engine concentrated on making it more reliable, and more refined. The finalised design, built for Volvo by Pentaverken, had a swept volume of 1,944 cc, and produced 28 bhp at 2,000 rpm. There was a long way to go to the smooth, powerful and sophisticated Volvos of the 1960s and 1970s, but by the standards of the day the Volvo was perfectly competitive.

In many ways the production cars had been influenced by North American thinking. The three-speed gearbox, with its central gear change, could have come straight from a Chevrolet of the day, as could the steel disc wheels of the prototypes (though these were changed for conventional European-type wooden-spoke 'artillery' wheels for the start-up of production). Mas-Olle's influence on the styling of the cars could only have been in detail and was mainly confined to trim and interior furnishings, for the basic style of the car was typical of so many other European cars of the day, and featured simple steel skin panelling on a seasoned wood-frame body skeleton.

What made the Volvo distinctive, however, was not just the fact that it was to be the first genuine Swedish series production car, but that it carried a unique and quite distinctive 'trade mark' on its vertical radiator. The diagonal brightwork slash across the honeycomb was a styling point carried forward into the 1970s and 1980s on modern Volvos, but in that slash, on the original car, was the circle and diagonal facing arrow which is, in fact, a Swedish sign indicating iron (and also the biological 'male' sign)—and there was a lot of that in the new Volvo.

The tourer and saloon versions both rode on the same 116.1 in wheelbase chassis, which featured half-elliptic springs at front and rear, and only had rear wheel brakes at a time when European manufacturers were fast turning to four wheel brakes for all their new models. The tourer was to be named an OV4 (Openvagn, four cylinders), while the saloon was to be a PV4 (Personvagn, four cylinders), with prices of 4,800 and 5,800 SKr respectively. At the time, incidentally, this put the price of the original tourer at about £270, or $1,300, though such comparisons are really academic as exports of Volvos were not to begin for some time.

Rudimentary assembly lines (but no question of moving conveyor belts) were in place by March 1927 and the frenzied assembly of the first production car, an open tourer, began in April. In the early hours of April 14 1927, the job was done. Hilmer Johansson, one of the Volvo pioneers, jumped into the car, engaged first gear, let in the clutch—and set off smartly backwards!

Pandemonium. What had gone wrong? A few seconds of agonised groping about with the gear lever established that *this* particular Volvo had only one forward gear (very slow) and three reverse gears. The problem was obvious—that the rear axle had been incorrectly assembled, with the crown wheel on the wrong side of the pinion. It took very little time to put matters to right, and later that day, in broad daylight, the first car was driven out of the factory building into the yard, a move recorded by the factory photographer. The Volvo saga was under way.

(It is not only Volvo who have made this sort of error. I hear that when the first four-wheel-drive Humber military vehicle was built in Coventry during the Second World War, it could not be persuaded to move off the mark at first, the reason being that one axle was driving forwards, while the other was resolutely driving backwards . . . ..)

Unfortunately, the new Volvo was not an overnight success. In spite of the fact that it was Swedish, and that it was backed by the mighty SKF organisation, there was no immediate and patriotic rush to buy. This was rather worrying for Assar

Who said hatchbacks were new? This Volvo Special of 1928 shows off the feature. Were all those boxes really meant to be stowed inboard?

Gabrielsson, the businessman who knew all about profit and loss accounts and, above all, about cash flow. He had not expected the initial sanction to sell out without an effort, but the slow response must have been worrying. History would show that Volvo trucks sold better than Volvo cars until the end of the 1940s, but in 1927 there was no truck ready to sell, to fill up the factory with work—the first would not be delivered until 1928.

In the remaining eight months of 1927, only 297 cars were built, many of them being the open tourers, which equates to an average production rate of a mere eight cars a week. It rapidly became clear that the decision to sell an open car in Sweden had been a mistake, for it was the wrong type of car for the climatic conditions. Accordingly, though the OV4 would be listed until 1929, it was rapidly superseded by the PV4 saloon. In the end, only 205 OV4s were delivered, some completed chassis being supplied for special coachwork to be added, and some for pick-up bodies to be added, but the balance of the 500-strong open bodies were scrapped; thereafter, all efforts went into building PV4 saloons.

Unlike the OV4, the PV4 saloons were not panelled in pressed steel (whose contoured panels could not readily be found in Sweden at the time), but was built after the fashionable Weymann style, which is to say that the conventional wooden body skeleton and doors were covered in padded leatherette or (200 SKr extra) in leather. It ran on exactly the same rolling chassis as that of the original OV4, which had always had a very generous wheelbase length. The performance was not, nor was ever meant to be, at all startling, but at least motoring could be done in comfort, well away from the biting winds of the Scandinavian climate. Heaters, of course, were not fitted to cars in the 1920s, but the other fittings were to a very high standard. The seats, for instance, had leather coverings, and were stuffed with horsehair, while the straps supporting the backrests of the separate front seats could be freed to allow the backrests to fold down, and for some kind of rudimentary bed to be provided.

Economically, things began to look up for Volvo in 1928, their first full calendar year of production. Not only were a total of 498 cars built (better, but still not good enough), but the original series of LV40 trucks (based on the car chassis, but with a payload of 1.5 tons) was released, and 521 were built. The company was still operating at a slight loss, but commercially at least they were beginning to look more settled. Four wheel brakes became available and, after the first series of PV4s had been built, the PV4 Special followed it. Already the first restyling had taken place, to modernise the shape of the Volvo car, and some early examples used a sideways-opening rear door, which must surely qualify them as very early examples, either of the hatchback, or the five-door estate car?

By 1929, however, the original four-cylinder cars had already been rendered obsolete. Not only different styles, but larger cars and a new six-cylinder engine, were all on the way. In motoring terms, the Volvo company was about to engage second gear.

Chapter 2

Six cylinders in the 1930s
The second generation

Even before the first Volvo production car was built, Gustaf Larson began to think about a six-cylinder engined machine to follow it. In the autumn of 1926, Assar Gabrielsson had invited Ivan Ornberg, a 45-year-old Swedish-born engineer, to visit him and report on Volvo's prospects. Ornberg had been a leading engineer at Hupmobile, in Detroit, since 1915, and it might well be significant that this successful North American firm had started with four-cylinder engines, but had replaced them with new six-cylinder designs in 1924.

Ornberg looked, talked, studied and asked questions, then left his recommendations with Gabrielsson and Larson. Based on these, and on his own growing experience of the cars which were doing so well in Sweden at the time, Larson reported to SKF in September 1926 that Volvo would eventually be wise to prepare a bigger six-cylinder car. In fairness to Larson, when work had begun on the design of the original Volvo, most US cars used big slogging 'fours'. Only two years later, however, cars like the latest Pontiacs had been introduced with six-cylinder power, and it was known that the Detroit giant, Chevrolet, was planning to follow suit. Ford, being Ford, and not being a trend follower, was about to replace the four-cylinder Model T, with the four-cylinder Model A, but Henry Ford was such a self-willed and eccentric tycoon that everyone expected him to follow his own whims and fancies.

Accordingly, and with the comforting thought that heavier Volvo trucks would also require more power than the four-cylinder engine could provide, Larson and his team settled down to produce their second major design. It would see the original four-cylinder car ousted in 1929, and it ushered in a stolid, but oh-so-reliable six-cylinder layout which would power every one of Volvo's cars of the 1930s and which would live on, in modified form, until the last PV832 taxi-cab left the Lundby works towards the end of the 1950s. Very few contemporary engines enjoyed a life as long as this.

Larson's team was still very small, but (in hindsight) extremely talented. Carl-Einar Abrahamsson, who had worked at Pontiac in the early 1920s, became the drawing office manager, Ivan Ornberg was retained as a design consultant and Erik Carlberg (who had been involved in the body design of the original OV4 model) continued to help out with body engineering.

The new chassis which Larson began to sketch out was more robust than that of the OV4, but of the same basic design. It had Bendix–Perrot type four wheel brakes right from the start and, as a real innovation, it was given a modern type of hypoid

Even in 1930, special-bodied Volvos had appeared. This was a PV650 with a so-called Fiskkroken *(fish-hook) coupé shell.*

bevel final drive. The tracks were widened to 56 in (142 cm), to allow a wider and more commodious body shell to be provided, but the suspension was still by heavy-duty half-elliptic leaf springs.

The secret of the new design, however, was in its engine—a massive six-cylinder side valve unit which Larson intended to be good enough to take on anything that Detroit should export to Scandinavia. Volvo, indeed, were looking to start exporting their own cars as well, and this more powerful type of machine was thought to be more suitable for more of the world's markets.

Although there was very little transfer machinery installed by Pentaverken at Skovde, 100 miles up-country towards Stockholm, the six-cylinder Type DB (the 'four' was Type DA) was laid out as if there was. In many ways, the DB's layout was the same as that of the original, with the same cylinder stroke, and L-head valve gear layout, but it had a larger cylinder bore to make up a swept volume of 3,010 cc (184 CID), a slightly higher compression ratio, and a lusty peak power output of 55 bhp at 3,000 rpm.

The first of the six cylinder cars, the Volvo Type PV650, was launched in April 1929, a year which, as it turned out, could not possibly have been less propitious for the expansion of a small company like Volvo, which had still to turn in its first operating profit. It was in 1929, of course, that the American Wall Street share market collapsed, in which many private investors were ruined, and in which the great American Depression erupted. Perhaps not in 1929, but certainly in the years which followed, Sweden—and Volvo—would suffer accordingly.

For the next decade, the ancestry of every Volvo private car, and specialised taxi-cab, could be traced back to the Type PV650 and, although there were many styling and engineering changes in the meantime, the philosophy of every car remained broadly the same. In his masterly overview of the period (*Cars of the 1930s*—now long out of print), the eminent motoring historian Michael Sedgwick has these biting, but essentially accurate, words to describe the new breed of Volvos:

'The Volvos of the 1930s were lacking in inspiration or technical interest, but they form a striking parallel with Australia's Holden of the 1950s . . . their products were hard to distinguish from the average American family saloon, except for the diagonal plated bars which graced radiators and grilles.'

If Gustaf Larson could have read those words, when they were printed in the 1970s, he might have been momentarily annoyed, but on reflection he might also have agreed with them. For Larson, the realist, would have admitted that, in the 1930s, Volvo deliberately set out to copy the marketing approach of the North Americans, so that they could appeal to the Scandinavian people who were still persistently buying so many such cars. And it was a strategy which worked, if only on a limited scale. By the mid-1930s, Volvo sales were creeping up towards the 1,000 cars a year level, which gave them perhaps seven per cent of the domestic car market. More important to Volvo salesmen like Olof Peterson was the fact that Volvo was the second strongest individual marque in the crowded sector—where Dodge (one of the Chrysler companies) outsold Volvo, but where cars like the Oldsmobiles and Pontiacs were already trailing.

It was the availability of the six-cylinder chassis, along with considerably more performance, and more roomy coachwork, which at last allowed Volvo to turn their attention to the limited, but commercially important, Swedish taxi-cab market. But Volvo was not merely content to provide a slightly modified version of the private cars for taxi operators; a special series was developed which used the same engines and transmissions, but which had lengthened wheel-bases, and noticeably different coachwork styles.

In wading through the mass of statistical information about 1930s Volvos, some of which is printed in the Appendices at the back of this book, it is quite easy to distinguish a private car from a taxi. A private car is always a Type PV . . . , where PV stands for *Personvagn* ('private car' in Swedish), whereas a taxi is a type TR . . . , where TR stands for *Trafikvagn* ('taxi' in Swedish).

Sorting out the various sub-derivatives, whether cars or taxis, is made no easier by the fact that Volvo were always willing to supply rolling chassis so that a customer could have his own choice of special coachwork and added after delivery. For that reason, therefore, although the Type PV650 is the lowest number in this six-cylinder series, it refers to rolling chassis only, and the first proper Volvo-built six-cylinder private car was the Type PV651 of 1929. In the next eight years there would be ten different PV . . . private cars, and no fewer than 14 slightly different taxis! In that time the engine size went up twice, from 3,010 cc, through 3,266 cc to the definitive 3,670 cc, peak power outputs rose from 55 bhp to 84 bhp, and wheel bases crept up from 295 cm to 355 cm (116.1 in to no less than 139.8 in). Synchromesh was added to the gearboxes in 1931, and the independent front suspension was added to some chassis types, but not to others.

The PV651, which qualifies as the 'father' of the series, was a strictly conventional car, with staid upright styling, a separate 'boot'—literally, a great luggage box—on the tail, double-blade bumpers, twin spare detachable rim wheels, the wheels still being of the old artillery-style wooden variety. Its top speed was claimed to be about 95 kph (58 mph), which was very creditable when the barn-door aerodynamics and the 1,500 kg (3,300 lb) unladen weight is considered. It was the rugged sort of

Above *An early example of the six-cylinder Volvo—a PV654 saloon, showing traces of North American styling influence.*

Below *'Carioca'—after a popular dance of the period—was the nickname of the 1935 PV36 model. It was the first 'streamlined' Volvo and showed rather disastrous similarities to the Chrysler Airflow of the day.*

PV51 of 1936, which followed the PV36 'Carioca', was much more simple and had more restrained styling. Consequently, it was more popular as well.

motor car which looked as if it could run and run, for the engine had a seven-bearing crankshaft, and no aspect of chassis and body design had been skimped. Compared with the PV4, too, the body construction had changed, for steel skin panels were used throughout. Volvo, like many other car makers, were finding that 'Weymann' construction had as many snags as advantages, not least of which was that local bird life seemed to like pecking through the skin coverings to get at the padding underneath.

PV652, introduced in 1930, was mechanically the same type of car as the PV651, except that the body interior was more luxuriously trimmed and equipped. More important than this, however, was that the PV652 eventually took on a more powerful 3,266 cc engine, which produced up to 65 bhp. The new engine, coded EB by Volvo, also celebrated their decision to buy out Pentaverken, and make it a wholly-owned Volvo subsidiary.

1929 and 1930 were momentous years for AB Volvo, for not only was the company continuing to expand, but it was also moving steadily into profit. Company archive records show that the first monthly profit was made in August 1929, and that after a set-back in September, the profitable trend continued for the rest of the year. The total corporate profit for 1929 was 1,956 SKr (or about £110)—tiny, but significant.

By the end of 1930, in spite of the deepening world-wide economic depression, production at Lundby was up to nearly 2,000 vehicles a year, the majority of these being trucks and truck chassis. It was still a long way (and a great disappointment no doubt) from the 8,000 vehicles which SKF had been hoping to sell by the end of the 1920s, but it was, at least, a step in the right direction. The first of the new buildings had already been erected at Lundby and more would soon follow.

PV653 and PV654 appeared in August 1933, as direct replacements for PV651 and PV652. Their chassis layout was basically the same as before, which is to say that front and rear suspension was by half-elliptic leaf springs, but there was a new cruciform X-bracing to add rigidity. The latest Type EB 3,266 cc engine (with down-draught carburettor) was standardised on both models, as was the synchromesh gearbox, while the standard specification now included hydraulic brakes, hydraulic lever-arm suspension dampers and modern wire-spoke wheels.

There was, of course, a completely new body shell, all-steel for the very first time on any Volvo, still very upright and conventional (one might almost say 'middle-class'), but now with a slight rearward slope to the radiator shell and the windscreen, more rounded corners and more shapely wings. Volvo's technical development had been helped along because Ian Ornberg had left Hupmobile to become Volvo's technical director (passenger cars) in 1932, working under Gustaf Larson, and the body style was mainly the work of Gunnar Borgert.

However, even though Volvo were making progress, and becoming more widely known, they were still badly hit by the Depression, which seemed to be trying to knock the stuffing out of the manufacturing industries. One result was that Volvo car sales slumped—only 591 complete PV653/654 cars were built, compared with 2,176 PV651/652.

One result was that Volvo decided to make startling and obvious visual changes to their cars' styling, the outcome being the controversial PV36 'Carioca' of 1935. However, although this car overshadowed the older-type '650 Series' car, it did not replace them, and for that reason I must defer its description until later in this narrative.

PV653 and PV654 had been unsuccessful—no-one denied that—but it was not entirely the fault of the cars. By 1935, when the new PV658/PV659 cars arrived, many more people were once again able to buy cars, and the future looked brighter.

When war broke out, fuel supplies were restricted, so Volvo developed a producer gas version of the PV53, which towed its fuel source on a trailer.

Six cylinders in the 1930s

It must have been hard for Volvo, therefore, to see that the new cars sold just as slowly as before. Even though they were much faster than before—the Type EC engine, with 3,670 cc and at least 80 bhp, endowed them with top speeds of about 7o mph—and smarter-looking, with V-radiators and more shapely lines, it was clear that they were becoming technically outdated. The last of all, a PV658, was built in 1937.

Running parallel to these cars at all times, were Volvo's famous TR . . . series of taxis. By the mid-1930s these machines were selling equally as strongly as the private cars. Throughout the period, the taxis shared the same basic mechanical designs and layouts as the PV . . . private cars although they all had longer wheelbases. I have always thought that sales of private cars were held back by this similarity to the taxis, because some form of snobbery must have deterred sales at times.

From 1935 the taxi pedigree progressed to Type TR701, when the machines were really the same as the PV658/PV659 models. However, the line was by no means dying out when the PV... cars were phased out in 1937. In fact, in 1938, the taxi lines were rejuvenated yet again as TR801 and TR802, this time with very up-to-date rounded body styles and a Lincoln/Ford-Detroit style of false 'radiator' grille. It was in this form, sometimes with Producer Gas power, that the Volvo taxi line kept going throughout the Second World War (in which Sweden was not, of course, directly involved) to 1947.

The upheaval in Volvo car design, however, had already occurred in 1935, when the PV36, nicknamed 'Carioca' after the then-popular American dance, was unveiled. The story really goes back to the Chrysler Airflow of 1934, an ugly but so-called 'aerodynamic' car which caused many otherwise blameless company stylists to lose their sanity for a time in an attempt to copy its shape. The Airflow,

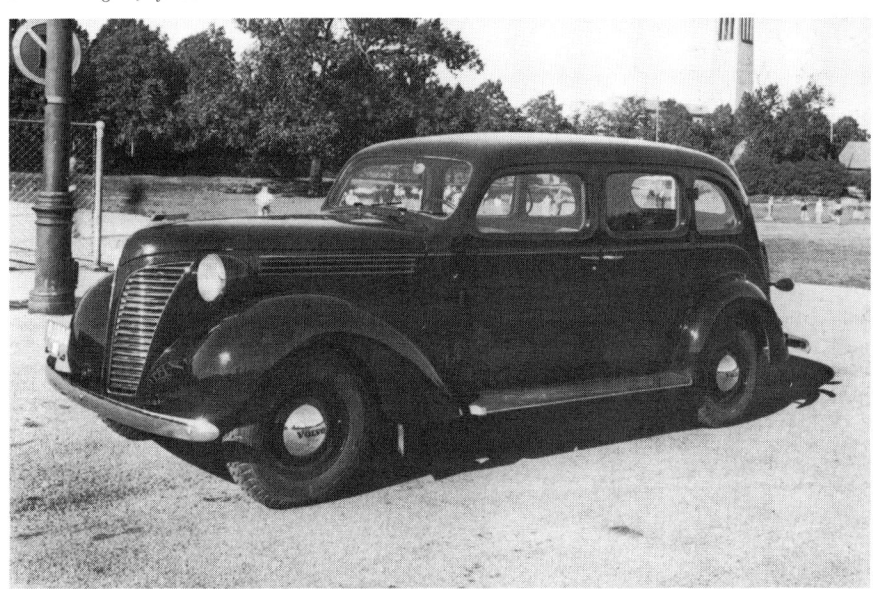

One of the famous line of Volvo taxis of the 1930s and 1940s—this was the PV802, complete with 3.7-litre engine, of 1938.

under the skin, was not a bad car, but its radically different front shape, incorporating, for the first time, headlamps faired-in to a full-width shape, was thought to be hideous by some and was certainly unsuccessful in the market place. The problem was that other companies, setting out to build 'look-alike' cars of their own, did not realise that the Chrysler was a commercial failure until it was too late.

One 'streamlined' Volvo prototype ('Venus-Bilo'—see Appendix D) had already been built in 1933, as a private-enterprise project, although Volvo had not felt that they wanted, or needed, to put it on sale as a production option. This did not, however, cause them to reject the new PV36 when it was first shown to them.

Development of the new style went ahead at great speed, with Ivan Ornberg in charge of the styling. He, apparently, realised that the shape would be controversial to his bosses—for by comparison with the sturdily upright 653s and 658s it was a startling model—and resolutely refused to let Gabrielsson or Larson into his studio until he was ready. Their first view of a full-sized wooden mock-up was also the occasion on which they committed it to production in 1935.

PV36 (the title could mean: 'New model for 1936') was not only a new shape, however, but a new chassis as well. The 3,670 cc Type EC engine and transmission was retained from the PV658/PV659 models, but there was independent front suspension, by coil springs and wishbones, and the latest type of pressed-steel road wheels. PV36 was meant to be a 'luxury' Volvo, so no attempt was made to trim the all-up weight below 3,660 lb. For the same reason, no doubt, only a limited sanction of 500 sets of components were ordered.

It was asking a lot, expecting the Swedish public to accept the styling of PV36, complete with built-in headlamps, a sweeping nose and a long smooth tail, when they had been used to more traditional shapes for so many years. Henry Westerberg, quoted in an interview after his retirement, said: 'This car was much too advanced in its bodywork and styling for its time. People were still rather conservative in their requirements . . ..'

The outcome was that the PV36 'Carioca' model was very difficult to sell, not only because of its styling, but because of its rather high price, which was 8,500 SKr at a time when the most expensive Volvo taxi cost only 8,200 SKr. Of the 500 cars laid down in 1935, only 475 could be sold up until 1938, and the last 25 of all were actually assembled and sold off in the car-starved days immediately after the end of the Second World War; series production, in fact, was really all over within two years, as only 47 cars were built in 1937, and a mere seven cars in 1938.

The 'Carioca', therefore, was a prophet without honour, like so many other advanced cars which later take on a 'classic' reputation of their own, and Gustaf Larson was happy to revert to the design and building of more conventional machines. Business, in the end, was all about making profits, and for that to happen the public, however conservatively-minded, had to be kept happy.

Before the PV36 was launched, Volvo were indeed making money which, when the diverse nature of the car production line-up is considered, was something of a miracle. In 1934, for example, cars of no fewer than 13 different types were assembled and yet total output was only 609 cars. The saving grace, however, which kept the accountants (and Mr Gabrielsson of course) happy, was that the first 26 series-production Volvo bus chassis were delivered and no fewer than 2,332 trucks were assembled.

SKF now seemed to sense that the time had come to cut AB Volvo loose and let it find its own way in the world. In 1935, therefore, SKF had Volvo shares quoted on

Six cylinders in the 1930s

PV60 was built for four years immediately after the Second World War, but had been designed for introduction in 1942; it was reputed to be inspired by the 1939 Pontiac.

the Stockholm Stock Exchange, then agreed to increase the company's capital from four million to 13 million SKr, and allowed control of its destiny to slip away. Larson was later quoted as saying that: 'It was a big and joyous day when at last we stood on our own feet . . ..'

To make up for the disappointment of the 'Carioca', the engineers worked away with great speed to produce the lighter, simpler and much cheaper Type PV51. Although it was not immediately obvious, much of the new car's body shell was actually that of the 'Carioca', with changes. There was a new and simpler front end, still with a sloping radiator grille, but with lower front wings and with free-standing headlamps at each side of the grille. The rear wheel covers had been discarded and there was a one piece, rather than a vee, windscreen, but many common panels remained.

The chassis, however, reverted to a beam front axle for the time being, and had a slightly shorter wheelbase, although the same 80 bhp-plus 3,670 cc engine was retained, along with the usual three speed gearbox. The interior and facia styling was more simple and all in all this allowed the PV51's selling price to be pitched at a mere 5,800 SKr, the more luxuriously equipped PV52 (following in 1937) costing 6,300 SKr.

In spite of the fact that the PV51's specification had been cut to the bone (only one windscreen wiper and no arm rests, for instance) it was well received and it quite revolutionised Volvo's sales prospects. In marketing terms, the PV51 was a whole class lower down the scale, where more customers were available, and it was facing up to competition from imported machines like the German Opels.

One comparison is startling. Whereas Volvo sold less than 500 PV36 'Carioca' models in four years, they sold 1,000 PV51s in the first full year (1937) alone. Total car sales in that year leapt to 1,815—double those of 1936—and it marked the point at which Volvo sales began to push steadily and (apart from the war years) quite unstoppably upwards. By 1938, Volvo were sixth in the Swedish car sales 'league' and about to swallow up their nearest rivals, Dodge and DKW.

In 1937, Volvo's share capital was increased once again, to 18 million SKr, Gustaf Larson reached his 50th birthday and yet more factory extensions at Lundby were brought into use. The company, no doubt, had stopped being something of a 'cottage industry' and was becoming big business.

Whereas the PV51/PV52 cars were to be as successful as the PV36 had been a commercial failure, stylist Ivan Ornberg died in 1936 before he could savour his turnabout in the company's fortunes. Accordingly, there was a period when no new styles were being developed or introduced, following Ornberg's death, and it was not until Olle Schjolin and Carl Lindblom both arrived from General Motors in the USA, to join Edward Lindberg, that the PV51/52 line could be sharpened up and modernised.

For 1939, therefore, the PV53/54/55/56 Series took over. Like the TR800 Series taxis introduced in the same year, this carefully graded range of four-door passenger cars retained the same basic 288 cm (113.4 in) wheelbase chassis, the side-valve six-cylinder 3,670 cc engine (now developing up to 86 bhp) and the existing passenger compartment and panelling from the PV51/PV52 cars, but it had a new and very transatlantic-looking nose, with the radiator now well hidden away behind the contoured grille.

These cars sold even better than those they had replaced (2,253 in 1939, compared with 1656 of the overlapping ranges in 1938) and the result was that Volvo's 1939 output rose to an all-time record, in spite of the fact that the Second World War broke out on September 3 and ruined prospects for the future. This was a great compliment, not only to the current state of Volvo design, but to the company's ever-growing reputation, especially as the latest cars had only ever been intended as an interim 'holding-the-line' measure until a brand-new chassis could be made ready!

The new design, started in 1938 and originally intended for launch in May 1940, was the PV60 Series. The war, and (in spite of Sweden's neutrality) Volvo's turn-over to the making of commercial and military vehicles, put a stop to that so that, in the event, just five prototypes had been built. In the event, the PV60 went on sale in 1946 and was phased out in 1950 but, as it belongs so obviously to the 1930s' pedigree of Volvo, it needs to be surveyed here.

Gustaf Larson's engineers were given a fairly free hand in some aspects of the new car's design but not in others. While they were encouraged to look at a new chassis, new suspensions and a new body style, they were told to use the same six-cylinder engine and transmission which had now been a familiar part of the Volvo scene for a decade.

Since Schjolin and Lindblom had both moved over to Volvo from General Motors, where latterly they had been working on the 1939 GM Models, perhaps it is not at all surprising to find that the PV60 scheme had so much in common with the general layout of the Pontiacs from Detroit for that year. The body style in particular, with its six side window layout, its 'fastback' shape incorporating a split-pane rear window, its horizontal grille bars and its podded headlamp cowls, was all so very typical of the cars from Detroit—the difference of course being that Volvo proposed to have it tooled up and built in Sweden, only for their own use.

The new chassis, which reverted to a familiar 285 cm (112.2 in) wheelbase—just

The 1950s Volvo taxis, in spite of their modified front styling, were still recognisably derived from a 1930s layout—even so they were built up until 1958.

3 cm shorter than that of the PV51 to 56 models—featured massive cross-bracing under the floor and a new coil-spring-wishbone independent front suspension. The rugged engine had been boosted, yet again, to 90 bhp, but every Volvo garage mechanic would have been familiar with its layout and its detail.

If the truth be told, the PV60 was already obsolete by the time it could possibly be put on sale, in 1946, but as all the production tooling had been ordered, completed and made ready, the ever-practical Assar Gabrielsson decided to put it on sale anyway. In 1946, after all, there was a huge demand for cars in Sweden (as in every other country in the Western world), the old models from the 1930s which had soldiered on through the twilight of the war years were well-and-truly obsolete, and the new-fangled PV444 was still not ready for production. So—why not?

Why not, indeed. In the next five years, Volvo easily sold out their planned sanction of 3,000 complete cars and 500 rolling chassis and, if they had not needed all available space at Lundby to build PV444s, they could undoubtedly have sold more.

In the meantime, between 1939 and 1945, Volvo—and Sweden—had to carry on as best they could. Even though Sweden itself was strictly neutral, it was geographically very tightly sandwiched between Norway and Denmark (both in German hands), Germany itself, and Finland (who had to make peace with the Russians in 1940) and it no longer had free access to some concerns which had supplied components from overseas during the 1930s.

Although commercial vehicle and military machine production increased a lot in the early 1940s, private car building was not closed down altogether. The only important technical change was that producer gas kits (either for direct mounting to the car itself or for mounting on light trailers) were made available. With the otherwise standard 3,670 cc engine, this reduced peak power from 86/90 bhp to about 50 bhp.

A detailed look at production statistics from 1939 to 1945 shows that there were no changes, or even deletions, from the last model year of the 1930s and that even luxury cars like the PV56 continued to be built in tiny numbers. Production, however, slumped from 2,834 in 1939 to as little as 99 in 1942 (when a mere five PV53/56 cars were assembled and the vast majority of the machines built were taxis) and only crept back to 335 in 1944 when the balance was shifting back slightly towards private cars.

During the war years, however, those Volvo engineers not tied up in essential military work were by no means idle. Sometime, somehow, things must surely return to normal and new cars would be needed. Perhaps, after all these years, Volvo could at last afford a new engine and a new type of chassis design. In 1944, at an exhibition in Stockholm, the public found out what had been going on. There, in all its non-running glory was the very first PV444!

Chapter 3

PV444—a 'world' car from Sweden

While the Second World War raged all around its borders and its long coastline, the Swedish nation concentrated carefully on its neutrality and on ensuring its own defences. Sweden's long-term commitment to non-belligerence (maintained to this day) never wavered and at least it meant that the people could face up to the postwar years in confidence, with their country and their people intact.

Even so, the Swedish armed forces had to be ready for anything. Accordingly, they asked for more cars, more lorries, more tractor units and many new types of military vehicles, to make them as mobile as possible. Volvo as a patriotic Swedish business, speedily ran down its production of private cars and turned Lundby to the temporary production of such machinery. The car designers, on the other hand, found themselves with a little time to reflect.

It was during the war years, too, that an ambitious technical engineer called Gunnar Engellau finally joined Volvo—finally, because he had first been approached by Assar Gabrielsson in 1941, though he did not actually join the group until 1943, after a great deal of nagging. Engellau, like so many other eminent men before him, had found that Gabrielsson could be extremely tenacious, and that if he knew what he wanted, then the odds were usually on him getting his way.

The two first met in 1941, when Gabrielsson was looking for ways to make the ignition and burning of his 'producer gas' Volvo fuels more predictable. Engellau, who had served in the Swedish Air Force, then worked briefly for the Swedish State Railway system (as a locomotive cleaner), spent seven years with Motala Verkstad (Sweden's old-established heavy engineering workshops), but became technical sales director of AB Electrolux in 1939. Electrolux, then as now, made vacuum cleaners and other domestic appliances. After the war they grew rapidly, and it must have given Engellau enormous pleasure, when he became Volvo's President, to see Volvo overtaking them.

When Volvo cast around, in Sweden, for ways to improve the producer gas process, Gabrielsson eventually approached Electrolux, and Engellau himself produced the right sort of switchgear which consisted of modified vacuum cleaner components. There and then, Gabrielsson tried to attract Engellau to Volvo by offering him the job of technical director at Svenska Flygmotor, a company partly owned by Volvo, making aircraft engines.

Engellau fended off this approach on the grounds that he was too committed to Electrolux and its problems to make the change. Gabrielsson, however, kept on nagging and kept on at Engellau. Eventually, in 1943, Gabrielsson 'caught his

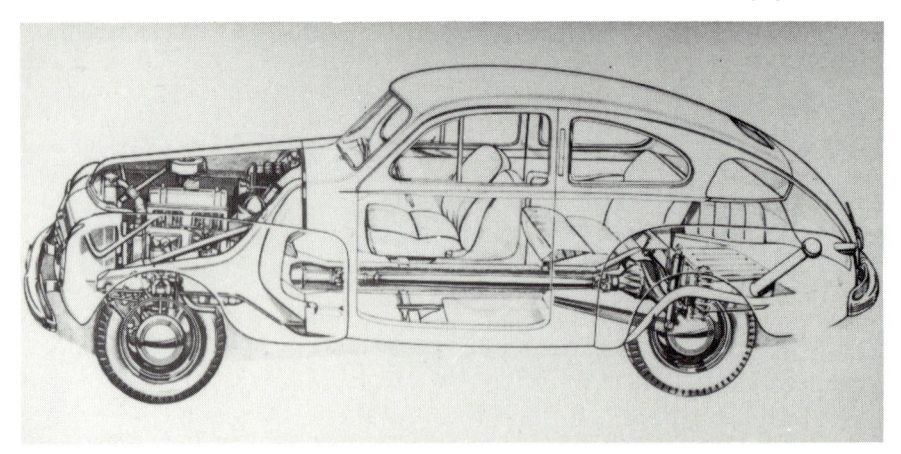

The PV444 of 1944 was simple, rugged, and the foundation for all Volvo's future growth. Only the two-door saloon was offered at first.

salmon' by making Engellau not the technical director, but the President, of Flygmotor. It was the start of an active association between Engellau and Volvo which was to last well into the 1970s.

In the meantime, the PV444 model was beginning to take shape. However, the story of PV444 really began with PV40 in the late 1930s. (I am sorry, but design and development stories often involve the quoting of project numbers and codes. The reader, I am afraid, will have to get used to it, for there will be many, many, more later in this book!) It started with the two ex-General Motors engineers, Olle Schjolin and Carl Lindblom, and with two advanced small cars (the AD-5 and the AD-8 prototypes) which they had designed in Detroit before moving across to Volvo.

Clearly, when Schjolin and Lindblom arrived in Gothenburg from Detroit, they imported quite a lot of typical North American urgency with them, not to mention the memory of designs left behind them in General Motors. In 1938 they not only inspired the updating of the PV51/PV52 cars into PV53/54/55/56 (as already related in Chapter 2), and began design work on the six-cylinder PV60 saloon, but they also began thinking about entirely new types of cars as well.

Gustaf Larson, I am sure, had realised that Volvo mechanical design had settled into something of a rut during the 1930s, with no new engines being introduced, and with chassis and suspension improvements proceeding on strictly conventional lines. These two 'whizz-kids' from Detroit, he must have reasoned, were the type of design engineers who could be encouraged to produce something new. In effect, they could set up their own 'Advanced Design' department, and built radically different prototypes, but at that moment there was no question of rushing them, unproven, into quantity production.

Like many other such projects (or, if I tell the brutal truth, like most such projects), the PV40 became too much of a 'designer's car' and not enough of a 'production engineer's car'. It looked like being clever, technically interesting, and way ahead of its time—but it was not at all the sort of machine which Volvo were used to building.

The AD-5 and AD-8 cars which Schjolin and Lindblom had left behind in Detroit had featured unit construction body/chassis units, all-independent suspension and rear-mounted engines. Not only that, but the engines had eight cylinders, in which four pairs were arranged in an X-pattern and they operated on the two-stroke principle. No doubt two-stroke operation was an easy way out of the camshaft and valve gear complications which would surely have afflicted such a layout . . . .

Exactly the same layout was provisionally adopted for the Volvo PV40 project. The first work was concentrated on the new engine layout, which was thought (correctly, as it transpired) to need the most work and, to maintain strict secrecy, the design and development began in buildings remote from the Lundby factory. Two engineers, Westerberg and Albinsson, detailed the 1.6-litre unit, which was more complicated than any other automotive engine of its day. Not only was the engine effectively ranged as a two-row radial engine, but the pairs of cylinders were linked by a common cylinder head/combustion chamber, all the inlet transfer ports were concentrated in the front cylinder of the pair, and the exhaust ports were in the rear cylinder. The inlet charge was supercharged by a Roots-type blower mounted between the upper pairs of cylinders which propelled the petroil mixture through a centrifugal fan at the nose of the crankshaft.

The very first test engine was run early in 1940—in other words, *after* the outbreak of war and *after* all Volvo's car production programme had begun to run down—and before long the 1.6-litre unit was producing up to 70 bhp and about 116 lb/ft of torque. This, frankly, was a disappointment, although Volvo have never actually said as much. By their own admission, it was only about 90 per cent as

The PV444 was the first-ever integral construction Volvo but, as this picture shows, the techniques of designing 'monocoques' were still not developed very far.

efficient as a four-stroke engine would have been and for that reason alone it was not acceptable to management; in addition, the Roots supercharger was noisy and the whole engine was complex, bulky and costly to build.

Even so, no fewer than 25 Type GA engines of this design were eventually built in 1940, and the design of the PV40 car evolved around them; like the engines, the car was different—very different. It had a 108 in wheelbase—shorter than any previous Volvo—and the target weight was to be about 2,000 lb (908 kg). The basic style of the car was something like the existing Volvo PV53/56 Series, with four side windows and a long sloping tail, though hindsight suggests that it was more inspired than this, and in many ways paralleled the shape of the rear-engined Renault 4CV which followed, or of the British Jowett Javelin.

Under the skin, the engine/transmission unit was behind the seats, which was advanced enough, but even more astonishing was the fact that the X-8 engine (I can think of no more graphic way to describe it) was ahead of the line of the rear wheels, tucked in behind the rear seat squab, and would have been the very devil to service and maintain. The chassis layout, designed by Sven Viberg, featured coil spring front suspension and torsion bars, VW-style, at the rear.

However, corporate enthusiasm for PV40 waned during 1940, even though a full-size wood body model was completed and two test body/chassis units were constructed. Both Schjolin and Lindblom returned to North America in 1940, as the war intensified, and with them went the drive to get PV40 on to the road. Gustaf Larson let work continue for a short time, but he was never convinced that PV40 was going to be a successful Volvo (if, indeed, it could be a successful *anything*), and by the end of 1940 he had cancelled the entire project.

For the next two years, at least, Larson and his designers could only think about,

Mechanical details of the PV444, including the front suspension on its separate cross-member, and the back axle located by radius arms, and sprung on coil springs. In principle, all future Volvos would follow this layout as well.

PV444—a 'world' car from Sweden

The original PV444 two-door style, complete with divided screen and divided rear window.

but not actually start building, new motor cars. Indeed, it was not until 1943 that a new project, PV44, was even vaguely considered, and even then it needed the influence of a forceful outside engineer called Helmer Petterson to get things moving. The sequence of events, inside and outside the Volvo archive, is well-documented and emphasises how quickly, and how strongly, Petterson became an important consultant—for I can think of no better word—to AB Volvo.

Petterson, born in 1901, had spent six years in North America in the 1920s, working with the Excelsior company in Chicago, where he looked after their cycle racing and was involved in motor cycle design. He returned to Europe in 1928, indulged in cycle speed record breaking, and eventually settled down as a service manager to a GM, and later a Ford, dealer in Stockholm.

Petterson met Assar Gabrielsson because he, as well as Volvo, was developing producer gas (charcoal-burning) fuel generators against the time when war would certainly lead to a petrol shortage. Petterson's design, being so efficient, was eventually taken up by Volvo as the Volvo-HP-1; it was fixed to the rear of the cars, and I need hardly point out that the 'HP' in the model name could either be construed as 'High Power', or 'Helmer Petterson' . . ..

In 1943, the Volvo company was, tentatively at least, beginning to look forward to the time when peace would return to Europe and when their private car business could be opened up again. Both Assar Gabrielsson and Gustaf Larson saw, not only that they would need new models (and, they suspected, smaller more economical models), but that they had a distinct shortage of experienced design engineers to develop those new cars. Ivan Ornberg, after all, was dead and both Olle Schjolin and Carl Lindblom were back in the United States.

Helmer Petterson, it must be emphasised, had absolutely no 'track record' as a designer of cars, but his wood-gas generators had been so successful that Assar Gabrielsson was inclined to respect his judgement on other matters. Petterson, it

Above *The PV444B, introduced in 1950, better equipped than the original.*

Left *Occasionally even Volvo descended to whimsy! But could they really have been serious about a vase of flowers on the dashboard of the PV444?*

PV444—a 'world' car from Sweden

seems, was driving Gabrielsson to the Skovde engine-manufacturing factory one day in 1943 when he happened to comment that Volvo would need a new small car for the post-war markets, and that he, Helmer Petterson thought he knew how it should be done.

It was presumptuous, to say the least, and a modern parallel might be for a 'special builder' to approach Ford or General Motors with the proposal that he should take over design and bring them profitably into the late 1980s. But for reasons which he never troubled to make clear, Gabrielsson was impressed and (presumably after consulting Gustaf Larson, who was, after all, the engineer in the partnership) suggested that Petterson should present his ideas.

It rapidly transpired that Petterson, although full of ideas, had not actually started to design a car. He had many talks with Gabrielsson about the sort of car he had in mind. Gabrielsson apparently said: 'I think we will make a small car, but we don't want a soap box.' This reference was almost certainly meant to be a swipe at the pre-war Germany DKW, a small car with a two-stroke engine, which was the fourth highest selling car in Sweden at the end of the 1930s; what Gabrielsson meant by 'small', however, was something smaller than the traditional-type six-cylinder Volvos, and certainly smaller than the American Chevrolets and Fords which were still flooding into Sweden every year.

By the spring of 1943, however, Volvo were ready to let Petterson get started on 'his' new car. They put a long-serving Volvo engineer, Eric Jern, at his disposal, not merely as an aide, but actually as the man who could translate bright ideas into reality. Petterson, it should be emphasised, was not so much a design engineer as something of a self-styled visionary, entrepreneur (and, later, a stylist as well).

The sketching up of possible layouts began in May 1943 under the code name PV44—the 44 relating to 1944, when Patterson and Jern expected the car to come to maturity. (Do not get too excited by such logical project coding—before long the car would become PV444, and a successor to it announced in 1958 did not have '58' in its nomenclature. The one sure thing about Volvo project codes is that they were never sure, never logical—and therefore impossible to predict. For years before the new 760GLE was launched, some motoring magazines were confidently dubbing it the 'new 400 Series'.)

At first, both Petterson and Jern favoured the idea of a front-wheel-drive car, drawing, no doubt, on the success of the front-wheel-drive DKW. Before they could detail this, however, they had to decide on a new engine. There was no way that they wanted to use an engine as large, heavy and as out-of-date as the Type EC side-valve 'six' used in the 1930s.

One engine, however, was already available to them—in theory. This was the X-8 two-stroke supercharged PV40 engine which had been lying around, unloved, since the end of 1940. Should they try it? Would it even fit in to a new general layout? History records that it was, in fact, mocked up in several different ways but, in the end, all of Gustaf Larson's old doubts reappeared and he killed it off, finally and totally. 'We will take a normal four-cylinder engine, because then we know what we are doing.'

But should the new car have front-wheel-drive or rear-wheel-drive, even if the choice of the engine type had been taken? The whole concept of the new car was still in the balance as the summer of 1943 gave way to autumn. Although Petterson was still sure that the PV44 should have the front wheels driven, many Volvo people did not. Even though Petterson went so far as to suggest that the engine should be laid flat on its side, with all electrical fittings and the carburettor uppermost (which would have made regular maintenance and repairs very easy), the doubts remained.

Perhaps a decision could have been made easier if there had not been a certain amount of disagreement between Volvo's two illustrious founders. Even after 20 years, Gabrielsson and Larson were not complete soul mates, for both had strong characters and did not easily defer to the other. The classic example was the final choice of rear-drive for PV44, after various front-drive mock-ups had been built. It was Gustaf Larson who finally shied away from the potential problems which might follow the layout of front drive, high-speed transmission shaft rotation, and the fact that Volvo would have to manufacture a considerable proportion of the installation. 'I don't want any troubles at all,' Larson told the team, 'Let's do it as a rear-wheel-drive.' Petterson later commented about this: 'I was hired by Gabrielsson, not by Larson, and each of them did not like anyone hired by the other. So I had to do my best to keep Larson happy.'

From the end of 1943, the concept of PV44 became more conventional than before—for it was to have a four-cylinder engine mounted up front, a normal drive line and a rear axle like other Volvos. In 1944, up to 40 men were involved in the design, building or testing of the project. Eric Jern headed the design effort, for by this time Helmer Petterson began to concentrate on the styling of the new car. Edward Lindberg was in charge of structural design, while Axel Roos' people made die models and the first prototype bodies.

One of Helmer Petterson's ideas which was retained, was that PV44 should have a unit-construction body/chassis unit, not only because it was likely to make the car stronger, but lighter, and, if enough cars could be made, cheaper to build into the bargain. Volvo archive material suggests that this design was partly inspired by a pre-war Hanomag two-door saloon, but there were many other influences abroad as well. Chassis-less cars had been developed widely in Europe in the 1930s, with the front-wheel-drive *traction avant* Citroën as one of the pioneers. We must not forget, either, that Schjolin and Lindbolm, who had made their mark, briefly, at Volvo at the end of the 1930s, had come from General Motors and that the Detroit monolith were well in with this particular aspect of design. Their European-owned subsidiaries, Opel and Vauxhall, had introduced unit-construction bodies in 1935 and 1937 respectively and other companies (like Hillman and Morris, in the UK) had followed them before 1940.

The styling of PV44 occupied Petterson for many weeks, and he admits to having been influenced by the pre-war Pontiacs—which is one more tenuous, but completely unofficial, link with General Motors in particular, and Detroit in general. I doubt very much if this style was eventually chosen with an eye to selling PV44s in North America (sales, after all, did not actually begin until the mid-1950s), although some writers, with the benefit of hindsight, have suggested that it was.

Certainly the general style of PV44—a two-door saloon with a long sloping tail, having no separate boot bulge, with a full-width nose and recessed headlamps, but only part-recessed front wings, and without running boards, was all very typical of some Pontiacs of the period, but they were not unique. A quick flick through 'Collector's' encyclopedias covering the early 1940s shows that Ford, Mercury, Lincoln, Buick, Chevrolet and Oldsmobile were all promoting the same theme. It seems reasonable that a tyro stylist like Petterson should have been influenced by all

After a long delay, PV444 production began at Lundby in 1947. In the next 18 years, 440,000 cars of this basic style would be built—it was the first truly 'mass-produced' Volvo.

these cars, particularly as many of these cars were still finding their way in Sweden as war tightened its grip on the world.

After several clay models had been produced, altered, viewed by Gustaf Larson and modified yet again, a full-scale mock-up was built up in wood, with solid window panes painted silver to make them look like glass. With the appropriate 16 in wheels and tyres bolted into place, but with no other mechanical equipment on board, the mock-up was put out into a country location near Gothenburg for Gabrielsson and Larson to inspect.

The viewing (which, by a study of the only pictorial record I have seen, must have been in April or May) was brief and decisive. Volvo's founders paced around the car, looking at it from all angles, and seemed to like what they saw. As Petterson was later to comment: 'In 15 or 20 minutes, it was all decided.' The race was now on to get prototype cars on the road, for Volvo were determined to show at least one at a special show they were planning, in the Royal Tennis Hall in Stockholm, in September 1944.

Unit-construction body design technology was not at all advanced at this time, and that chosen for the PV44 actually used a pair of strong longerons extending forward from the scuttle/toeboard (which my American friends would call the firewall) following the same paths as might have been chosen for traditional separate frame members. One feature of the shell, of course, was that both the windscreen and the rear windows were divided by central strips, and at the front this certainly made it easier and cheaper to produce the windscreen panels.

Although the 'chassis' of the new PV44—which, in this and all future Volvo design concepts means suspensions, steering and mechanical layout, all to be attached to the unit-construction hull—was entirely new, with no carry-over parts from Volvos of the 1930s, it was a straightforward and conventional layout. Like most new models—then and now—the original concept had been considerably more 'way-out' than the car which actually took shape in 1944. The new four-cylinder engine was vertically mounted, up front, with a three-speed synchromesh gearbox bolted up directly to it, and there was a single-piece propeller shaft driving the rear wheels by a spiral bevel rear axle which was to be sourced from Spicer. Independent front suspension was by coil springs and wishbones (reputedly copied from a Plymouth), while the steering was a Ross worm gear (even though Petterson had recommended rack and pinion—such refinements did not find a place on Volvos until 1974, when the 240/260 Series cars were revealed).

The rear axle was located by twin trailing arms which angled well in towards the centre line of the car, pivotting near the propeller shaft itself, and anchored to the body shell on the right side by a Panhard rod. For the first time on a Volvo, however, the rear springs were coils, rather than half-elliptic leaves, these being positioned behind the line of the axle, and telescopic dampers being mounted ahead of that line.

I had forgotten just how thoughtful Volvo designers could be until I looked underneath a PV444 production car at rest in the magnificent exhibition hall at the Torslanda factory near Gothenburg. Not only was the underside of the body shell relatively smooth and uncluttered, but the propeller shaft itself was cossetted by a panel underneath it, as well as by the conventional tunnel. The brakes, incidentally, were 9-in drums, and were almost the same as those used on current-model Studebakers, and would be built for Volvo by Wagner Electric.

The really major investment in this new car—apart, of course, from the body/chassis unit—was the engine itself. Petterson, having been rebuffed in so many ways over his design concept, was determined to stick out for the very best type of four-cylinder engine he could achieve, and in doing so he inadvertently made sure that it

By 1955, the PV444 (in its 'K' derivative) had acquired a new grille and a more powerful 51 bhp engine, along with a one-piece rear window. The white-wall tyres betray this car's destination—the USA.

would live not just for years, but for decades. Cost-conscious Volvo engineers, steeped in Volvo tradition, wanted to stick with a side-valve layout, but both Petterson, the consultant, and Jern, the actual design chief, insisted on an overhead valve layout, which would place Volvo at least on a par with most of the forward-thinking car makers of Europe.

As Volvo historical material puts it: 'To be sure their detail designs followed the best practice, the Gothenburg engineers studied the latest overhead-valve engines made by Opel, Hanomag and Fiat, the model 508C engine in the last-named case. In the bottom end design, with three main bearings and crankcase sides that extended down past the crank centre-line, the Fiat influence was strong.'

Quite. And Volvo had nothing to be ashamed about in doing this. Since they had not previously designed any sort of overhead valve power plant for a private car, the engineers could have spent much time and money in making their own mistakes and learning by experience—the same mistakes and the same experience already gleaned by their potential competitors. To short-cut those pitfalls, they chose to buy, study and learn from the competition. Everyone did it in those days—and you may be sure that everyone does it today.

The engine which evolved was a rugged three-bearing design with (at first) a bore and stroke of 75 × 80 mm and a swept volume of 1,414 cc (86.3 CID). Coded B4, where the '4' certainly indicated the number of cylinders, it looked rugged and *was* rugged—a characteristic which was to endear it to hundreds of thousands of Volvo customers in the next two decades. More important than this, however, was that there was some built-in 'stretch' (the engine, in other words, could be enlarged in future), though I doubt if Eric Jern thought too carefully about that in 1944.

Because the cylinder head was cast iron, the combustion chamber simple and 'bath-tub' shaped, and Volvo had plans for awful fuels with a mere 65 octane rating, B4 was no ball of fire when first run, but it was immediately obvious that it was very strong indeed. At 45 bhp, its bhp/litre figure was only 32, but as PV44 was certainly going to be the lightest Volvo ever made, it was sure to be enough at first.

Parts for the first three prototypes were manufactured during 1944, but it was only possible to complete one in time for the opening of the show in Stockholm, and even that car was still a non-runner at the time. Incidentally, it was this show that the car suddenly and irrevocably took on another name—it lost its PV44 project code, and was badged up as a PV444 instead. Its significance? Lost in the mists of time now, but it's a fair bet that '444' indicated '1944 model, with four-cylinder engine'.

It would not be overstating the case to say that the 1944 exhibition was sensationally successful for Volvo. Not only was the company able to show off its brand-new PV444 (though they made it clear that it was by no means ready to go on sale at that time) but it also displayed the six-cylinder PV60 model (the car which had been designed before the war closed down Volvo's private-car operation) of which the first five prototypes were built by 1942.

There never seemed to be any doubt that Volvo's new small car was likely to sell very well indeed. If for no other reason, the tentative 4,800 SKr price tag would see to that—for this was exactly the same as asked for the PV4 in the late 1920s, and was a lot less than any other Volvo had cost in recent years. Price, in fact, would not have held it back at first, for in Sweden, as in other European countries, there was a huge pent-up demand for new cars, which had been growing steadily since industry had converted itself into makers of armaments during the war.

Above *The only style derivative ever offered on the PV444 was this three-door station wagon which, in modified form, was built until 1969.*

Below *In 1958, when most pundits were sure that the PV444 design was doomed, Volvo announced the greatly revised PV544, distinguished here by the new grille, the one-piece windscreen and different decoration.*

Although no promises could be made for delivery of the new PV444 (it was certainly not possible until peace returned to Western Europe, and even then there would be further delay), orders were taken for the new car and sales contracts issued. Volvo, if they had only realised it, were backing themselves into the same sort of corner as VW had done in the late 1930s—but Volvo were to get out of it with more honour. No fewer than 2,300 firm orders were placed, all under the assumption that the provisional price of 4,800 SKr would stay firm.

The story of the PV444's protracted development phase has been told several times before. Testing and tooling dragged on, and on, so that it was not until February 1947, 29 months after that show in Stockholm, that the first production cars left the Lundby factory. The first prototype was not actually ready for driving until March 1945, the whole of Sweden's mechanical industries were virtually shut down by a strike which lasted from February to July 1945 (six months—what was that about 'The English disease'?) and all three prototypes were not running reliably until 1946. None of this was helped by the acute shortage of fuel, and of tyres, both directly due to the war, of course.

There were long delays in signing up suppliers to provide thousands of components to Volvo, not least because Volvo was little known, or because it had not previously had a reputation for building so many cars as were now planned. Assar Gabrielsson re-hired Carl Lindblom in 1945 to urge the car into production, and it was only a personal visit to the United States in one of the precious running prototypes which helped the most vital contracts to be signed.

In the meantime, the delay was working to Volvo's advantage in one direction, for there was plenty of opportunity to test the car on all road surfaces, in all weather conditions, and with many drivers at the helm. In particular, Sweden's rugged unsurfaced roads, and the rigours of a Scandinavian winter, were both tackled by the test cars, and their specification gradually improved. It was this delay, no doubt, which helped turn the PV444 from just another good new Volvo into a truly remarkable machine.

I really cannot take seriously the idea that Volvo actually meant to deliver PV444s complete with the flower vase attached to the rather garish green-and-ivory facia, but I can quite believe that Volvo eventually honoured their original sales contracts for the car, signed in 1944, when the cars began to be delivered in 1947. The first nine PV444s were built before the end of 1946, but series production actually began in February 1947. The first two cars went to customers in Alingsas and Boras on February 8 1947, but only another 14 cars were shipped in that month as a great deal of handwork was still needed on the early models. Thereafter the pace increased and output went ever upwards. In 1947, as a whole, 1,920 PV444s were built, followed by 2,176 in 1948, 3,614 in 1949 and 4,782 in 1950; at that point PV444 production took over completely at Lundby and the Volvo private-car output soared to previously undreamed-of heights.

In the meantime, and even before deliveries began, the cost of everything throughout the world had risen sharply and it seemed that there was no way in which the original 'Stockholm' price of 4,800 SKr could be held. This meant that frustrated motorists, instead of waiting patiently in a queue, could sell their order contracts to the highest bidders, and newspaper advertising columns were spattered with such offers. Those who held the original contracts, for which they had paid very little money, found that they could sell the contracts—*not* the cars, mark you—for up to 12,000 or 13,000 SKr.

Even so, in spite of this money-grabbing excess, Assar Gabrielsson decreed that Volvo should honour its original commitment if it was to retain the customers' long-term loyalty. Accordingly, the first 2,300 PV444s were delivered to original contract holders for a mere 4,800 SKr each, when they should have been selling for 8,000 SKr. The 'true' price of 8,000 SKr, incidentally, was equal to $2,160, or about £450.

The PV444, in truth, had been a long time in the gestation period. It hung around for so long that it acquired one easily remembered nickname—Jesus! Why Jesus? 'Oh, that's easy,' Olof Peterson told me, 'the PV444 was just like Jesus. Everyone had heard of it, but no one had actually seen one!' Assar Gabrielsson also got into the habit of sitting down at public meetings, parties or dinners, turning to the guest on each side of him, and saying: 'Have you ordered a PV444?' If he got the answer 'No' from both of them, he would visibly relax, smile broadly, and announce: 'Thank goodness. Now I can enjoy myself!'

In their early advertising for the car, Volvo used to describe the PV444 as 'A Swedish Beauty'. Perhaps it was no bad thing that there was no Trades Description Act in Sweden at the time, for the shape of the PV444 was certainly not likely by everyone who saw it. But demand for the car was huge and seemed to grow with every month and year which followed. Certainly, the story of Volvo cars in the late 1940s and early 1950s is also a story about numbers. The nail-biting days of the 1930s, when Volvo had struggled to build up to 1,000 cars a year, were long gone. Now it seemed to be a case of expanding Lundby and hiring more workers, in a constant and unavailing attempt to make as many PV444s as the sales department demanded.

Peace had returned to Europe in May 1945 and, in spite of shortages and actual rationing in many countries, day-to-day life was nearly back to normal by the end of the decade. Once the war was over, Volvo rapidly ran down their military vehicle building commitments, tried to sort out the sprawling inefficiencies of Lundby, with its inefficient mixture of old and new buildings, and started to look like quantity-production car makers at last. Before 1939, Volvo might have been tempted to get out of the private car business from time to time, because it often looked to be a struggle to survive; after 1945, there was never any question of this. Before the war, Volvo had been commercial vehicle builders who also made cars—from 1949, when production of PV444s at last overtook those of trucks and buses, the situation was reversed.

Even so, the PV444 was only outstanding in its reliability, for it was not dramatically fast, nor super-economical. The first English-language road test was published by *The Motor* in March 1950 when a car supplied directly from Gothenburg was found to have a top speed of 74 mph, while it provided a creditable overall fuel consumption of 33 mpg (Imperial). *The Motor* also quoted a price of 6,490 SKr for the 1950 model (less than when the true economic price was established in 1947/1948), which was the equivalent of £448. It is interesting, also, to reprint the magazine's final comments about the car: 'Avowedly designed as a small car with American characteristics, the Volvo is an extremely creditable example of how excellent orthodox modern engineering can combine the conflicting qualities of speed and fuel economy, comfort and modest manufacturing cost . . . The Volvo should continue to reflect great credit upon the Swedish engineering industry.'

When, in the course of the same trip to Sweden, *The Motor* also took the opportunity of looking round the Lundby factory, and saw the PV444s being assembled, they noted that more than 8,000 cars had been built, all in black, and that: 'The range is shortly to be extended to include cars painted in colours and with "de Luxe" body furnishing (at slight extra cost).'

The 'Volvo way' of doing things was still different enough to arouse comment, notably the fact that about 15 per cent of the PV444's content was sourced outside Sweden, and *The Motor* also picked up the fact that although the Sweden of 1950 was more prosperous than most other Western European countries, the demand for large American-style cars was falling.

This was interesting, because Volvo were already finding that their six-cylinder PV60 was becoming somewhat hard to sell and there appeared to be no export prospects for it at all. During 1950, the last of the 3,500 PV60s (complete and rolling-chassis types) was built; Volvo were not to re-enter the private car market with a six-cylinder car until the Volvo 164 arrived in 1968.

Although the PV444 was built in what looked like the same basic form from 1947 to 1958, there were thousands of changes, some major, some minor, made to the vehicle as the years evolved. Before the PV444 gave way to the similar, but much changed, PV544, it went through eight derivatives known internally by such suffixes as PV444B, PV444C, right up to PV444L. Such cars not only included more power (which would eventually go up to 60 bhp—a figure Helmer Petterson had suggested, right from the start), but enlarged 1,583 cc engines, a hypoid-bevel axle, different facia, different decoration of the car, and many other details.

All the time, production of PV444s, and the capacity to build more, was being increased. In 1951, private car production exceeded 10,000 a year for the first time, more than 25,000 cars a year were first made in 1954, and the 50,000 mark was approached by the end of 1957. This was not only because the saloon car itself was becoming more and more popular (the last series, the PV444L, built only in 1957-58, sold no fewer than 64,087 examples, which was nearly five times the total production of *all* Volvos built before the end of the 1930s), but because other derivatives had been developed as well.

Even in the 1940s, Volvo's sales force had seen that the car could be sold in other guises, such as vans, light trucks or estate cars, but to do this there would have to be major changes to the structure of the machine. Quite simply, it was not possible to provide such derivatives from the existing unit construction body/chassis unit, so the engineers, under Ing Tor Berthelius, took what might look like a technological leap back into the 1930s, by developing a separate-chassis version of the original design, which was not at all as simple to do as it sounded.

Work began in 1949, but it was not until 1950 that the first PV445 chassis was available for sale, originally to independent coachbuilders. The rear suspension of this type was different from that of the saloon, because there was no longer a logical place for the saloon-type radius arms to be pivotted; instead, the back axle was sprung and located in the classic 'Hotchkiss' style, which is to say that conventional half-elliptic leaf springs were used. The original PV445 van had a high roof and a raised bonnet line, and was bolted down to the new separate frame; later, as production rose, and the estate car came on stream, tooling was installed to weld the two items together, and the design was almost back to a 'chassisless' construction once again. The estate, called the Duett, was finally launched in 1953 and would be built until 1969.

The original specified PV444 gave way to the 444B during 1950, when there was a new facia with circular instruments, more shapely bumpers and new direction indicators mounted on pylons, which helped give the car its nickname of 'kuckoo'. The 444C of 1951 (a year, incidentally, in which the 25,000th 444 was built) not only had larger-section tyres, but colours and a 'Special' trim version, but the first obvious change to the customers came with the 444H of 1954, which had a single-pane rear window and a slightly larger windscreen.

By this time, however, really big changes were on the way. In 1954, Assar Gabrielsson had visited the United States to assess Volvo's prospects in that vast continent. Not only did he come back with the idea of building a sports car (the P1900, which I describe later in the book), but with the conviction that there was enormous potential for his company. But to sell Volvos in North America would not only need more attention to the style and equipment of the cars, but to their performance as well. It must also be pointed out, too, that Gabrielsson was not only wanting to sell 444s in North America, but he wanted to convince himself that the still-secret 120-Series Amazon would also be right for the Americans.

The upheaval duly took place in 1956. Assar Gabrielsson retired in favour of his protégé, Gunnar Engellau, the Amazon made its bow, and Volvo sales to the USA began in earnest. Gabrielsson had reached his 65th birthday and (like Gustaf Larson, who still acted as a part-time engineering consultant, though he had officially 'retired' in 1952) thought it was high time that he stepped down, though he was to remain as chairman of the board for another six years.

With the US market in mind, therefore, the engineers not only boosted the performance of every 444K to 51 bhp (the first-ever power increase for this engine type), but they also produced a sporty twin-carburettor high-compression version, dubbed the B14A, which produced 70 bhp, and endowed the car with a top speed of more than 90 mph. But this was only the start. Sales of all Volvo cars leapt to 48,940 in 1957, and it was in that year that the 444K, complete with egg-box grille, gave way to the final 444L version, complete with enlarged 1,583 cc engine, 60 or 85 bhp, and yet more detail style changes. The reward was a boost in 1958 production to 63,204, some of this due to the build up of Amazon sales—but there was also the talking point of a new-style PV544 to keep interest at its peak.

PV544, however, did not come into the world without trauma, for several other cars, modifications and style-changes had been proposed while the PV444 was still being built. Most of these cars are described in some detail in Appendix D (and much of the activity stems from the era ushered in by the arrival of the young artist, Jan Wilsgaard, in 1950), but PV454 logically takes its place here.

Wilsgaard's 'Philip' prototype and very promising PV179 two-door model had both been built, and found to need a lot of investment before they could be sold to the public, when Helmer Petterson once again got the ear of Assar Gabrielsson, told him that in his opinion the 444 ought to be face-lifted—and that he was once again the man to do the job. Gabrielsson was never averse to introducing a bit of competition to his staff, and agreed.

Petterson's solution, in 1953, was to utilise the same basic floor pan and running gear as the PV444, and not to face-lift at all, but to style a completely different two-door saloon body shell on top of these, much lower and sleeker than the original. Author Karl Ludvigsen avers that it was influenced by the Loewy-styled Studebakers of the period, with a divided-nostril front grille, front wings which flowed smoothly back into the main body, but still with separate rear wings. Although Petterson retained a divided front screen, there was a much-enlarged rear window, and a lot more side window area, with a waistline which sloped down towards the back.

Assar Gabrielsson, who had not told Gustaf Larson what he and Petterson were cooking up, liked PV454 so much that he approved it, and a start on the production of tooling at the Olofstrom factory, even before his partner first saw the car. At this point, however, *he* found out that Larson was cooking up successors to the abandoned PV179 project, and that there was a conflict of interests. The result was the PV454 was frozen out, went into a styling competition with cars like the '55' and '65' models, and lost out. It was never seen again.

When the PV544 appeared in 1958—effectively a thoroughly overhauled and partially updated PV444—it astonished almost every pundit in the motoring business. The PV444 had been around for 14 years, nearly 200,000 of the same two-door saloon style had been built, and it had really been rendered out of date by the smooth new Wilsgaard-styled Amazon of 1956. The Amazon, however, was a much more luxurious, larger and more expensive car to make than the PV444 type, and Gunnar Engellau was convinced that Volvo could go on selling tens of thousands of each, without harming profitability or overall prospects.

Engellau therefore ordered a revision of PV444, although he wanted the minimum change to the body sheet metal, which would have cost a great deal of money to revise. Styling changes, therefore, were confined to the use of a one-piece windscreen, slightly curved, a larger rear window, yet another new facia with Amazon-style strip speedometer and revised seats, with a new-type mesh grille as the most obvious feature from the front. There was also the option, for the first time in this body, of a four-speed gearbox, which had just been made available on Amazons. However, it was not until the autumn of 1960 that the van/estate car types were brought into line with these changes (the estate car was P210). The 1.6-litre engine, of course, was standardised (it was called B16) with the same engine tunes as offered for North America on previous PV444 models.

Thus equipped and launched, the PV544 gave the original 1944-type body a new lease of life, and sales rushed ahead; nearly 100,000 of the original PV544A model were built in just two years, and Gunnar Engellau's decision that Volvo should have two product lines had already been proved justified. The 50,000th PV444/544 car for the United States left Gothenburg during January 1960 and, by this time, 20 per cent of all Volvo production was going to that market. It was also in 1960 that the European Free Trade Area (EFTA) was set up, as a counter to the original Common Market of six countries, by which time the selling operation in Britain had also begun.

There were no Volvo sales in the UK until 1958/59, mainly because the PV444/PV544 models were never made in right-hand-drive form (it was possible, but Volvo management never thought it to be justified), but essentially because the combination of booming sales at home and elsewhere, and tariff barriers across the North Sea, all made things rather difficult. The factory actually took stand space at Earls Court Motor Show in 1956 to exhibit their four-door Amazon saloon, but went no further as the Suez crisis then erupted, and petrol rationing was inflicted on the British for the next six months. They did not come over in 1957, but in 1958 they were back again, this time with more confidence, and this time quoting prices.

It was Charles Singer, a director of a garage in the Lex group, who had contacted Volvo during the year, tested their cars, and signed a contract to take 100 cars from them in the next 12 months. History now tells us that Lex sold 250 cars in that period and that they have never looked back. The British market is now nearly as important to Volvo as is the Swedish market, and only surpassed by that of the USA.

The PV544, however, was never officially imported to the UK, which was a pity in many ways, as the later models were very sporty indeed. The major up-rating of the PV544 came in the autumn of 1961 when the PV544C cars came on stream, one of which was called the PV544 Sport. The most important improvement was the standardisation of the enlarged B18 1,778 cc engine (it was also fitted to the Amazons and the P1800 sports coupés by this date), but there was also a 12-volt electrical system for the first time.

The three new versions were the 'Favorit', with a 75 bhp engine and three-speed gearbox, the 'Special' (75 bhp/four speeds) and the very impressive 'Sport', which had a twin-carburettor 90 bhp engine, allied to the four-speed gearbox. It was the sports saloon which the rally drivers like Gunnar Andersson and Tom Trana had been waiting for, and it gave US drivers a lot more speed with which to tackle their own domestic monoliths on turnpikes and freeways.

As far as the average showroom visitor was concerned, however, this was really the last change made to the PV544 design, even though the factory nomenclature progressed to PV544G in 1965. Although Amazon production and assembly was progressively transferred from Lundby to the brand-new Torslanda plant, a few kilometres further out of the centre of Gothenburg, by 1964 the PV544 was left to complete its long and distinguished sales career at the old Lundby factory.

Although the public were never able to see this, the factory stylists, led by Jan Wilsgaard, made one further attempt to change the 1944 shape. In 1959 and 1960, soon after the PV544 went on sale, they produced one example of a car—dubbed PV644—which was quite distinctively changed, but still retained many standard panels. At the front, there was a prominent type of vertical grille—one they had already tried on the massive P358 (see Appendix D) and one which would appear again on the six-cylinder 164 of 1968—but otherwise the familiar bonnet and front wing contours were left untouched. So, too, was the windscreen and the doors, but at the rear the tail was extended and squared off, the rear window made a little more vertical, and longer rear quarter windows were neatly incorporated in sweeping sail panels, joining the modified roof to the longer tail.

PV644 was interesting and, from certain angles, it looked good, but in the end it was turned down by management. The existing two-door PV544 (there never was a four-door version) therefore ran on until 1965, and the increasingly old-fashioned-looking P210 station wagon was not phased out until 1969. The last PV544 of all rolled off the old Lundby production line on October 20 1965, just over 21 years after the original car of its type had been shown in Stockholm, and the career of the car (which had projected Volvo from their staid image of 1930s into their worldwide frame of the 1950s) was over. Nearly 244,000 PV544s were built in seven years (1958 to 1965)—a production rate far in excess of that achieved by the original PV444s—and exactly 440,000 of all types of the two-door saloons were built between 1947 and 1965. The grand total of all derivatives, including PV445/P210 estates, was 526,509 vehicles, a wonderful achievement by any standard.

But all such statistics and records are just made to be broken, as far as Volvo are concerned. Even while the PV544 was at the height of its popularity, another car was working on that. In 1950, Jan Wilsgaard had joined the company and, in 1953/54, his 'Amazon' style was approved for production. The real Volvo world-beater was on its way.

Chapter 4

The mighty Amazon

Perhaps it was divine providence which made sure that Volvo would eventually build the Amazon. If Volvo had not decided to build up a proper styling department in 1950, they might never have visited one particular art college in Gothenburg. If Jan Wilsgaard had not taken a very big gamble and abandoned sculpture, he would not have been tempted to go into the motor industry. Without Jan Wilsgaard, for sure, the next Volvo new model would not have looked the way it did. And without the Amazon, Volvo's future might have been very different.

'In the spring of 1950,' Wilsgaard told me, 'my teacher told me that Volvo were looking for a designer, and that he was thinking of me. I was only 20 years old, and still had one year to go at the school. The head thought I should go—so in June 1950 I started work at Volvo. There was really no styling house at Lundby, then. There was only one other designer, who had been there a few months. He was designing interiors and I designed exteriors.'

The working environment was less than ideal. Wilsgaard, though still a novice, was convinced that he should be working in clay, not in wood, as the PV444 had originally been shaped. But where to buy the clay—tons of it? 'We got that clay from a Swedish company that was making it for children,' Wilsgaard recalls. It was too stiff to be worked ideally and since Wilsgaard was his own model man at first, it meant that he spent a lot of time with dirty hands and a pain in his back. Thirty years on, he hasn't changed completely—if you were to call at the smooth new styling studios in the Torslanda complex today, the chances are that the styling director will have to wash the modelling clay, or the sketching charcoal, off his hands before he can shake hands and settle down to a meeting.

Nor did Volvo provide him with a spacious studio. At first there was only one room and, as Wilsgaard says: 'It was very small—we had just one extra metre of space around the car.' It was years before a proper studio—and, equally as important, an outside viewing area—was made available.

Wilsgaard's first effort, with no strings attached, was the 'Philip' of 1950, his second was the PV179 of 1952 and his third was the '55' of 1953, all of which are described in great detail in Appendix D, but it was not until later in 1953 that he started work on the car which would eventually be called 'Amazon'.

However, the roots of the 'Amazon'—which has always been known, more prosaically, as the 120-Series in all countries outside Scandinavia—lie in the PV444 for some of the running gear, and in the P179, where certain new suspension components were first tried. The style, however, was completely new.

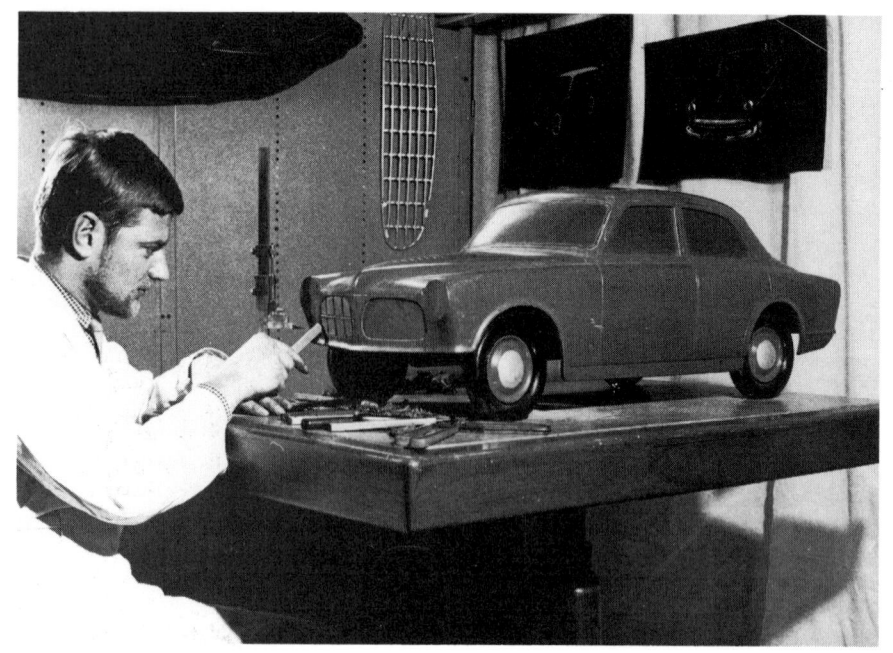

Shaping the Amazon at Volvo—though I have an idea this was a publicity picture, posed well after the style was approved.

As my study of the prototypes makes clear, Wilsgaard's original effort with 'Philip' was clearly a derivative of the 1950/51 Kaiser, and it was not only spiritually intended to take over from the PV60, just being killed off, but it had a 3.6-litre V-8 engine as well. PV179, however, was much more pure, though Assar Gabrielsson was eventually persuaded that it was too large and too heavy for the PV444 engine to be used.

A great deal of creation, however, took place in 1953. Not only did Helmer Petterson persuade Gabrielsson to let him produce the PV454 fastback, and not only did the Swedish businessman Gosta Wennberg have Vignale design him a two-door coupé on the basis of the PV445 separate-chassis structure, but Gustaf Larson had sent both Wilsgaard and his companion stylist, Rustan Lange, off to the body tool-makers at Olofstrom to work separately on PV444 successors; his instructions were that they should each produce ideas for him to view—Wilsgaard's car being coded '55', and Lange's '65'. Larson, as already mentioned in a previous chapter, had not even told Assar Gabrielsson what was going on, just as Gabrielsson had not revealed the existence of Petterson's PV454 project to his old friend.

Once this muddle was exposed, it had to be resolved, and quickly. The founders therefore decided that all three projects—PV454, '55' and '65'—should be brought together for viewing, and that management would then decide what to do. The problem was that opinion at this viewing was sharply divided—some liked PV454, and some liked Wilsgaard's '55', but few wanted to see any refinement of the American-style '65'.

The board's decision was typical of the way so many of these meetings go, all

The mighty Amazon

By the end of the 1950s, the original Lundby factory was bursting at the seams. In this aerial shot, the old SKF building can be seen in the centre.

round the world. Jan Wilsgaard was given a very restricting specification for the new car—he had to work from the basic elements of PV454, and add features from his own '55' style. It was the type of assignment which makes seasoned designers wake up in the night and worry . . . ..

Wilsgaard, however, still only 23 years old, and without a great deal of industrial experience behind him, buckled down: 'But while I carried out my instructions,' he says, 'I also started work on another car, which became the Amazon. I could only work on it in my free time, early mornings, lunchtime, evenings and weekends. I was *very* tired for a long time, but I wasn't yet married, so there was no home life to dislocate.'

'A few days before the show was due, Anders Rydell, who was technical director by this time, saw the Amazon, liked it very much, and decided to put it up along with the other car . . . .'

What happened was pure theatre—and quite vital to Volvo's future. 'When the day for the show came, Gabrielsson, Rydell and myself were all present, but not Mr Larson, because he had really retired by then. Gabrielsson concentrated on the model built to his specifications—he was Boss, and a Demi-God, you know—but after half-an-hour there came a knock on the door, and who should come in but Gustaf Larson. I could see the reaction in Gabrielsson's eyes, which said something like, "What the hell are you doing here?". Anyway, Mr Larson marched straight up to the Amazon clay model, and said: "*This* is the car for us!". That, at least, swung Mr Gabrielsson to look carefully at the Amazon model.'

It was at this point that Gabrielsson, the stolid businessman, revealed some of his own character and his taste in cars: 'Yes, it's good-looking,' he said. 'In fact it looks like a pin-up girl. It's too good-looking. It should be ugly!' But he could not decide, so the sales director was sent for, and asked his opinion of the two cars. When he, too, chose the Amazon style—the 'unofficial' project—Gabrielsson looked quite angry for a time.

There was no decision taken at that meeting, but a few days later Gabrielsson made up his mind and gave in gracefully to the majority opinion. Instead of the PV444 being replaced by a new car, it was to continue as a two-door saloon. The new Amazon, which had actually been styled as a two-door saloon, was to become a four-door car, and the two models were to be built in harness at Lundby. Both cars would be built on the same wheelbase of 260 cm (102.4 in), but their chassis details, and of course their body shells, were entirely different.

At this point, in 1953, the style still did not have a name, and I have called it 'Amazon' merely to establish familiarity. It became Amazon in time for its launch in 1956—no one now remembers who invented it, but almost everyone agrees that it was sound and memorable. The Amazons, of course, according to Greek mythology, were a race of warrior women from the Caucasus. We will skim over the legend that they were supposed to cut off their left breasts so that they could use bows and arrows more efficiently, and merely note that they were strong, brave, and often of striking appearance.

Jan Wilsgaard's new car was certainly all of that. He wanted the style to have life, like a face, to have some bulk behind it, almost to look as if there were rippling muscles just under the skin. In truth, it was not at all difficult to improve on the PV444; nevertheless the distinctive shapes he sculpted for the 'Amazon' were his own, his very own, without influence, or dilution, from anyone else.

The chassis and running gear of the new car had already been designed before the new four-door body shell had, having originally found a home under Wilsgaard's PV179 prototype of 1952, the car which Assar Gabrielsson and his artistic consultant, Mas-Olle, had liked so much, but which the *eminence grise*, Helmer

As Jan Wilsgaard, Volvo's noted stylist, told me, the Amazon was shaped as a piece of sculpture, to look as if it had a body with muscles underneath. Judge for yourselves.

The mighty Amazon

The rear view of the original P120/Amazon of 1956.

Petterson, had not. Sound commercial common sense had dictated the use of the PV444's engine, gearbox and basic back axle, but the layout of the suspension was quite different.

At the front there was conventional coil spring and double wishbone independent suspension with ball joints, allied to cam and roller steering. At the rear, however, the location of the back axle was different. Instead of having radius arms angled in towards the centre of the car, PV444 style, the Amazon had a new twin radius arm location at each side, the arms running nearly parallel to the propeller shaft line. As with the PV444, there was also a Panhard rod for sideways location of the axle but the coil springs, instead of being placed behind the axle, were actually on top of it.

It was, of course, a larger and heavier car than the PV444, so it would certainly require a more lusty engine even to match that car's performance. The PV444, as currently built, was 14 ft 9 in long, 5 ft 2 in wide and weighed 2,130 lb, featuring a front suspension track of 4 ft 3 in; the Amazon would be 4 in shorter but with much more interior space, 5 ft 4 in wide and showed all the signs of weighing up to 2,350 lb.

To deal with this, Volvo's engineers enlarged the rugged overhead-valve four-cylinder engine. By boring it out from 75 mm to 79.4 mm, the swept volume was increased from 1,414 to 1,583 cc, and the engine changed from the original B14 to the B16 unit. There were to be two versions—the 60 bhp B16A unit, with a single carburettor, and the much more sporty and powerful 85 bhp B16B, for which two British SU carburettors were specified. At first, at least, the 85 bhp engine would only be fitted to 'Export' Volvos with a particular emphasis on the North American market.

Much of the new design was modern, if not exactly trend-setting, so it came as a surprise to some that the three-speed gearbox of the old PV444 was retained, a fitting which rather took the edge off the performance possibilities of the 85 bhp model.

The body shell, apart from being sleek and attractive, was also immensely strong—so strong, in fact, that many of these cars are still in use, a quarter century after they first went on the road. The techniques of designing unit construction body/chassis units had advanced a lot since the PV444 had been laid out ten years earlier, and this meant that the torsional rigidity was almost excessively high—11,000 lb/ft per degree compared with the excellent 7,000 lb/ft per degree already achieved in the PV444—and this was with a four-door shell inherently less strong because of the big holes in the sides!

This was just one of the features which set up the Amazon as a very safe car and there is no doubt that it was this car which set Volvo on the road toward world supremacy in the building of 'safety' cars. Among the fittings were a collapsible steering column, a recessed hub steering wheel, padded sun visors and a padded facia crash roll.

By the time the Amazon was ready to meet its public, in August 1956, a lot had been done at the Lundby factory to prepare for it. The PV444, as already mentioned, was going from strength to strength, and the first exports had already been made to the United States. The company had initiated, and confirmed in spite of complex legal action in Sweden, a far reaching warranty, and in 1953 a large assembly hall had been completed for the trucks and buses to fill. This marked the end of the expansion possibilities at Lundby, which meant that Volvo could not contemplate making a new sports coupé themselves (this explains why the P1800 was originally assembled in England) and that they would soon be looking round for new premises altogether. Sales were still expanding well and production was continuously being pushed up to match.

Only one thing had been forgotten. When the name 'Amazon' had been chosen, the question of trade marks had not been settled conclusively—it was, after all, the first time that any Volvo had had a name, rather than a number. I can do no better than quote from another writer's view of what happened next: 'A German motor cycle and moped manufacturer called Kreidler claimed that the name [Amazon] was his, and had been patented by him, and solicitors' letters and threats of law suits flew back and forth between Germany and Sweden.'

The outcome of this crisis was that Volvo could only call their car 'Amazon' in Scandinavia, but had to find new titles for the car in the rest of the world. Because of this, they instigated the very first of their self-explanatory model-coding series of titles—self-explanatory, that is, if you know how the logical Swedish mind is working.

Right from the start, the new car had been coded P120, as a secret Volvo project, and it was already known as the 120 Series by many employees. To name it for the world, therefore, Volvo called the basic single-carburettor car a 121 (the final '1' referring to the carburettor), while the 85 bhp version became the 122S (the last '2' being twin carburettors and the S standing, I guess, for sporting).

'This was all very well at first, but when Volvo finally produced a two-door version of the car, and then an estate car, they had to think again. (The numbering system was not always logically carried out for the Amazon-type car, and when the time came to supplant them by new models, a great deal more thought was given in advance!)

The new car, whatever its name or title, was undeniably very handsome. Even so,

The mighty Amazon

Jan Wilsgaard's original idea for the Amazon was that it should have a two-door body style, like this 1961 example. Officially, two-door Amazons were P130 Series cars—Volvo were well into their 'identification by numbers' era.

Assar Gabrielsson, I'm sure, was quite wrong to call it a 'pin-up girl', because it was not at all voluptuous or—in the more recent idiom—'sexy'. It was smart and quite unmistakable, for Jan Wilsgaard had not copied features from any other car in the shaping of it.

In profile, the Amazon was the smoothest car which Wilsgaard had yet designed, for it had a wing crown line which elegantly connected the headlamps to the taillamps, a really large and useful boot and a wrap-around rear window which did not look as if it was a fashion (which, indeed, it was not) but a genuine aid to better visibility. There was a boldly-stated double-nostril front grille, with the name 'VOLVO' proudly picked out in individual lettering on the nose of the bonnet above it. Helped along by its wider-section 15 in wheels and tyres, the Amazon looked altogether more squat and purposeful than any previous Volvo had been.

With the introduction of the new car which, henceforth, I should really call by its world-wide name, the 120 Series, and with the arrival of the new chief executive, Gunnar Engellau, it was almost as if Volvo had slipped into a higher gear and was becoming more assertive. Before the new car arrived, Volvo had a traditional reputation, with long-established management, and a way of offering sober, even anonymous-looking, cars which were not likely to excite anyone.

The style of Gunnar Engellau's management and the character of the new car changed all that. No one troubled to spell it out loud (and such antics would have been quite alien to Volvo at the time), but the definite impression offered around for the world to see was that Volvo was *here*, Volvo was suddenly *modern* and Volvo was on its way to *greater things*.

In spite of the fact that the new car was launched prematurely—before the cars were actually in production—and in spite of the fact that the first deliveries were made early in 1957, when the fuel shortages caused by the first Suez War were at their height, the Volvo company never missed its step. Indeed, in the next ten years, with the 120 Series as the most important model in their range, Volvo private car production increased every year except one, and even that dip (of 5,800 cars, from

Plenty of space under the bonnet of the Amazon, here seen in its simple single-carburettor form.

1960 to 1961) was directly attributable to a short-lived recession which afflicted North America and Western Europe.

There are many ways of describing Engellau, almost all of which emphasise his forceful character and his salesman's zeal, but I must really start by quoting one Volvo pensioner, who told me: 'Engellau certainly came as something of a shock to most of us—especially to the telephonists! But he certainly jolted Volvo and moved the company into more modern times.' Before he became Volvo's boss, Gunnar Engellau is credited with having gone over to the United States, on Assar Gabrielsson's behalf, and recommended a really strong sales push; as soon as he took control, he was quite clearly determined to take Volvo into every available, and viable, world market.

Not only was Volvo taking much more of an interest in the outside world, but the motoring world (particularly the press) were beginning to take much more interest in Volvo. Early in 1958, for instance, that flamboyant character Laurence Pomeroy, technical editor of Britain's *The Motor* magazine, made a visit to Sweden, not only to look at the country itself, but mainly at the Volvo company. Apart from the fact that Pomeroy misquoted the boss' name as Walter Engellau, he had many interesting things to say about Sweden and its most important car manufacturing company.

Pomeroy started by making the point that Sweden is perhaps three times as large as England, but that at the time there were 60 per cent more cars per head of population in Sweden, and that the standard of living was the highest in Europe. An even more accurate pointer to the type of cars Volvo had to build, to keep their domestic market happy, was this comment he made when he reported on the trip in May 1958: 'With one car for every nine persons, over half the passenger miles covered in Sweden are made on private cars over roads of which only 10 per cent have a hard surface and in the extremely rigorous climate experienced every winter'. The fact that he had arrived in a Sweden gripped by snow, with a temperature of 30 degrees of frost, must have made Volvo's task even more obvious.

By 1958, of course, Volvo's long-life reputation had already been established, for

This is typical of Volvo as many of us know it—with one of the long-running Amazons being pushed along snow-bound tracks in Scandinavia.

Pomeroy commented that: 'Sales are sustained by the fine reputation of the car; it is claimed, for example, that it is normal for a car to go for ten years without being repainted despite the fact that most of them are left out night and day, with snow and very low temperatures in the winter and dust and abnormally high temperatures in the summer. The makers also offer a unique "guarantee" in which each PV444 model sold in Sweden is freely insured in perpetuity against damage resulting either from mechanical failure or accident.' In an interview, Gunnar Engellau let slip that the PV444 'would go on for some years', while he also said that it had cost £2 million to invest in new body dies for the 120 Series.

There was also the question of Volvo's early and growing success in selling to North America. Engellau quoted his agents' satisfaction with the low depreciation of the cars and that they thought some credit was due to 'the absence of styling changes, as in the case of the VW'. Now that really *was* important—Volvo were already convincing the public that long runs could work to their advantage, as well as to the company. It was an impression which intensified as the years passed by and Volvo's policy in this respect has never wavered.

However, even though the Amazon/120 Series saloon was very well received by all who saw it, there was a long delay in getting it into true volume production. Less than 5,000 of these cars were built in 1957, which meant that the ageing PV444 outnumbered it by a factor of nearly nine to one at this stage. One reason was certainly that Volvo were cautiously feeling their way in the build-up of an entirely new body/chassis unit (only the second, of course, which they had ever done since the end of the Second World War), but it was also true that there was a certain amount of consumer resistance to the three-speed gearbox.

Early in 1958, however, Volvo introduced the first changes—to a car which had only been on sale for a year. Not only was a four-speed gearbox offered as an option to the original three-speeder, but the bonnet release was now located inside the car, and the rear suspension was lowered by about an inch to improve the car's 'stance' on the road.

Thus equipped, the 85 bhp 'Export' model was very spritely indeed, and one Swedish journalist was moved to call the car: 'a wolf in sheep's clothing'—hardly original, but to the point. When Britain's *The Autocar* magazine borrowed a Dutch-registered car for tests in the spring, they were surprised and pleased to note a maximum speed of 94 mph and overall fuel consumption of 26 mpg (Imperial). The price in Sweden, it was noted, was 12,600 SKr, equivalent to £868, or $2,430 in American currency. Their summary, so typical of so many who tried the car in its definitive 1958 form was: '. . . if one were to put into competition all the comfortable family four-seater cars of up to 1,600 cc engine size, the Amazon would quickly take itself a clear stride ahead. To that comment no addition or qualification is required.'

Once the good word had gone around, demand for new 120 Series cars began to rise, and rise again. Since 1958 was also the year in which the PV444 was displaced by the slightly restyled, and considerably more refined, PV544 model, it was soon clear that Volvo had a problem—and one of the most pleasant kind. They were rapidly running out of space at Lundby. Even though the building layout had been modified several times since the war, and even though truck and bus chassis production had been moved out, the end of the expansion process was now in sight. In 1951 Volvo had planned to expand to 50,000 cars a year by 1955, and then decided to upgrade that to 80/90,000 by 1957—now there was no scope for more.

Even though Volvo car production was already somewhat fragmented (engines from one factory, bodies from another, axles, wheels, brakes and many other details from England, not to mention steel from Sweden and from other European countries), Gunnar Engellau and his directors decided to look round for another site. This would be brand new—a 'green-field' site to start with—would have to be much larger than anything contemplated by Volvo in the past, and was to concentrate on the assembly of private cars.

In 1958, several locations were considered, but soon the planners began to favour

The mighty Amazon 63

an undeveloped area in a region called Hisingen, just a few kilometres further from the centre of Gothenburg, towards the open sea. Some archivists insist on calling Hisingen an island, but this was only geographically true because on one side it was bounded by the sea, and on the other sides by branches of the same river. To all intents and purposes, the area, soon renamed Torslanda by Volvo, was on the mainland, and it was ideal for its purpose. Not only was it close to the sea, and the docks which were becoming more and more important to Volvo's expanding shipping and exports, but (according to a Volvo old-timer): 'it was also a cheap site, and it was nice and flat!' By 1959, the deal was done and building work started. In the long term, the plan was that the old (original) Lundby factory would be given over entirely to the production of Volvo's commercial and related vehicles, while Torslanda would build private cars.

But not, for the moment, *all* its private cars. Even as the Torslanda site was being purchased, Volvo were heavily involved in the development of the new P1800 sports coupé, and there was absolutely no way that this car, and its near-unique body shell, could be made in Sweden for the next few years. This juxtaposition of events and dates explains why the first batch of P1800s were assembled in England, but it is such a long and complicated story that it deserves a chapter on its own.

While the Torslanda factory was being planned and built, Volvo were busily laying the foundations for more, faster, better and plushier derivatives of the 120 Series models. In the next few years, not only would there be larger and more powerful engines, different transmission options, and the adoption of disc brakes, but the two-door saloon body shell always planned for by Jan Wilsgaard would be put on stream, and the long-forecast big estate car would also make its appearance.

1959 was a somewhat momentous year for the company, not only because of the start at Torslanda, but because the 500,000th Volvo was actually built (on November 17) and the 120 Series cars were finally introduced to the United States; this introduction had been delayed for a couple of seasons after the car's birth, at

Left *Most of the time, Volvo played down the 'Amazon' link with that fearsome race of Asian ladies—but sometimes it was irresistible....*

Right *Gunnar Engellau, who became Volvo's president when Assar Gabrielsson retired. He was the architect of Volvo's huge expansion in the 1960s.*

The 220 Series station wagons, so clearly and closely developed from the P120/Amazon design, sold in large numbers in the 1960s and established Volvo's 'large-estate-car' traditions.

Engellau's behest. He wanted to see the car right before he committed it to such a large and prestigious market; history now shows us that he was right, even though there were dealers all over the 49 states champing at the bit and anxious to get their hands on the modern-looking car.

The truly major developments in the 120 Series models in the next few years were, of course, to the engine, and to the available body styles. It is worth mentioning at this point that the B8B V-8 engine (of 2.5-litres) developed for the 'Philip' prototype of the early 1950s, had been tried in Amazon/120 Series test cars, but had not been committed to production. Accordingly, when more power was needed, not only for the saloons, but for the forthcoming P1800 sports coupé, the B18 four-cylinder unit was developed.

The B18 was not simply an enlarged B16 unit, though it had much in common with it, including the same 80 mm stroke and the same type of overhead valve gear, plus a cylinder bore increased from 79.4 to 84.1 mm. The major difference was that the B18 had a more robust cylinder block and crankcase, not only with a full five-bearing crankshaft for the first time on a four-cylinder Volvo, but with scope for further enlargement of 2 litres in future years. Erling Kurt, the Danish engineer who had much to do with the B18's development, once commented that it had always specifically been designed as a 2-litre unit, then had started its life as a 1.8-litre unit.

Over the years, therefore, this meant that the 120 Series' performance could be pushed up quite noticeably. From the 60 bhp and 85 bhp units originally on offer, the B18 provided 75 bhp and 90 bhp from the autumn of 1961 (by which time the engine had already been put into the P1800 coupés with a rating of 100 bhp). Four-door saloons never advanced on this, but the two-door cars, which took on a somewhat more sporty and specialised image after the PV544 disappeared, were given a choice of 85 bhp, 100 bhp or full-house 115 bhp for 1967, and when the engine was at last enlarged to its always-intended 2-litre capacity in time for the 1969 season, the most powerful derivative of the car had 118 bhp, and a top speed of well over 100 mph.

As I pointed out earlier, when discussing how the shape of the 120 Series came to be settled, Jan Wilsgaard had always planned it as a two-door saloon from the very beginning. It was the *four*-saloon, however, which held court at Volvo until 1961, when it was finally joined by the two-door car. Engineering differences were slight, and even in side view one had to look closely to see the differences, so neatly had the conversion from one type to the other been achieved. Front seats folded forward of course, but in all other aspects the space and comfort of the interior was the same as before.

The estate car variant which followed (it was announced in February 1962) was a much more significant machine, and it set all sorts of standards for Volvo's own future. Previous Volvo station wagons, on the PV445 base, had been rather staid, rather upright, and clearly van-derived models, lacking in creature comforts, and more 'commercial' than 'private'. The new big estate car—the 220 Series—was closely based on the body chassis of the four-door 120 saloon, not only looking good, but having a cavernous loading space into the bargain. Its wheelbase was the same as that of the saloon, and it took up the same amount of room on the roads; Wilsgaard's styling department had kept many major panels unchanged, even including the rear door skins and the rear wing outers, but there were new square-rear door frames, and a simple extended cabin, with a two piece (upper and lower) tailgate. Britain's *Autocar* called it 'chunky and practical', and pointed out that there was a 6 ft long loading space when the rear seats were folded down. Their test of a 1962 model, complete with 1.8-litre B18 engine, proved that the body style, even though not wind-tunnel developed, must have been smooth and aerodynamic, for even the massive estate car style allowed an 88 mph top speed when fitted with the single carburettor 75 bhp engine.

By the early 1960s, Volvo were not only selling two different types of car—the PV544 and the 120 Series families—but several derivatives of each, and the final assembly lines at Lundby were taking on a many-varied aspect, not only in colours but in shapes as well. There were two-door PV544s and two-door 121s, four-door 120 Series cars, two-door P210 (old-type) station wagons, and 220 Series four-door estates of the new type. There were single-carb and twin-carb engines, and many other detail differences.

The new Torslanda factory, it was hoped, was going to sort out this propinquity and make further ordered expansion possible. (I will not call it confusion, for it was not that.) In 1962 Volvo built 94,570 cars, and in 1963 they pushed that up to 106,775—the first time the six-figure yearly total had ever been achieved. In 1962 the press were shown round Torslanda for the first time, though it was still not complete, and in 1963 final assembly of the 120 Series began there, though some processes were still carried out at Lundby, and components were still flooding in from all over Europe, being trucked hither and thither in Sweden by trains and huge Volvo lorries. However, the move away from Lundby of the big saloons, allowed P1800 coupé assembly to be moved back *to* Lundby from England, in circumstances explained in the next chapter.

Even though the Torslanda factory was still not quite complete (the body pressings division would not open up until 1966), every main assembly process was complete by April 1964, and the building was ceremonially declared open by King Gustaf Adolf on the 24th of the month. Unhappily, Assar Gabrielsson was not there to see this proud day, although his long-time colleague Gustaf Larson was. Gabrielsson had been stricken by cancer, and died in 1962, when only 70 years of age; he had remained as chairman of Volvo until the beginning of that year, forthright and businesslike to the last.

Even though Gustaf Larson was already 77 when the King of Sweden opened Torslanda, he was proudly able to make a tour of the new plant with the King, seated in the front passenger seat of the historic open Volvo OV4 of 1927, which is now preserved for all time in the company's collection of past models. He was to live until 1968, and 81 years of age, finally fading away just as the next major phase of Volvo's new-car programme was revealed.

In the meantime, much had been done, not only technically, but to make recognition of the cars somewhat easier. By the time the PV544 was about to disappear, in 1965, Volvo had resorted to badging their Amazon/120 Series cars on the front wings to make more logic of a complex situation. Each car was given a three number title, the first number referring to the body type, the second to the number of passenger doors and the third to the number of carburettors. A single-carb four-door saloon was a 121, whereas the twin-carburettor equivalent was a 122; two-door versions were 131s and 132s, respectively, while the single-carb estate car was a 221.

All this, however, was thrown up into the air and found to be unsatisfactory, when the most powerful two-door 'GT' saloon was made available, effectively to replace the PV544 Sport. Logic suggested that it should have been called a 132GT—but it actually appeared, and persisted, as a 123GT. Things got better—they *had* to get better—when the 140 Series cars arrived in the same year.

Even though the 120 Series cars seemed to change very little, visually, during the 1960s (for there were no external 'sheet-metal' styling modifications of any type before the car was dropped), Volvo always seemed to have something new to offer when model-year change-over time came round; 'new' Volvos were habitually revealed in the autumn, so that the all-important North American market could be stocked up ready for New Year sales to begin.

During 1960, new all-synchromesh three-speed (M30) and four-speed (M40) gearboxes were introduced, while the British Laycock overdrive was made available behind the three-speed box; later on, of course, it would also be mated to the four-speed box, and become a very popular Volvo extra.

In 1963, however, came the big improvement which made USA customers, in particular, very happy. As a further option, at first only on four-door saloons, Volvo offered fully-automatic transmission, the box being built by Borg Warner in Great Britain. This increased Britain's involvement in Volvo even more—both Sweden and Britain were still outside the European Common Market, but the burgeoning two-way 'Volvo' trade (components to Sweden, complete cars coming back to Britain) helped the motor industry forget about the tariff barriers stopping their products from getting into Western Europe.

It was in the areas of safety and comfort, however, that Volvo made so many advances with the 120 Series cars. There were always headlines to be generated, even if it was not always clear that new sales were also being gained. First of all, in 1959, there was the introduction of three-point safety belts in the PV544 and 120 Series cars for all markets—a world-wide innovation, although some US firms had dabbled unsuccessfully with lap belts a few years earlier.

It was for 1962, however, that Volvo not only introduced the two-door body shell, the B18 1.8-litre engine, a four-speed gearbox as standard (with optional overdrive)

The mighty Amazon

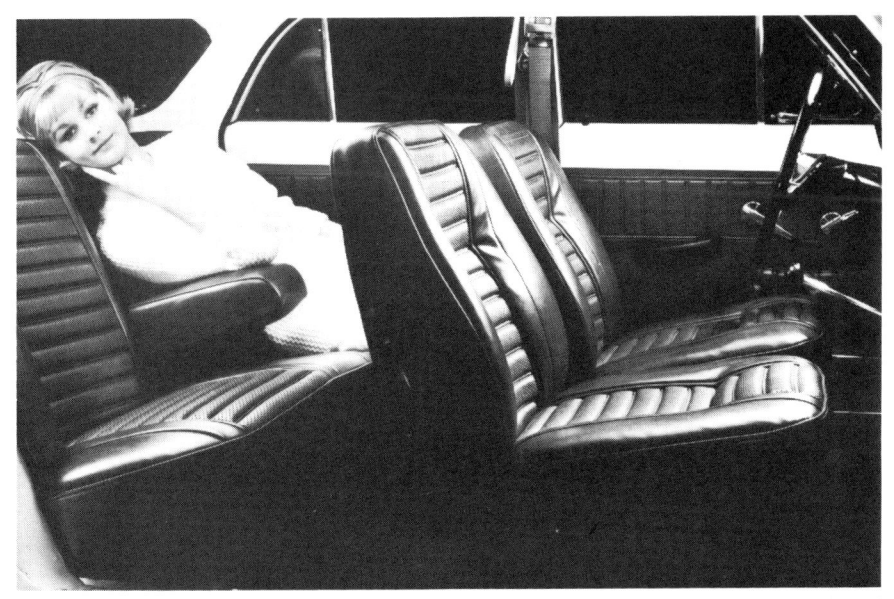

Above By the mid-1960s, the Amazon's interior had got positively plush, with well-contoured seating.

Below The side view of the station wagon version of the basic Amazon design shows how easily the lines of the saloon car were adapted, and the size of the loading box.

and a 12-volt electrical system, but they also fitted Girling disc brakes—another contract going to Great Britain for this job.

For 1965 there were the new-fangled and ultimately famous 'medically-idealised' seats, which incorporated an adjustable lumbar support, while for 1967 the 'safety-first' attitude was taken a stage further by the introduction of a two-part steering column, designed to collapse in a head-on crash, and therefore not to injure the driver.

Nor was this all. Even after the 120 Series had received its eventual 'notice to quit' by the arrival of the smoother, more squared-up 140 Series cars of 1966, there were more improvements to be introduced. In 1968, when the B20 2-litre engine was made available, Volvo began fitting steering column locks to their 120s, along with the much-acclaimed twin-circuit, triangle-split hydraulic braking system. The last significant changes of all, made in 1969, were to phase in front seat headrests (more on safety grounds than to make the car look good) and to begin fitting safety belts for rear seat passengers as well.

At its peak, in 1965 and 1966, more than 2,000 of the 120 Series cars—saloons and estates—were flooding out of Volvo's car factories every week, but it would have been quite impossible for Torslanda to achieve such figures on its own. All over Sweden, smaller 'satellite' factories were building Volvo parts but, more important still, new Volvo assembly factories were also springing up in other countries.

The first of these was opened in Canada—at Halifax, Nova Scotia—in 1963. Like everything ever done by Volvo, this new venture was carefully planned. It was in North America because that was where Gunnar Engellau saw scope for expansion in the next few years, and it was at Halifax because that was the nearest feasible port to Gothenburg. You couldn't get nearer to Sweden, and still be in the North American continent, without setting up shop on Newfoundland island!

However, if the Halifax plant was important, that opened up at Ghent, in Belgium, in 1965, was vital. Here, for the first time, Volvo were able to manufacture cars (partly from local components, partly from items shipped in from Sweden or Great Britain) on the mainland of Western Europe and—more significantly still—inside the barriers of the Common Market.

Neither overseas assembly factory, at first, was large, nor likely to dominate the Swedes themselves. Assembly, almost entirely from kits, at Halifax, was but a few thousand cars a year, all for the US and Canadian markets, while Ghent's planned capacity was 14,000 cars a year at first. But both ventures have been successful—in 1981, the last year for which I have complete figures, the Canadian factory built 10,400 cars, and the Ghent plant no fewer than 40,600. This compared with a total of 151,400 Volvos actually assembled in Sweden, and was nearly 34 per cent of that achievement. Other smaller assembly plants, notably in Malaysia, were to follow in future years.

Once the new-style 140 Series cars, analysed in Chapter 7, came on to the market in 1966, the 120 Series range slowly but inexorably began to run down. Logically enough, the 144 four-door displaced the four-door 121s and 122s almost straight away, but neither the two-door 142s nor the roomy and so attractive 145 estate cars could kill off the demand for two-door 120 Series saloons and the practical and versatile 220 Series estate cars though the last of the estate cars was built in 1969. Nor was it merely a matter of letting these cars die slowly away at an uneconomic

The mighty Amazon 69

rate—after the 140 Series was announced, nearly 150,000 more two-door 120s and 29,000 estates took to the roads.

By 1970, it was nearly all over, and the last 120 Series cars to be built were two-door saloons, some with 90 bhp and some (the 123GTs) with 118 bhp 2-litre engines. When the last of those cars dropped off the Torslanda assembly lines on July 3 1970 (effectively, at the end of the 1970 model year run), no fewer than 667,323 of all types had been built. It was yet another new record for Volvo, far surpassing that set up by the well-loved old PV544 when it bowed out in 1965.

Even by previous PV544 standards, it was an amazingly successful car—the breakdown encompassing 234,208 four-door saloons, 359,918 two-door saloons (including the so-called 'GT') and no fewer than 73,197 estate cars. Collectors looking for the most powerful of those many cars will want to know that the last 47,418 two-doors and the last 2,897 estate cars had the B20 two-litre engines.

It was, indeed, a new record, but it was not to last for long. Before the last of the 140 Series cars was built in 1974, they would have doubled the 120's achievement. In the 1960s, however, lovers of pedigree cars had more to do than concentrate on the myriad variants of the graceful 'Amazon'. In 1961 a smart coupé, the P1800, had gone on sale, and its birth and evolution make a particular enthralling tale.

The last Amazon of all, number 667,323, was finally built in 1970. It was a record then but the 140 Series surpassed it later.

Chapter 5

Sports cars and coupés
P1900 and P1800

The history of sports car production at Volvo is short, but by no means simple. Even though the first open P1900 was shown in 1954, and the last 1800ES of all was built in mid-1971, the events influencing their development, and their subsequent careers, were complex and fascinating. Indeed, it was the events, and the people behind the cars, rather than the cars themselves, which made this period in Volvo's history so interesting.

For many years after the birth of Volvo, there was no place for sports cars, or even high-speed cars, in the development of the company. Neither Assar Gabrielsson nor Gustaf Larson had any interest in such cars and, until the post-war years, they did not pretend their cars were exciting to drive. There was also the undeniable fact that many companies found it very difficult to make money out of sports cars—and far too many had gone bankrupt in the attempt. Gabrielsson, who was above all a businessman and not a gambler, was not tempted to join them.

Then the PV444 came along. Although the car, as developed for production, was once again a strictly orthodox Volvo, the small team of designers at Lundby tried all manner of things before that specification was settled. As Rune Gustaffson, Volvo's current director of Vehicle Engineering, told me not long ago: 'We even found time to design a car with hydrostatic drive, using hydraulics. It was not a success, though, there were too many oil leaks. At Volvo, some people had strange ideas—yes, really—in those days.'

However, even though there was no lack of talent in the small design department, there was no actual experience of sports car design at Volvo, and no demand for such a car to be built from the sales division. Something therefore happened to change the company's thinking—Assar Gabrielsson made one of his first fact-finding visits to North America, to assess the prospect of selling Volvos in that market, and was apparently impressed by the sports-car fever currently raging in the USA. I should point out, incidentally, that MG had been cultivating this fever for some years, and that both Triumph and Austin-Healey were both rushing new cars through to get their own slice of this expanding business.

Mr Gabrielsson visited the USA in 1953 at a time when the Anglo-Italian-US Nash-Healey was selling well, when Kaiser said that they were going to start building Kaiser-Darrins, and when (most importantly) Chevrolet were just preparing to launch the Corvette. Gabrielsson made a visit to Chevrolet's factory at Flint, Michigan, where he saw that the Corvette body shell was built in glass fibre.

It was the material, rather than the car itself, which really sparked off his interest.

Sports cars and coupés

The short-lived P1900 sports car, put on sale in 1956, used PV444 mechanical components in a tubular frame, with a glass fibre body shell.

Not only was glass fibre cheap and easy to work, but very little production tooling was needed to build body shells in limited numbers. I need hardly emphasise that Volvo's current problem, in Sweden, was not a lack of demand for its products, but a lack of body-making facilities of its own.

Volvo's president then paid a visit to the small Californian company of Glasspar, which specialised in glass fibre bodywork, and which had started building the prototype Kaiser-Darrin shells. Gabrielsson was reputedly interested in the potential of glass fibre for truck cab construction as well as for sports cars, but the immediate result of his visit was that he got together with Bill Tritt (Glasspar's president) and general manager Jerry Niger, and started talking about a sports car design for Volvo. The basic problem—that Volvo did not have a suitable separate chassis on which to evolve such a car—was not allowed to get in the way.

Volvo's president worked out an agreement even before he left California for home. Bill Tritt of Glasspar was not only contracted to style a new open sports car for Volvo (without reference to Jan Wilsgaard, back in Gothenburg), but Glasspar were also to make a prototype body shell, prepare the rudimentary moulds and tooling needed to build a series of cars, and to instruct Volvo's body engineers in the proper and efficient way of building these bodies in Sweden.

Even while Gabrielsson was still in California, Bill Tritt drew up the shape he had in mind, on the shortened (240 cm or 94.5 in) wheelbase which had been agreed, and utilising the PV444's front suspension, rear axle and tracks. The original style was very American, as was only to be expected, and featured a sculptured front end incorporating a large, rounded, front grille opening, two seats and a wrap around windscreen.

Gabrielsson, who was not a stylist (his comments at the viewing which led to the finalisation of the new Amazon spring to mind again) took this shape, unmodified

A few P1900s of the 67 built survived into the 1970s. This shot was taken comparatively recently— that is Gunnar Andersson standing outside the car.

and unqueried, sent Tritt's plans back to Sweden with the crisp request that the engineers should begin designing a chassis to suit, and also air-freighted back a proprietary Glasspar shell for them to inspect. One of his staff, Ake Zachrison, was nominated to move to California to learn about the new process.

It is not going too far to suggest that these decisions caused something of a disturbance at Volvo, but because Gabrielsson was, after all, The Boss, few were disposed to argue with him. Jan Wilsgaard was not at all happy with the Glasspar-designed body style and sent some of his own sketches over to California with the first Volvo people to visit the company in preparation for the new car. In particular Wilsgaard did not like the nose of the original, or the screen, and the car first shown to the public in mid-1954 had a neater front end, with a conventional, nearly-flat windscreen. In addition, Volvo designed a much smarter facia panel of their own, which not only included a matching speedometer and rev-counter display ahead of the driver's eyes, but also no fewer than five auxiliary instruments over the propeller shaft tunnel.

Gabrielsson was anxious to progress this scheme as quickly as possible, even though the small design office in Gothenburg was already heavily committed to Amazon/120 Series work. Raymond Eknor and Eric Quistgaard therefore had to work many hours of overtime to develop the running gear though, as the PV444's engine, transmission, front and rear suspensions and the steering were all to be used, intact, this really meant that their task was centred on the chassis frame itself.

There was no detailed product plan for the new car (which did not even have a name at that time), except that it was only expected to sell in limited numbers. Accordingly, there was no question of large capital sums being allocated for chassis frame tooling, which meant that channel or box section members could not be used.

Sports cars and coupés

The chosen design, therefore, used tubular members, and the layout was similar in some respects to the latest generation of Allard sports car frames currently making their names in North America.

To give proper beam strength, there were side members sweeping out under the body sills, composed of two 1.5 in tubes, one above the other, joined together by sheet steel, well drilled to keep the weight down. There were six major cross members, also tubular, stiffening gussets at strategic points, and a double-tubular cruciform member to add to overall rigidity. All the PV444 parts bolted easily up to this frame, and a big 12 gallon (Metric—55 litres) fuel tank was in the tail, taking up much of the potential luggage space.

To propel this 1,875 lb sports car, the latest twin-carburettor 70 bhp 1,414 cc engine was chosen, backed by the usual Volvo three-speed gearbox (and direct-action central change, with a long willowy lever), and a 4.56:1 back axle ratio. At first, incidentally, Volvo proposed to sell their car without a spare wheel, for great and wonderful things were then being claimed for the puncture-proof abilities of the new (Scandinavian) Trelleborg tyres; it was not a policy of which the customers approved!

Volvo built the first three prototypes, but sub-contracted the building of the production frames to Motala Werkstad of Sweden. Two of the cars—one open, and one with the detachable glass fibre hardtop in place—were shown off in June 1954, before development or preparations for production had been completed, although a top speed of 96 mph was claimed, and it was suggested by the company that one car a day would start to be built from September 1954.

It was a premature and, on hindsight, unwise sneak preview. Not only was a lot of development work still needed, particularly to stiffen up the bodyshell and make it rattle free, but to prove out the new tubular frame, and to assess the merits of the Volvo three-speed gearbox against five-speed ZF transmissions tried out as an alternative. Even the engine could not be taken for granted, for the 70 bhp tune had not, at that time, yet been offered as an option in the PV444—it would first be fitted to cars destined for North America in the 1956 model year. Prototypes went as far afield as North Africa during the test trials.

The new car, now named P1900 for no good and obvious reason, made its public debut at the Brussels Motor Show in January 1955, though it was still not ready for sale. Not until 1956 were the first few cars delivered to customers, though the car did the round of the early-season shows (including Brussels and New York) to keep up the interest. The production-type body shells, made down at the Volvo Penta works in South Sweden, were better than the prototypes, but still not as good as Volvo management would have liked. At least, by this time, the car was to be supplied with a spare wheel after all.

The P1900 was, to be frank, a commercial disaster for Volvo, and if they had committed large capital sums to the tooling it would have cost them a lot of money, and probably put them off sports cars for the next 50 years. A mere 44 cars were built in 1956, and 23 more followed in 1957, before production was closed down in March; almost all of those last cars, which never even approached the hoped-for 'one-car-per-day' rate, were sold in the United States, though Volvo have retained one of their own for posterity.

As ex-sales manager Olof Peterson says: 'It gave us experience of glass fibre—and made us decide not to do it again!' Designer Eknor admitted that it was a failure, not because the chassis didn't work, but—by inference—that the body material and its looks had let the car down. But the man who killed P1900 off, without mercy, was the newly-appointed chief executive, Gunnar Engellau.

The new president, who had only taken over from Assar Gabrielsson in 1956, the year in which not only the P1900, but the Amazon saloon, went on sale, never hid his feelings about the car. He hated it. In his own words: 'That car was one of the first things I destroyed. I killed that car! I drove it one weekend for 750 kilometres, and I thought the doors would fall off, and it was noisy and I didn't like the wheels, and in any case we were losing huge sums on each car we made, so it was a poor deal and had to go.'

Volvo, therefore, had been in and out of the important North American sports car business for just one year, and retired leaving almost no traces. But this did not last for long. Not only were North American sales, spearheaded by the PV444, and later by the 120 Series cars, beginning to boom, but the dealers were itching for something with which to fight back at the MGA or the Triumph TR3. And by this time that forceful character, Helmer Petterson, had come back on the scene once again . . . .

Petterson, though still not a salaried employee of Volvo, and not at all involved in the design of the 120 Series, was still a confidante of Assar Gabrielsson and Gunnar Engellau. I know of no other individual who had as much outside influence on the Swedish company at this time. Petterson had taken a prototype P1900 on some of its long-distance proving trials, and he was one of its most vocal critics.

On the other hand, he was certainly not blind to the potential of the North American market in particular, and at the end of 1956—well before Gunnar Engellau had killed off the P1900, incidentally—he suggested that Volvo should try again. Naturally he was not doing this without a personal interest, as Engellau well knew. The result was that Engellau looked at his sketches, recalled his previous forceful involvement in the PV444 project, and suggested that Petterson should travel to Italy to see which of the coachbuilders could tackle a new project.

The P1800 sports coupé, as built by Frua/Ghia, and as exhibited in prototype form in 1959.

Sports cars and coupés

Above *Lots of transatlantic glitter around the facia of the original P1800 coupé.*

Below *In spite of the lower, sleeker, lines, there was still plenty of engine room under the bonnet of the P1800.*

Above *An early UK-built P1800 coupé, posed in Sweden. The early cars were easily identifiable by their 'cow-horn' front bumpers.*

Below *Assembly of the coupés began in Sweden in 1963, after which the cars were called P1800S, or—later—just 1800S. This is a UK-built car. The lines were distinctive, but the cars were strictly two-seaters.*

Sports cars and coupés

Engellau did not ask his own stylists to produce a new sports-car shape (not because they were too tied up with the Amazon, as other authors have suggested—the Amazon work was all over by the beginning of 1956, and this project did not arise until the end of the year, or even early 1957 . . .) which suited Petterson down to the ground, because he had an ulterior motive of his own; his son, Pelle, was a 23-year-old graduate, currently studying industrial design in the United States, and father wanted to launch him into an automotive career.

The elder Petterson, therefore, did not go off on an absolutely complete tour of Italian stylists, but took some of the younger Petterson's sketches of cars (done with the encouragement and the guidance of his father) to Ghia, which was one of the most notable styling houses of the day. Detailed contractural arrangements have never been revealed, but the result was that Petterson, acting on behalf of Volvo, put the business of shaping a new car to the Torinese studio, and the younger Petterson also started working there. Some say that Pelle was not actually working for Ghia, but for his father, but one thing is absolutely sure—that Gunnar Engellau did not know that Pelle was involved at all!

At this point in the evolution of the Italian motor industry, the coachbuilding section, which was largely centred in or close to Turin, was a very incestuous business. Stylists moved from job to job, companies like Fiat or Lancia patronised not one, but several, and a lot of sub-contracting went on between them. That said, the rather murky events surrounding the birth, development and finalisation of the new Volvo become easier to understand.

It is certain, however, that the Pattersons, *père et fils*, presented their ideas for a two-seater Volvo coupé with a fixed roof (an open version was never, apparently, considered) to Ghia, and commissioned this company, led by Luigi Segre, to work up a full size style. Ghia, at this time, were at the height of their reputation, having done much-publicised work for both Chrysler and Ford USA in this period.

Almost immediately, however, Ghia ran into other contractual problems, for they also had links with VW to develop a new Karmann-Ghia coupé, and were bound not to develop a potential competitor to that car at the same time. The outcome was that the whole project—drawings, Petterson family and all—was moved over to Frua, also of Turin, for completion.

That, however, was not the end of the story. By mid-summer there were five distinctly different paper proposals—two by Ghia, two by Frua and one by Pelle Petterson. In August, all five proposals were shown to Gunnar Engellau, in the presence of Helmer Petterson and Ghia's boss, Luigi Segre, at which point Volvo's president unhesitatingly chose the young Petterson's proposal. It was only at that time that Segre had to admit that neither Ghia, nor Frua, had prepared it, and that Patterson's son was to be credited with the design. Engellau was apparently angry that such a subterfuge had been committed, but was so impressed by what he had seen, that he regularised the situation. Ghia would back gracefully out of the project, Pelle Petterson would carry on working with Frua, now on an official basis, and Frua would not only refine the chosen style, but would build the first prototype cars as well.

At this point, I have to say that I still find the process by which the style was chosen to be a little convoluted, especially as I think that the P1800, as we know it, bears some resemblance to Ghia coupé sytles of the period, rather than those from Frua—Pelle Petterson, clearly, had been much influenced by what he saw at Ghia in

Above *The 1800E coupé had a 2-litre fuel-injected engine and 130 bhp at first. The cast wheels were a recognition feature of the new car.*

Left *Quantity production of the 1800S in Sweden was originally centred at the old Lundby factory, even though most Volvos were being built at Torslanda by this time.*

Top right *If you could get close enough to the boot lid of an 1800E, there was a badge to tell you why it was going so fast!*

Right *Although there was talk of an occasional rear seat, in the 1800E it was really only useful for stowing luggage when the backrest was folded down.*

Sports cars and coupés

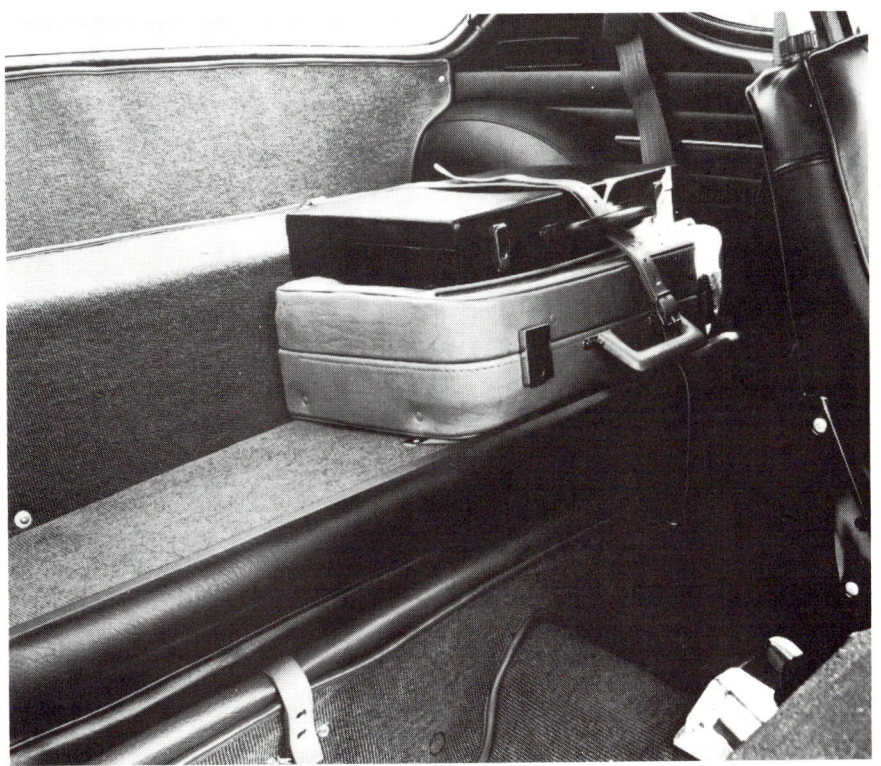

the spring and summer of 1957. Jan Wilsgaard, who kept a dignified distance from all his manoeuvring, merely says: 'It wasn't me.'

In the beginning, the P958 (as it was known at first), was supposed to be engineered around the shortened floor pan of the new Amazon/120 Series saloon, with an entirely special hull but, as in so many other cases in other companies, it became more and more specialised as detail design progressed. For the record, however, I should point out that the wheelbase of the saloon was 260 cm (102.4 in), while that of the new coupé was 245 cm (96.5 in)—both of which should be compared with the 240 cm/94.5 in of the ill-fated P1900.

In many ways, therefore, the P1800 was an easier car to engineer than the short-lived P1900 had been. The chassis layout was entirely familiar—for the Amazon's front and rear suspensions, steering and basic running gear were all used. It was never intended to be anything other than a fixed-head coupé and, although an upholstered shelf was provided behind the separate front seats, there was very little headroom, and virtually no legroom for them to be other than very occasional '+2' seats. In detail—engine, gearbox, brakes and tyres—the P1800 was going to be much different from the existing Amazon (or, at least, it would have been, if it had not been delayed for so long on the way to production), but its basic heritage was obvious.

At first, progress was rapid. The first complete body shell was ready in the autumn of 1957—Italian coachbuilding companies could be very rapid indeed when their volatile workforce was actually in residence, rather than indulging in the 'metalworkers' strikes' which were to afflict Italy so badly in the next few years—and the original prototype of three, XI, was driven out of the gates in Turin before Christmas of that year.

It was at this stage that the first major delay to the P1800 occurred. Even while the shape of the car was being finalised, and while Frua and Ghia were still co-operating on the project, Volvo had encouraged Ghia's quantity-production partners, Karmann of Osnabruck, in West Germany, to become involved. At Helmer Petterson's recommendation, Gunnar Engellau had agreed that Karmann, who had extensive facilities, should be invited to tender for the press tooling and production of P1800 body shells in large numbers. Karmann had shown that they were quite capable of doing this for VW, and their factories were ideally placed for the spreading autobahn system to allow the bodies to be transported up to Sweden, via Denmark and the short sea crossings.

But it was not to be. Just when it looked as if Volvo might have struck a good bargain for all concerned, Karmann were 'warned off' by VW, who had better things in mind for them. The irony of this was that the convertible VW1500 which Karmann were to have built at the beginning of the 1960s was cancelled immediately after its birth . . ..

Volvo now had a problem. Their engineers, and the sales force, were now thoroughly fired up by the possibilities of this new coupé, which was undeniably attractive looking, and showed every promise of being a 'real Volvo'. But there was nowhere in the Volvo Swedish empire that this special body shell could be produced (and because it was all in pressed steel, the investment and the complication was going to be considerable)—it would *have* to be produced by an outside supplier. But which one? The whole of the European motor industry was booming away in 1958, and spare capacity was limited. The fact that a Swedish newspaper published a sneak picture of the prototype in the summer of that year didn't help.

Sports cars and coupés

Above *From 1964 the 1800s had more luxuriously trimmed seats with pleated leather facings.*

Below *The grilles on the rear wings of the 1800Es were to encourage through-flow cabin ventilation.*

Further efforts by Petterson to find a supplier in West Germany were in vain and, in the autumn, T.G. Andersson, who was Engellau's assistant managing director, was instructed to find a solution. Eventually, Raymond Eknor was sent to Great Britain, where Volvo were already buying many components for their cars. 'Don't come back until you have the answer,' Andersson is reputed to have said, 'and don't forget that I like to play golf!'

Eknor who, by this time, had a good working knowledge of the British motor industry, soon hit on a solution. He arranged for the giant Pressed Steel Co to build the bodyshells and, better yet, he arranged for Jensen Motors to look after the final assembly of the complete cars.

This was a real breakthrough. Up until this moment, Volvo had always been resigned to assembling their own P1800s, though on the basis of body shells supplied from outside Sweden. Now, if they could guarantee that the quality was going to be right, they could actually sub-contract the entire manufacturing process to another concern. At first sight, it was an ideal arrangement, for many of the parts which would normally have been supplied from Britain could merely be diverted to Jensen, and the major Volvo-made items, like engines and transmissions, could be shipped over along with the new cars which were just beginning to go in to that market.

If Britain was to be the source of bodies, then Pressed Steel, which was still independent, and one of the largest builders of pressed-steel bodywork in Western Europe, was an obvious choice. Not only was the PSC closely linked with the Nuffield part of the BMC group (its main factory was cheek by jowl with the Morris Motors assembly plant), but it was also currently supplying shells—bare, or painted and trimmed—to Rootes, Standard, Rover, Jaguar, and even to Rolls-Royce. They had three major factories, the one chosen for Volvo P1800 production being at Linwood, just west of Glasgow. And Scotland, as Andersson well knew, was wonderful golfing country . . ..

The choice of Jensen was intriguing. Until the 1950s, Jensen, a privately-owned company with a factory in West Bromwich, just a few miles west of the city of

Volvo's own fine cutaway drawing of the 'square-back' 1800ES. The amount of 'rear seat' leg room is emphasised because the front seats have been pushed forward.

Sports cars and coupés

Birmingham, had been small, but they then took on the important contract of supplying complete painted and trimmed body/chassis units for the Austin-Healey 100 (the 'Big Healey', as it was always affectionately known by motoring enthusiasts). By 1958 their business had so expanded that they were building up to 150 shells a week for BMC, as well as making a few exclusive GT cars of their own.

Agreement with Pressed Steel and Jensen was reached at the end of 1958, a year in which the evolution of the car from prototype to production machine had effectively marked time. Pressed Steel would build the body shells in Scotland, transport them down to West Bromwich, where Jensen would paint, trim and complete assembly. To do this, Jensen needed more factory space so, in 1959, the Jensen family sold out to the Norcros Group, the money was found to build an extra 70,000 sq ft, and a further 100,000 sq ft was planned.

In the meantime, development continued, and the car's specification settled down. As planned, the chassis specification was mainly adapted from the Amazon/120 Series, except that springs and dampers were all different, and a different front cross member allowed the front of the car to be dropped by about one inch. The five-bearing B18 1,778 cc engine was to be in twin SU carburettor form, producing up to 100 bhp, while the latest four-speed gearbox was not only given an optional Laycock overdrive, but a very neat and sporting remote control gear change. Front wheel disc brakes (by Girling) were standardised, along with servo assistance.

Volvo released the first details of the car in May 1959, when it had still not been given a name, showing pictures featuring the Frua-type road wheels, and suggesting that production would start in 1960. The first public showing was forecast for 1960, and a tentative price of 15,000 SKr (about £1,050) was mentioned. At this stage the link-up with Pressed Steel was made clear but, although Volvo announced that the car would be assembled in Britain, Jensen's name was withheld.

After that, it seemed to take an age actually to get the new coupé into the showrooms and out on sale. The car was shown proudly at the Brussels exhibition in January 1960, by which time it had been named P1800. Only the three prototypes

Later models in the 1800 Series could be supplied with Borg Warner automatic transmission. The facia design, incidentally, is that of the 1800ES.

Practicality in the layout of the 1800ES 'estate coupé' of 1971-73, with a flat load floor made available by folding down the backrest of the occasional rear seat.

still existed, the show car being one of them, and at last the Jensen assembly agreement was made public; up to 100 cars a week, it was suggested, would be built. Production, originally to have begun in the autumn of 1960, was delayed while body shell tooling was completed and proved out, and finally the line began to move in January 1961.

During the spring, the production lines at Linwood and West Bromwich began to fill up, such that *The Autocar* announced that the first 300 had been finished at Jensen's factory by the end of May 1961, with the first 200 cars already in Gothenburg for checking and approval. At first, all cars were built in left-hand-drive, and the Swedish price had been fixed at 16,950 SKr (equivalent to £1,171), while in the USA the P1800 was to sell for $3,800.

If the information released to the press by Jensen and Volvo was to be believed, there were ambitious plans for production of the P1800 for, in August, *The Motor* reported that the 1961 target was for 3,000 cars and that this would rise to 7,500 a year in the future. *The Autocar*'s technical analysis, published a few weeks earlier, had mentioned production rates of up to 150 cars a day, which was a real howler— neither Jensen's factory capacity, nor the market place, could deal with this rate, which would have been equivalent to at least 35,000 cars a year!

Although the P1800 was well received by the motoring press, who found, in road tests, that the car could achieve nearly 105 mph in overdrive form (and that, incidentally, it was nearly as fast and more economical than the MG MGB which was announced in 1962), there was no doubt that the quality standards being

Sports cars and coupés

Above *The square-back 1800ES had an enormous rear window/hatchback, in which the hinges were fixed direct to the glass. Almost all the original sheet-metal had been retained from the 1800E.*

Below *Jan Wilsgaard's re-shaping of the 1800 coupé, into a square-back, was very successful, making an elegant car even more practical.*

achieved were below Volvo's expectations. As Peter Browning wrote in his history of Jensen, published in the 1970s: 'The Volvo contract, however, was not without its trials and tribulations, for there were constant disagreements on inspection standards between Pressed Steel, Jensen and Volvo, who finally sent over their own inspector to be resident at Kelvin Way, West Bromwich. The main problems stemmed from the condition in which the bodies arrived from Linwood . . ..'

Within a year, it seems, Volvo had concluded that this original deal had gone wrong, and even though their original contract with Jensen was for 10,000 cars to be built, they hastened to find some way out of the problem. As 1963 approached, two developments made a change not only possible, but desirable. In the short term, production and assembly capacity would become available at Lundby, as Amazon production was progressively transferred to the new, and still incomplete, Torslanda plant, while in the long-term there were fears that Pressed Steel would not be able to continue the supply of body/chassis units; in 1963 the Hillman Imp was launched, with body production concentrated at Linwood, and final assembly in a new Rootes Group factory literally across the road—the likelihood being that Pressed Steel would become more and more dependent on Rootes patronage in future years.

In March 1963, therefore, the last P1800 coupé was assembled at the Jensen factory and, from April 1963, the assembly of the cars began at Lundby, close to, but not intermingled with, the old PV544 saloons. Now Pressed Steel continued to build the body/chassis units, in spite of Volvo's misgivings about product quality, and shipped them over to Sweden for final assembly; chassis number sequences now mentioned the '1800S' series, with 'S' standing for Swedish-built.

Jensen, by the way, found themselves with an empty factory building, but their historian, Peter Browning, writes that: 'It was an amicable agreement, and Jensen was paid a considerable sum in compensation for the lost work, although it continued to supply components and make a number of small items for Volvo for a considerable period afterwards.' As far as Jensen were concerned, in any case, some good came out of misfortune, for shortly they were approached by Rootes to take on work connected with production of the Sunbeam Tiger sports cars—and it just so happened that they had space, and idle workers, to do the job. (The Tiger, incidentally, was built until 1967.)

Clearly, Volvo and the customers were happier to see the 1800s built in Sweden, for sales began to increase as improvements were made, and soon settled down to between 4,000 and 4,500 cars a year, not spectacular, but certainly profitable, and great as an image-builder for Volvo in the all-important North American market.

The original style of the 1800 coupé ran for ten years, in which literally hundreds of changes, some major but most were minor development improvements, were made. Until the end of the 1971 model year run, all 1800s had the same elegant two-door coupé body style (a convertible was never offered) in which the passengers sat low, in which the car's natural 'waist-line' was high, and in which the vestigial rear fins were an obvious recognition point.

Until the start-up for the 1969 model year, very few mechanical changes were made to the car, except that the peak output of the 1,778 cc B18 engine was boosted to 108 bhp for 1964, and boosted once again to 115 bhp for 1966—in the first case with a new camshaft profile and a higher compression ratio, in the second by a more efficient exhaust system.

All the time, however, the sales force, aided by the engineers, were working away

Sports cars and coupés

Work going ahead in Volvo's styling studio on the very smooth P172 coupé, which might have replaced the 1800 coupé at the end of the 1960s.

on the detail specification of the car. The original Lundby-built cars were identical to the Jensen-assembled machines, but for 1964 there was new badging, leather facing for the seats and the standardisation of 120 Series wheel covers. For 1965 the medically-influenced 'Volvo seat' was introduced, the 'bull horn' bumper style was abandoned in favour of straight bumpers, while for 1967 there was a new grille style and straight, instead of curved, side mouldings.

The major change to the 1800's performance came in the autumn of 1968, for the 1969 model year, when it was given the enlarged B20 engine of 1,986 cc which was actually being standardised across the whole range of 120 Series and 140 Series cars as well. This enlargement was simply achieved with a larger cylinder bore of 88.9 mm, for which the five-bearing cylinder block had always been intended. Because of exhaust emission limitations imposed by certain markets, notably the United States, the peak power output was only pushed up by 3 bhp, but peak torque was increased to a lusty 123 lb ft at 3,500 rpm. There was higher gearing (4.3:1 instead of 4.56:1 final drive, when overdrive was fitted) and many other minor, but useful, upgradings of equipment.

Nevertheless, this activity was just a prelude. For the 1970 model year, not only did Volvo complete arrangements to build the cars entirely in Sweden, but they boosted the performance even more, by specifying Bosch fuel injection in place of twin carburettors. Perhaps, if Pressed Steel had not been taken over by BMC (the giant British company building, among other things, Austin and Morris cars) in 1965, and if BMC had not then sold the Linwood factory to Rootes, Volvo bodies might have continued to be built in the UK but, as they had to be moved out of Linwood, the decision was taken to transfer press tools and assembly jigs to the Olofstrom plant in Sweden, though final assembly continued at Lundby.

The 1970 model, called 1800E (E for Einspritzung, the German word for 'fuel injection') looked similar to the displaced 1800S, except that externally it had new badging, a new black grille, cabin air outlets in each rear wing, above and behind the rear wheel arches, and smart new wheels with cast-alloy centres and steel rims. The engine itself produced up to 130 bhp (or, in Volvo's new sweeping mood of honesty, 120 bhp net) at 6,000 rpm, and torque was also up, to 130 lb/ft at 3,500 rpm. Not only was there Bosch Jetronic fuel injection to provide the boost, but the

Above *P172 was shaped by Jan Wilsgaard during his 'sabbatical' stay in California. It was bigger, wider and more assertive than the existing 1800 coupé.*

Below *Among others at this secret viewing of the P172 coupé project, lined up against an 1800 coupé, is Per Gyllenhammer. The car was not put into production because investment costs would have been too high.*

latest, more robust, ZF-manufactured Type M410 gearbox (as already fitted to the six-cylinder 164 saloon) was fitted behind it.

Even though this gave a boost to the 1800's sales, the fashion-conscious North Americans were beginning to resist the purchase of a car which still looked like those which had been on sale since 1961. Volvo's problem was that they were not selling enough to make the capital expenditure on new press tooling worthwhile, and if they did not provide new styling they would not be able to sell more cars—it was a real 'Catch 22' situation . . . .

Jan Wilsgaard's styling department had not ignored the car, however, it was just that the public had never been allowed to see what was brewing. Even as early as 1964/65, when he spent some time working in California, Jan had produced some sketches of a bigger, cleaner and more 'international' shape of car, which was to be a 2 + 2, to use the new Volvo 164's six-cylinder engine, and might have replaced the 1800S by the end of the 1960s. This was the P172 project, a car described more fully in Appendix D. Later, in 1966, the styling staff looked at the 1800S once again, this time improving it by converting the shape to a fastback style, still with the same basic bodyshell, but only one prototype was ever built.

What followed it, in 1967, was much more fruitful. Styling were asked to consider a facelift for the existing car so, under project P183, one of Wilsgaard's designers evolved the bare bones of a square-back conversion, something which Jan Wilsgaard calls a 'hunting car'. However, as this had been styled on the 'minimum-change' principle, Wilsgaard thought it would be interesting to offer a more radical restyle, and evolved a much more shapely proposal, which he called the 'Rocket' car. Whereas the 'hunting car' retained existing rear wings, the 'Rocket' was really all new behind the doors, and would cost a lot more in press tooling; the 'hunting car' kept a conventional rear bumper, while the 'Rocket' had a bumper built in to the curve of the tailgate. Both cars were intended to have a large tailgate, mostly comprised of glass. At the final clay stage, incidentally, the 'Rocket' had distinctly different side window profiles, though only the rounded profile was approved by management. 'They decided to make a prototype of the "hunting car", and I also got permission to make one of the "Rocket" as well,' Wilsgaard says. 'So we must have caught Mr Engellau on a good day!'

Originally, Volvo were going to ask Frua to build both cars, by converting standard 1800S cars shipped down to Italy for the work, but this was later modified. Jan Wilsgaard had known Sergio Coggiola when he was working for Ghia in Italy, then found out that he was branching out on his own, and decided to put work his way. Frua was to build the square-back 'hunting car', while Coggiola built the 'Rocket'—that way Volvo got the job finished faster.

It is important to realise that both these styles existed in 1967/68, well before Reliant showed the Scimitar GTE at the 1968 Earls Court Show, for many pundits have suggested that Volvo merely copied what Ogle Design had done for the British company. Jan Wilsgaard is adamant that both hatchback 1800 styles were done in 1967, and the dates on archive photographs reproduced here bear this out.

When the cars came back to Gothenburg in 1968, there was a difficult decision to be made, for the 'Rocket' was very appealing, just as the 'hunting car' was neat, smart, understated *and* relatively undemanding of investment. In the end, the more conservative style was chosen, and the single 'Rocket' prototype was consigned to the 'might-have-been' store.

Because it takes so long to have new tools prepared, the square-back change could

The story of Volvo cars

Above *This was another 'might-have-been' proposal—this time by Sergio Coggiola on an 1800E underframe.*

Below *3000GTZ—by Zagato—yet another idea of the way that the life of the 1800 coupé might have been extended.*

Sports cars and coupés

Torslanda, where Volvo cars have been built since the early 1960s—close to Gothenburg, and close to sea ports.

not be made to the 1800 until the autumn of 1971, in time for the 1972 selling season in North America, but it was well received even at that late stage. In the meantime, the 1971 1800E coupés had been given the option of Borg Warner automatic transmission (which went down well in North America), and had reverted to a strengthened Volvo-built four-cylinder type M41 gearbox, so for 1972 the last sanction of 1800E coupés (1,865 of them) were built alongside the first season's 3,070 1800ES 'sporting-estate cars'. The 1800ES, of course, not only provided a potential 5-ft loading platform at the rear, but unrivalled visibility through a tailgate which was entirely glass, to which the hinges at the top, and the T-handle at the bottom, were directly attached. For management, and the production engineers, the beauty of the 1800ES was that the entire nose, scuttle/ screen, doors, rear wings and most of the floor pan were retained, unchanged. Although the rear '+2' seat was really no more practical than before, it was fully upholstered, and the extra load carrying capacity was much appreciated. Under the skin, too, the engine had been boosted by a further five bhp (gross), the wheel rims had been widened to 5.5 in, and larger 185/70 section tyres were fitted. Tinted glass, inertia reel safety belts and other safety fittings all helped to keep the same image which Volvo were promoting for their touring cars. On the other hand, it was considerably more expensive—£2,638 compared with £2,238 for the 1800E in Great Britain, for instance.

Although the two different styles of 1800 were made together for some months, the last conventional coupé was built in June 1972, after which the 1800ES soldiered on alone. But even as the public began to get the message, that the

1800ES was a much improved car, it fell under sentence of death from the factory. Volvo, like all other European manufacturers, were beginning to reel under the new safety legislation which was flooding out of the United States at this time. Like Triumph with the GT6 and the Stag, and MG with the MGB GT V8, Volvo were finding that sending the 1800ES to North America in restricted numbers was no longer profitable, now that so much extra gear had to be fitted, and so much exhaust emission work had to be done. The final straw, no doubt, was when it became clear that new, large and probably ugly bumpers would have to be fitted for 1974. Accordingly, Volvo discreetly let it be known that the 1973 models would be the last.

As one might expect, demand for these cars perked up immediately! In spite of the fact that a Swedish newspaper quite wrongly stated that the 1800ES was out of production in November 1972, the 1972/73 sanction of 5,008 was the largest of any in the career of the 1800, all the last few months' supply going for sale in North America. The last 1800ES, indeed the last 1800 derivative of all, was built on June 27 1973.

The statistics of 1800 sales and production make creditable reading for all at Volvo who believed in the car throughout the 1960s and early 1970s. All in all, 47,585 cars were assembled, 6,000 of these originating from England. There were 30,093 P1800s and 1800S models with carburettor engines, 9,414 1800Es with Bosch fuel injection, and 8,078 1800ES 'sporting estates' with the square-back body style.

There was no natural successor to the 1800ES and to this day no compact, specialised, Volvo coupé has ever been made, for the Bertone-built 262C of 1977-80 falls into an entirely different, more costly, category. Since 1973, indeed, Volvo have been far too busy building more and more large, comfortable, long-lasting and ultra-safe saloons and estate cars to indulge themselves in a sporting car once again.

Yet the urge, the corporate feeling, about such cars is still present at Torslanda. No less an authority than Rune Gustafsson, commenting sadly that his engineers no longer really 'have time to play', also admitted that there *is* still a demand for this type of car. Perhaps, one day, we might see a new sporting car from Volvo. Perhaps . . ..

Chapter 6

Safety fast!
The factory in competitions

Memories are short. You really couldn't look at a current-model big Volvo, then look at the glamorous world of modern rallying, and link the two. But there was a time, less than 20 years ago, when a Volvo could be a formidable force in international competition—and not merely in those events requiring sheer brute strength. For a time, at the end of the 1950s, and in the 1960s, the Volvos were also among the fastest of the rallying saloons.

There have, in fact, been many major successes, but I could summarise these merely by quoting Gunnar Andersson's European Championship victories in 1958, Tom Trana's double outright wins in the RAC Rally of 1963 and 1964, and the amazing success by Joginder Singh in the 1965 East African Safari—in a second-hand car!

In truth, there was really no Volvo capable of winning a speed contest before the 1950s. None of the original Larson-inspired cars were nimble enough, or fast enough, and in any case the Volvo company was not at all interested in promoting its products in this way. However, if you ever saw that splendid film, *Monte Carlo or Bust*, you may have noticed a rather smart PV4 saloon. Knowing how good film companies are at faking things, I was amazed to discover not only that that particular car was real, but it was only one of two such machines that could be discovered in 1968, when the film was made; Volvo have the other, and they firmly refused to have anything to do with the filming, which might have been hazardous to their priceless relic. (But if you believe that the Mercedes-Benz SSK and the Peugeot competing against the Volvo are real, you'll believe anything . . ..)

Even as late as 1955, when the PV444 was already in its prime, the factory showed no interest in rallying, even though their car-making neighbours, Saab, were becoming prominent. Even in 1956, when Saab took three of the top five places in the Rally to the Midnight Sun (Sweden's qualifying event for the European Rally Championship) and were outright winners of the Norwegian Viking rally, there was still no interest—nor, it seems, such effort by Volvo private owners.

But for 1957 the PV444 had more power than before, and the factory should not have been surprised when the Jansson brothers won the Midnight Sun outright, and Messrs Grondal and Bernsten also won the Viking. This was only the beginning—for 1958 belonged to Gunnar Andersson.

'I had started rallying with a Jaguar XK120 in 1953,' Gunnar says, 'then moved to a Fiat 1100TV, and in 1957 I bought my first Volvo—a PV444. A Volvo engineer helped me change the engine, from the Swedish-spec unit to the 75 bhp American-

Above *Jumping high on the Swedish Midnight Sun rally—Gunnar Andersson in his own PV444 in 1958.*

Below *Gunnar Andersson's PV544 in the French Alps in the 1961 Tulip Rally, in which he was second in his class.*

Safety fast! 95

Above *The most famous Volvo victory of all? The Singh brothers (driver, Joginder, on the right) at the end of the 1965 East African Safari rally which they won in an ex-works 1964 PV544.*

Below *In 1963, Tom Trana put up a truly virtuoso performance to win the RAC International Rally outright in this 'works' PV544.*

Left *Gunnar Andersson (left) and his protégé, Tom Trana, who were Volvo's principal rally personalities in the 1950s and 1960s.*

market tune. But I was still rallying privately—I had a small crash-repair business—for Mr Gabrielsson had no interest at all in competitions.' In 1958, Gunnar's immediate plans, finance permitting, were to take his PV444 to the Acropolis, Midnight Sun, German and Tulip rallies, even though he had never rallied outside Scandinavia before.

In his very first event, Andersson took third place overall in the Acropolis rally which was a rough and fast race around Greece—an event in which he was only beaten by ex-Grand Prix driver Luigi Villoresi's Lancia, and a local Greek's big Chevrolet. It was during this race that his pace astonished the opposition: 'The French and the Italians were quite convinced that I had a racing engine, and even though I had the homologation papers with me, they didn't trust those either. They actually had the engine stripped, and borrowed a private Volvo from the dealer in Athens, so that they could compare it!'

Although Gunnar led the Tulip rally outright for a time, he dropped back—but the event was won outright by another private Volvo, that of G. Kolwes, and other Volvos took sixth and ninth places. He was back in the results within weeks, however, when he took third place in the German rally, behind the nimble Alfa Romeo Giuliettas of Bernard Consten and Riess. 'After this I was called up by Mr Engellau, who asked me if I would like to start working for Volvo. The result was that I started at the factory on 15 June 1958, but in the meantime I had also won the Midnight Sun rally on 13 June!'

It was, in fact, something of a fairy-tale start for Volvo's first 'works' driver, because he defeated the cream of Scandinavia's cars and drivers at exactly the right time, and gained enormous publicity for the car, and for himself. Peter Harper of Britain, in a 'works' Sunbeam Rapier, had been leading the European Championship at half-distance, but in spite of winning his class in the ultra-tough French Alpine rally (when Andersson crashed after his Volvo's brakes gave trouble on the last night), he did not score again.

Right *Gunnar Andersson, who started his Volvo rallying career by winning the European rally championship in 1958, initially using his own car.*

Below *Canada's longest and toughest rally was the Shell 4000, which completely traversed the continent. In 1964, Klaus Ross and John Bird won the event outright in this Canadian-assembled Amazon.*

Andersson, however, clinched it all in July, when he took another PV444 to the Adriatic rally, held in Yugoslavia, and again won outright, from Wolfgang Levy's DKW and Alex von Falkenhausen's BMW. Even though it was a low points-scoring event (because of the lack of starters in this rough and remote event) it was enough. Having started from nothing at the beginning of the year, Gunnar Andersson had become European Rally Champion for 1958 by a considerable margin, leaving eminent rivals like Harper, Consten, Pat Moss and Maurice Gatsonides, trailing behind. Not that he stopped rallying at that point, however, for he also went off to the Norwegian Viking, and took second place (behind Ingier's PV444!). In one season Gunnar had had two wins, a second place and two thirds—and the PV444, in various hands, had won four European Championship events outright, which was more than any other make of car. And yet, at this stage, there was nothing at all special about the 'works' cars, which were prepared in one corner of a factory workshop and had little engine tuning, but the usual sump guards, extra driving lamps and modified brakes.

It was almost as if the reaction to such a magnificent first year had set in for, in 1959, Gunnar, now not only Volvo's 'works' driver but its team manager as well, barely figured in the results. However, even more glittering success was achieved this season by a spectacularly beautiful young lady called Ewy Rosqvist, who used PV544s to win the European Ladies' Championship, after a great struggle with Annie Soisbault ('works' Triumph TR3A) and Pat Moss' various 'works' BMC cars. She won the Ladies' cup in the Midnight Sun, Adriatic and Viking rallies, and added her name to a list of leading ladies which included Greta Molander, Shiela Van Damm, Nancy Mitchell and Pat Moss. It was also a year in which Volvo outright wins were achieved by Callbo (Finnish 1000 Lakes) and Ingier (Viking).

The 140 Series was theoretically ideal for the East African Safari rally, but Bengt Soderstrom and Torsten Palm had no luck with this 142S in 1971.

Safety fast!

In 1960, Volvo's reputation was enhanced when the drivers, now using more powerful 1.6-litre PV544s, achieved one outright victory (Gunnar Andersson in the German rally), second overall in the Ladies' Championship (Ewy Rosqvist behind Pat Moss' very fast Austin-Healey 3000s), and no fewer than 12 class wins in the European Championship again, finishing second, close behind Hans Walter's Rootes, who spent far more money on their Sunbeam Rapiers, but who usually could not beat the Scandinavians. Gunnar himself also took a couple of third places (Midnight Sun and Viking) and a fourth in the 1000 Lakes.

The team were back in business in a big way in 1961, for not only did the glamorous Ms Rosqvist win the Ladies' Championship by lifting the ladies' prize on seven of the 11 rounds, but Gunnar Andersson himself so nearly won the European Championshp again, finishing second, close behind Hans Walter's Porsche Carrera. Even so, Volvo did not take a single outright win, not because the PV544s were being outpaced (with more than 100 bhp from their rally-tuned engines there was no danger of this), but because they often suffered from handicapping, or from competition from out-and-out sports cars like the Porsches and Austin-Healeys.

Gunnar Andersson himself had bought a Ferrari 250GT 'for fun', and used it, with Volvo's permission, to win the Italian Mille Miglia, which had once been a race, but was now a rally. Apart from this, it was a year of 'nearly-wins', with second in Greece, third in Germany, fourth in Poland, and fifth in the 1000 Lakes. It was of this performance that John Gott, Britain's rallying *doyen*, wrote in *Autosport*: 'Gunnar Andersson, the 1958 Champion, was in brilliant form, but the Volvo PV544 is now getting a bit long in the tooth as a championship-winning tool.'

In later years, Volvo have concentrated on rallycross, and on performance equipment for customers' cars. This is an example of the powerful 16-valve twin-cam cylinder head developed by Gunnar Andersson's R-Sport department, on the basis of the B19/B21 bottom end.

He may have had a point, but Andersson and Volvo really had little choice, as the Amazon was a bigger and heavier car, using the same engines, and could not be expected to perform any better. There had been an attempt to blood the P1800 sports coupé, which had held down second place on the Midnight Sun for a time when being driven by a pale but brave young man called Tom Trana—but as this car would have to compete against the Triumphs, Porsches and Austin-Healeys if sent out into the world, it was an experiment not repeated.

1962 was not a year which Volvo will remember with much pride, as Ewy Rosqvist had eloped to Mercedes-Benz (perhaps there was an excuse, for later she married Baron von Korff, who helped manage that team . . .) and there were no outright victories to celebrate, though the redoubtable Andersson took second place in the Tulip (in an Amazon) and sixth in the Acropolis—there were six European Championship class wins in the year.

In 1963 and 1964, however, Tom Trana crowned everything the PV544 had ever achieved before, by winning the prestigious British RAC rally outright, twice in succession. It was an astonishing pair of performances, especially since many journalists observing the wins in Britain had thought the PV544 to be dead and buried some time ago. The fact was that in 1.8-litre form, with about 135 bhp in 'homologated' and tuned-up form, the PV544 was an extremely effective rally car, in spite of its design age.

1963 was the year in which the authorities suspended the European Rally Championship for a year and in which team manger, Gunnar Andersson, could only achieve two seconds overall (in the Acropolis and in Poland, in an Amazon) and a third in the Tulip (also in an Amazon), but it was also the year in which Volvo cars won eight major classes, five of them with Amazons. On this occasion, when reviewing the 1963 season, John Gott's *Autosport* comment was that: 'Andersson, the 1958 Champion, has remained at the top a long time, and although now shouldering the responsibilities of managing the Volvo team as well as leading it, had a good year indeed . . .', and he went on to rate Gunnar only marginally behind the two other acknowledged superstars, Erik Carlsson and Eugen Bohringer.

For 1964, Volvo's big effort was in the East African Safari, an event noted for its high speeds and rough roads—but also for the enormous publicity reaped by cars which gained results. Erik Carlsson's tiny Saab had already gained world-wide headlines in 1962 and 1963, even without winning, and Volvo (like other European teams before and since) became convinced that with all their rough-road experience, they could surely win. There was a team of no fewer than four cars, all PV544s, for Tom Trana, Gunnar Andersson, Carl-Magnus Skogh (ex-Saab team driver) and for Silvia Osterberg.

Unfortunately for Volvo, they were drawn to run well down in the field (whereas the six 'works' Ford Cortina GTs were at the very front) and not a single car finished. Trana's car, in fact, was crashed in the first few hours, but was sold off to a Kenyan-Indian motor trader called Joginder Singh . . . which was one of the luckiest, or wisest moves, which Gunnar Andersson ever made.

In Canada, while all this was going on, Klaus Ross drove a Canadian-assembled Amazon to outright victory in the Shell 4000 trans-Canada rally (with GP-driver Olivier Gendebien fourth in a sister car) and the Volvo team won the team prize, but even greater successes were gained in Europe. Tom Trana won the Acropolis rally and the Midnight Sun outright (both in PV544s), in addition to winning the RAC rally, and also finished second in the Finnish 1000 Lakes—no wonder he was

Safety fast!

The Volvo rallying team before the start of the Acropolis rally. The four principal drivers were Tom Trana (black hair, kneeling), Joginder Singh (in turban), Carl-Magnus Skogh (in safari shirt) and Gunnar Andersson (far right).

acclaimed as European Champion, ahead of the other Scandinavian star, Erik Carlsson. It was a year marred, however, by serious injury to Gunnar Andersson, when in a non-competing car, following the Polish rally, from which he happily recovered.

The next season will always be remembered as 'The year of the Safari', when the ex-Trana 1964 PV544, now with more than 40,000 miles on the clock, was re-prepared by Joginder Singh and won the event outright! This, mark you, was only a matter of weeks before the PV544 was due to go out of production, so there was no sales kudos to be gained from this phenomenal success. None of which should detract from Trana's fine win in the Midnight Sun or Skogh's victory in an Amazon in the Acropolis.

It was, however, the high-water mark of Volvo's rallying successes, for the 'homologation specials' from other concerns—specialised saloons with high power outputs, made in small (sometimes illegally small, by competitions standards) quantities—were taking over. Not even Tom Trana's undoubted genius could make up for the weight penalties inflicted by the sturdy Amazon body shell, so in 1966 his best performances were second on the 1000 Lakes, and third place in the Swedish rally, plus another third (after two victories) in the RAC Rally of Great Britain.

As Gunnar Andersson himself said when I talked to him in 1982: 'We became less interested, as a company, as the "homologation specials" arrived. We had always tried to compete in nearly standard cars and now, too, we had the new "safety" policy at the factory. I never asked for a special car—and I know I would never have got one anyway.'

In 1967, for sure, Volvo's rallying fortunes were on the decline, for the 'works' team had virtually been disbanded and the best single performance was by a then-unknown young man named Hannu Mikkola, who took third place in the 1000 Lakes rally in an Amazon. By 1968 it was all over. For some years after this, Volvo were officially out of rallying, though Gunnar Andersson stayed on as competitions manager, to provide a service to hundreds of private owners. In fact, Gunnar had been very loyal because, when he was at the height of his fame at the beginning of the 1960s, Mercedes-Benz had made him a very lucrative offer, for a three-year deal, to drive alongside Eugen Bohringer and Ewy Rosqvist—and he turned it down. That, in rallying terms, is the equivalent to shrugging off the offer of a Grand Prix car contract with Ferrari.

For the next few years Volvo built up their supply of kits for Amazons, 140s, and even for the older PV544 models, but it was not until the mid-1970s that a real chance to get back into 'works' competition came along. It was in 1974/75, of course, that Volvo took a controlling interest in DAF and it was in 1975 that the first 'Dutch Volvo' was announced. Once the 343 came on the scene, Gunnar Andersson and his 20-strong staff began to sit up and take notice.

It was not rallying this time, but the newly-popular TV-sport of rallycross. Rallycross was just as fast, and potentially even more costly, than the building of rally cars, but at least the rules were much less strict and the publicity potential was enormous. It also helped Andersson's cause that, at the time of the 343's announcement, the average DAF 'customer profile' showed buyers of high average age and that a high proportion of them were women. Rallycross, with a suitably

It may say Volvo 343, but the power unit is much more powerful than that—Per-Inge Walfriddson is driving, on his way to yet another European rallycross victory.

Safety fast!

modified 343, might be enormously successful in convincing other sectors of the market that such a car would interest them.

In 1977 there was little time for more than experiment but, in 1978, Volvo had a competitive 343—but it was like no other 343 being built. 'Just for fun,' Andersson says, a little wistfully, his mechanics had built one 343 with a 2.7-litre PRV V-6 up front and this, with about 260 bhp, could have been a real giant-killer. 'But we would have needed to build a small series and no one here was willing to see that happen. So—it was just a crazy idea from Gunnar Andersson, and only one car was made.' What happened to this car? 'Oh, we still have it, in a store room—it could be yours, for the right price!'

Although rallycross cars were (and are) built to very free engine regulations, they had to retain the original cylinder block and the engine had to remain in the same part of the car as that of the production machine. Even so, there was plenty of room for change. The R-Sport department (R = rally, or rallycross) started by moving as much weight to the rear of the car as possible, to optimise the weight over the driven wheels (which meant moving water radiators, cooling fans, battery, tanks and everything into the boot), while the 1.4-litre Renault engine was thoroughly revised, enlarged to 1.55 litres (the absolute maximum for this particular cylinder block) and turbocharged. At the time the work was started (1977), there was no such turbocharging experience in France, so Volvo had to tackle it all themselves.

Even in 1978 the engine produced 210 bhp and was competitive (the specially adjusted Variomatic transmission was remarkably versatile for rallycross use) but, at the end of the 1980 season, three years after a 'works' 343 had first appeared, the

One way to defeat the works-sponsored competition from Ford is to sandwich it on the way into the first corner, as these two Volvo-engined 343s are doing so effectively.

Volvo 343 + Walfriddson + massive Volvo engine power = very competitive rallycross car in the late 1970s.

same engine was churning out 280 bhp and was just about unbeatable. Andersson's bosses had allowed him three years to get to the top and this had certainly been achieved. In 1980 the bearded Per-Inge Walfriddson, who had once been the brave and under-rated driver of 140 Series cars in European rallies, had won the European rallycross championship, and the 343 had won the Swedish series in two of those years.

It was always a very limited programme—there were only two 'works' 343s at first and two extra cars were also sponsored in later years. These were easily distinguished by their yellow and blue Volvo 'R-Sport' livery, and in case any spectator did not believe that they were 343s, there was a huge '343' logo on the nose, where the conventional front grille and air intake should have been.

The DAF Variomatic transmission, incidentally, was only used for the first season, when a turbocharged 343 won the Swedish series, and after that the manual Volvo gearbox (as introduced for the production car by this time) was adopted instead. Nevertheless, Gunnar Andersson recalls that it was possible to put up to 240 bhp through the belt-drive DAF system, but that the main problem was in working out new settings to match the transmission to the high torque and the much higher revving engine, which peaked at 6,500 rpm.

After 1980, Volvo had no more to prove with the 343, for not only had Walfridsson won the European series from Martin Schanche's Escort, but three other 343s

Safety fast!

had taken third, fourth and fifth places. The emphasis then changed completely, with Andersson's team performing an engine transplant, slotting in the 2,315 cc B23 Volvo engine (the same basic engine as used now in the 360GLT, of course), and giving that a newly-developed 16-valve cylinder head, fitted with turbocharging and two large Solex carburettors. The result, in 1981 form, was a 300 bhp machine even faster and more driveable than before. Although the cylinder head was designed at Volvo, machining and air-flow development was carried out by Weslake, and later by Ricardo, in Britain.

By 1982 Volvo were no longer officially in motor sport again, which brought them back to their withdrawal of 1966, and Gunnar Andersson's little R-Sport division, which has a staff of 35 (including, in 1982, ex-rally stars Carl-Magnus Skogh and Tom Trana both working for him), operating from separate premises some kilometres away from mainstream factories, now concentrates on the sale of sport parts, and other Volvo tune-up kits.

If I wanted a full-house 16-valve B21/B23 conversion in 1982, it would have set me back more than £4,000, but I might have settled for a simple (by 16-valve standards) turbocharging kit instead, for about £700. Incidentally, if the sale of turbo kits sounds esoteric, I should point out that more than 1,000 of these were sold every week in 1982, and that Gunnar's operation is not only profitable for Volvo, but turned over more than 20 million SKr (£2 million) worth of parts in 1982.

Perhaps, however, we may never see Volvo returning to 'works' rallying or even rallycross, for the change of regulations effective from the start of 1982 made it very difficult indeed for them to sustain the interest. New supercars like the four-wheel-drive Audi Quattro, the mid-engined space-frame Lancia Rally, the mid-engined Renault 5 Turbo, and the rear-drive Ford Escort RS1700T have converted the new Group B category into a million-pound budget operation.

Andersson stated very firmly that Volvo would never get into that sort of power and money-spending race: 'After all, we make good cars, and we don't have to prove anything with specials. But I like the idea of Group A (5,000 cars to be built in a year) much more. Of course it would be very easy to build so many 343s with fuel-injected B23 engines—faster 360GLTs really—and I think we could do well with those . . ..'

It may be 25 years since the young Gunnar Andersson won his European Championship but the competitive fire is still there. What next from Volvo?

Chapter 7

140s, 240s and safety
Leading the world into the 1970s

Volvo never seem to do anything in a hurry. It took them ten years to produce a successor to the Amazon/120 Series range, and no one was unduly surprised. It had, after all, taken 12 years to produce a partner for the PV444. But such delays did not indicate corporate sloth—they merely confirmed that Volvo were becoming quite fanatical about the detailing of their cars. In the 1950s and 1960s the world of motoring—and, in particular, the buying public—were happy to wait; if it took ten years for Volvo to perfect a new car, so be it. The wait would almost certainly be worth while.

In any case, this all helped to confirm Volvo's growing reputation for painstaking work—most obviously as they collected more and more praise on two fronts, for the longevity of their cars and the primary safety built in to them. Early claims for the potentially long life of Volvos were greeted with a predictable 'let's wait and see' response—it was only when survey after survey showed that a Volvo did, indeed, last longer than its rivals that the critics were silenced. At a time when most pressed-steel family cars lasted no more than a decade, the fact that VP444s were still happily thundering around the roads of Sweden approaching their 20th birthday was obvious.

The 'safety' aspect of a Volvo was, and still is, very difficult to turn into a handy sales feature. For many years, indeed, North American manufacturers said that advertising their cars as 'safe' merely turned the customer away to a more excitingly presented machine; many motoring journalists, influential if not important in the scheme of things, still confess to stifled yawns when car companies begin their 'safety' pitch.

Volvo, however, had not been working on the *same* new car since the arrival of the Amazon in 1956, as Appendix D makes very clear. Immediately after the lines of the Amazon had been approved, the company's stylists played around with a tentative PV444-replacement shape called the 'Wood Rocket', then they produced the PV544 'facelift' instead. A little later a lot of time was spent on the development of the large and luxurious P358 project, which was intended to be a new Volvo 'flagship', and along with yet one more attempt to update the PV444/PV544 style, dubbed the PV644, they were fully occupied until 1960. And that was only on the cars side of the business; we must never forget that Volvo were also in the business of building trucks and buses, and that new styles of cabs and noses for these large vehicles were also under development.

Work on a new project, coded P1400, really began in 1960, and full size clay

140s, 240s and safety

Above *An early clay being developed for the 140 Series. This picture is dated 1961 and there are definite signs of Opel influence in the cabin shape.*

Below *Gunnar Engellau (left) and Per Gyllenhammar, who directed the fortunes of AB Volvo throughout the 1960s and 1970s.*

Shaping the 140 Series Volvo in the early 1960s—two views of the clay model in the styling studios.

models which began to approach the final shape were already being refined in 1961, as an exclusive picture supplied to me by Jan Wilsgaard makes clear. However, as happened with the Amazon in the early 1950s, the shape finally approved by management was not the one which they had requested in the first place, and as before it was a combination of Jan Wilsgaard's artistic instincts and his stubborn belief in them which produced a satisfactory result.

In 1960, Wilsgaard and one of his colleagues, Vic Hammond (an Englishman who also worked for Standard-Triumph for a time) began to produce layout drawings for a new car. 'At first,' Wilsgaard recalls, 'the specification was very dry, very tight—just as before. This time it was so detailed that we were even told what glass angles there had to be in the doors. I told people that this was too tight, and asked if I could do another one. OK, so then we built two models—one that was thought to be too 'wild', and one not 'wild' enough.'

Wilsgaard's problem—and I am sure that no one at Volvo would disagree with

Above *The 1966 144's 'chassis'—showing the very simple engineering of this long-running car.*

Below *The 140 Series rear suspension, which was used on the 240s as well, featured twin trailing arms, a Panhard rod and coil springs. It was different from the Amazon/120 models, but with a similar general layout.*

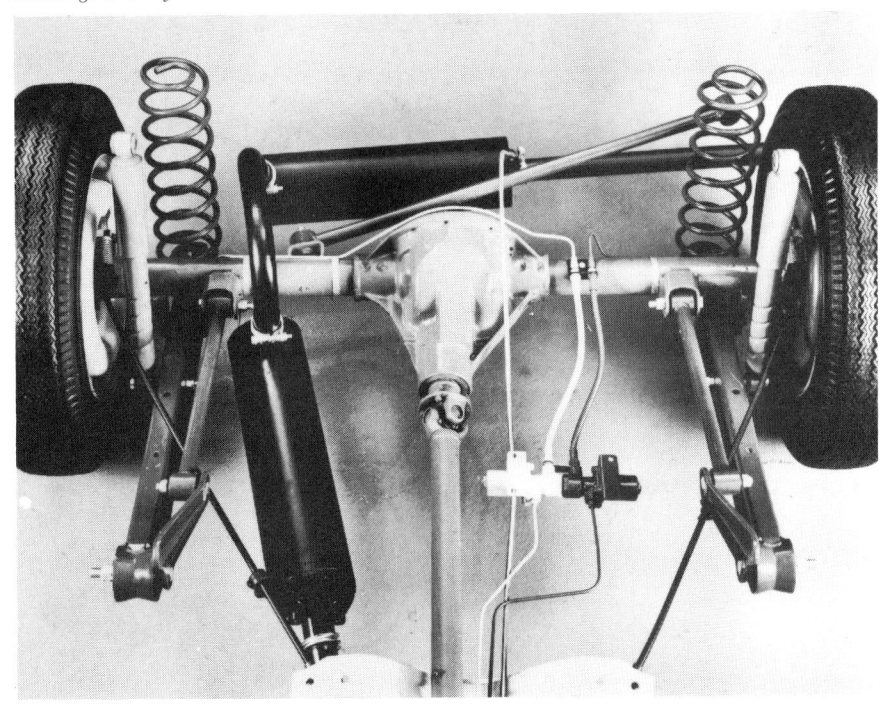

Volvo's 'safety first' image really came to fruition with the 140 Series. Here is a production car being crashed into the concrete block, at 30 mph. Afterwards, even the front doors could be opened.

this—was that new styles had to be approved by management, none of whom were as aware as he was of trends and acceptable fashions. Nor could they always express themselves adequately, as the consultant Mas-Olle's remark about the P179 and the PV444 makes clear.

The car which began to take shape in 1961 was, in Wilsgaard's own words, more of an industrial design than a sculpture. 'I had become an industrial man by then,' he now says. Tor Lidmalm, Volvo's technical director at the time, was quite convinced that this was a very practical machine, so a final viewing by the directors was keenly anticipated.

'We had been very careful with this car,' Wilsgaard says, 'and we built two mock-ups, to test entrance and exit, headroom, luggage space, everything. I remember that when the viewing was arranged on the studio floor, it took only 45 minutes before Gunnar Engellau suddenly banged on the table, looked around among his colleagues, and said: "Let's go!" The decision was taken so fast, that I was actually scared—I thought that something would go wrong.'

Wilsgaard was worried, for instance, that the design was so clean, that it might have lost interest over the years, but he need not have been troubled; in essence, the passenger box and tail of the agreed style was still being used, and built in large numbers, with the 240 Series cars being made in 1982 when I talked to him. Following Amazon practice, the car had always been laid out as a two-door or a four-door saloon, but in those very early stages no estate car had been modelled, and there were certainly no thoughts about a larger, long-wheelbase car which eventually became the 164. The style of the 164 was not completed until September 1964, more than two years after the basic design of the new P1400, or 140 Series, had been frozen.

The 140 Series was built with the new Torslanda plant in mind, for now Volvo

The driver's crash helmet is for test driving, not for competitions—but this was an original 144, being put through its paces for publicity purposes.

were looking forward to a large increase in production capacity. So much land had been purchased, incidentally, that it would have been perfectly possible, if financially difficult, for a 'mirror-image' or duplicate plant to have been built alongside the original factory, just a little further away from the centre of Gothenburg.

There was nothing adventurous about the mechanical layout of the car—by this time, observers would have been very shocked if Volvo had taken a great leap forward into the unknown—which was all, quite plainly, a development, and derivative, of the existing models. I should point out, at this stage, that the new 140 Series car was due to be launched in 1966 and that the building of the wonderful old PV544 would end in 1965. It would have been asking too much of Volvo's dealer network to market three different types of car and, as the PV544 was down-market of the existing Amazon/120 Series, and the new 140 Series was going to be larger, and more expensive, this would clearly alter the company's stance entirely.

Historians and motoring archaeologists, therefore, will readily see that the 'chassis' of the new car took some features from the Amazons, which were to continue in production, and some from the 1800S coupé, which was coming up to the prime of its life. The engine/gearbox/back axle were all common to the existing cars, in that the five-bearing 1,778 cc B18 engine was to be offered, in single carb (75 bhp net) and twin carb (100 bhp) guise, though on the basic engine a side-draught Zenith-Stromberg carburettor took the place of the down-draught Zenith instrument used on older models.

The gearbox, like that of the Amazon, retained a long but sturdy direct-action gear lever, but on this car there was the option of Laycock overdrive, or of Borg Warner three-speed automatic transmission. The independent front suspension, by coil springs and wishbones, was like that of the Amazon, while the rear axle location was much the same as before. The wheelbase of the new body shell, in fact, was the same as before, though both front and rear wheel tracks were wider—the 260 cm/102.4 in wheelbase now being quite traditional to Volvo, as the PV444 had been treated to this dimension way back in the mid-1940s.

Apart from the fact that all components were designed to last seemingly indefinitely, and the steering column had a collapsible joint in it to make sure that the steering wheel did not move back into the driver's chest in the unfortunate instance of a head-on accident, the most excitingly advanced feature of the chassis was the braking system. Not only were four wheel disc brakes fitted for the first time on any Volvo, but the split hydraulic circuits were so arranged that each circuit operated on both front wheels and one rear wheel; this meant that if one circuit was ruptured, or otherwise damaged, up to 80 per cent of normal braking effort was still available from the surviving circuit. It was a typically neat Volvo touch that at the rear there was a separate drum-type handbrake rather than the inefficient mechanical clamping of the disc adopted by some other concerns. The drums were tucked away inside the hubs of the rear discs themselves.

The 'chassis' of the new 140 Series car, however, was not the major advance, compared with the Amazon, nor was it ever intended to be. Not only was the style crisp and new, safe and protective of its occupants, but it was also more spacious than its predecessor. When I analysed the new car for *Autocar* in March 1967, I see that I commented: 'Though one is immediately struck by close styling similarities with such up-to-date European cars as the Hillman Hunter, the revised Cortina and even the Ford Taunus 20M, the 144 is a completely home-brewed design', which was only as it should have been, as Jan Wilsgaard could have had no idea of what Ford and Rootes were planning when he finished shaping the 140 Series; I now know, indeed, that neither British company had even started their own studies when the shape of the 140 Series was approved for tooling to commence.

Compared with the Amazon, the 140 Series was 19 cm (7.4 in) longer than the earlier car, and 11 cm (4.3 in) wider. Not only was there considerably more width between the pillars (a consequence of Wilsgaard's advance from the 'full of life' shape to a more 'industrial' style—his description, in each case) but the rear seat had been pushed back as much as decently possible and a lot more glass area had been provided. The two-door car (to be called 142), when it appeared, would have four side window glasses, as usual, but the first car to be launched, the 144 four-door derivative, had the new Volvo feature of three side windows—one for each door and a rear quarter glass alongside the rear seat squab.

Another factor which helped make the car longer was the storage boot, which was enormous. It had a very high sill, which was a nuisance when bulky or heavy loads had to be hoisted aboard, but this was retained for the good and simple reason that it helped stiffen up the structure, and keep the body shell intact in the event of a rear-end collision. It would not be until the early 1970s that a minor styling and engineering rethink allowed this sill to be dropped by an important, but barely noticed few inches.

The nose of the car, like the tail, was very bluff and vertically styled, but it could not have been too awfully un-aerodynamic, for the first independent road tests showed that the first 100 bhp 144S types were capable of more than 100 mph in non-overdrive form; later, in the mid-1970s, the outwardly smoother 240 Series cars often struggled to reach the same speed. On the other hand, the new car looked

140s, 240s and safety 113

Above *As with the 120 Series, Jan Wilsgaard made provision for two-door and four-door derivatives of the basic 140 Series shape. The nose style of this car was a later-model face-lift.*

Right *There has to be a story behind this, but nobody told me what it was! Seven 144s playing piggy-back, to prove how strong the structure was.*

Above *In 1968, Volvo announced the 164—really a long-wheelbase 144 with a six-cylinder version of the long-running four-cylinder engine.*

Below *The 164's grille carried that characteristic diagonal motif found on the original Volvos of 1927.*

140s, 240s and safety

heavy, and it *was* heavy. At about 2,550 lb, it was the heaviest Volvo car for some years, and this showed in the fuel consumption figures recorded by the magazines and the customers.

But Volvo were not at all perturbed, for there was a reason for it. The secret of the new car, after all, was not what it looked like, but what was in it. Perhaps many people never noticed, but there were big and sturdy bumpers with rubber inserts, a laminated windscreen, three-point safety belts, a hidden 'roll-over' bar in the roof, more of that crash padding which was going to minimise injuries in accidents and a very rigid structure indeed. Volvo had also come to terms with the fact that their cars would not only have to live in Sweden, but in North America and Canada, where the winters could be very severe. Electrical systems were more robust, batteries were large and heating systems more comprehensive. Even in 1966, Volvo's standard system included warm air fed through tubes hidden under the propeller shaft tunnel towards the rear seats, and ducting through the sills towards the rear window, to keep that clear of ice and condensation. I will never forget the first time I borrowed a 144S from Volvo to follow the Swedish rally of February 1967 and being astonished at the speed with which the inside of the car became bearably cosy, even when temperatures down to -40 degrees (Centigrade or Fahrenheit, they coincide at this mark) were being recorded outside.

The first of the Volvo 'bumper cars'—for 1974. The USA market soon made such fittings mandatory, but Volvo standardised them all over the world.

While the new car was being developed, however, there was something of a race to get a new and super-modern administrative building ready at Torlsanda ahead of it. Due to the company's growth in so many ways, it had long outgrown its ancient headquarters at Lundby, and even though the old ball-bearing building had long since ceased to see the actual manufacture of cars or trucks, it was quite incapable of accommodating a large staff. By the early 1960s, office workers were being accommodated in no fewer than 17 other different locations, dotted around Gothenburg and its suburbs.

A commanding site at Torslanda was therefore chosen, planning began in 1964, and actual construction of a forward-thinking open-plan office complex began in 1965. But the 140 Series won in the end—that was revealed in August 1966, whereas the new office building was not ready until 1967.

Volvo production, in the meantime, was still pushing ahead. The first 100,000-a-year figure was recorded in 1963, when the PV544 was still selling well, and while Torslanda's halls were still being completed. A year later, with Torslanda complete, that figure rose to 118,464, and in 1965 it moved up again, to 133,239. It was a time for new records to be set and broken. In 1963 the annual turnover of the Volvo Group exceeded two *billion* SKr for the first time, in 1965 Volvo products (cars and trucks) were being assembled in eight different countries, and at the beginning of 1966, the millionth Volvo car was built.

Well before the 144 model was ready to be shown to the world, there were test cars on the road, and before the end of 1965 carefully disguised production-standard prototypes were being driven on the open road, carrying badges proclaiming their identity as 'Mazuo ZT92' models. What did that name mean? Nothing at all—and it might have fooled a few people into thinking that something Oriental had travelled all the way to Sweden for appraisal.

As with the original PV444, and the Amazon of 1956, the 140 Series was only just ready to go into production when it was announced. In 1967, when I surveyed the Scandinavian scene for *Autocar*, I quoted Volvo's achievements for 1966, the year in

A 'ghost' view of the 164's layout, showing the long straight-six cylinder engine. From the screen backwards, the 164 and the 144 were virtually identical.

140s, 240s and safety

which the 144/144S cars were presented, and the statistics were completely dominated by the Amazon: more than 103,000 Amazon saloons had been built, compared with a mere 4,700 140 Series cars. But the surge was already under way—first the body derivatives and then the progressive upgrading of specifications.

After the four-door cars, the two-door saloon (142) and the five-door estate car (145) followed on in quick succession, thus completing the line-up planned from the very beginning. Compared with the Amazon/120 Series cars, the numbering policy for these cars was much more logical. All were basic 140 series cars, with the third number indicating the number of doors on the body shell. If the engine fitted was the single-carb unit, no further suffix was added to the name, but if it was a twin-carburettor unit the letter 'S' (S for sporting or special—Volvo never really bothered to explain) was added. A 142, therefore, was a 75 bhp, single-carb, two-door saloon, while a 145S was a 100 bhp, twin-carb, five-door estate car.

The two-door saloon, which in all other respects of seating, size and stowage accommodation, was the same as the four-door, had been planned and styled right from the start in 1961/62, and only followed *after* the four door because there were practical limits to the amount of tooling and new-model 'shake-down' activity which Volvo could tackle at once. The estate car was different. It was a shape and package on which Jan Wilsgaard and his colleagues lavished a great deal of time, so successfully that it has since become *the* large estate car with which most of the others are still compared, and in upgraded 240 Series form is still in quantity production as this book was being completed.

Wilsgaard's brief was that the estate car should use the same basic 'chassis' and underpan, nose, scuttle, screen and doors as the saloons—a normal limitation, as far as modern product planning is concerned. He was encouraged to provide a really huge stowage space, and one of his favoured schemes included a near-vertical tailgate, and went so far as to use a new shape of side window glass channel to blend in with the swept-straight-back roof line. Even today Jan thinks that he should have been allowed to use those reshaped doors, though he admits that the finalised estate

For 1972, Volvo matched the fuel injection system of the six-cylinder 164E (back to the camera) with fuel injection for the 144 as well. This made good cars even better.

Above *Hundreds of bits and pieces go into a modern car, as this display of 145 estate components shows.*

Below *In 1967 Volvo added the five-door (hence 145) estate car to their 140 Series, which became enormously popular.*

140s, 240s and safety 119

The 145 estate cars offered enormous extra stowage space, which tens of thousands of customers found irresistible. The same basic body/passenger compartment was carried forward into the 240/260 Series, and was still being built at the time of writing this book.

car rear end was well-balanced and very practical. Which explains why complete saloon rear doors are used on the big Volvo estate cars—management looked at the alternatives, looked at the cost of it all, and decided that a minor styling compromise was worth saving money for; in the motor industry, particularly in the 1980s, there is a lot of this about.

Even before the first of the 140 Series cars was announced, however, design work on a 'big brother' was well advanced. Gunnar Engellau realised that a truly big Volvo would probably not sell in sufficient numbers to make the investment worthwhile, but he and his senior colleagues not only missed seeing the large six-cylinder engined cars around any more, but they kept harking back to the big, impressive, P358 project which might have done so much for the company's image, world wide.

This, and other market pressures (particularly from North America, where Volvo thought they would need more performance to face the domestic competition, and from Europe where their cars were often being flatteringly compared with the products of Daimler-Benz) made the concept of a larger-engined car attractive once again. It was no coincidence that when production machines were installed for the new B18 engine at the end of the 1950s, they would be capable of producing six-cylinder as well as four-cylinder components.

Because of the huge expense (and delay) involved in producing press tools for steel panelling, there was no question of having an entirely new body style for a large new Volvo 'flagship', so the technical department, in conjunction with the stylists, were asked to find a way of grafting a longer six cylinder into the basic body/chassis unit of the 140 Series model. This was done by the relatively simple method of retaining the basic passenger compartment intact aft of the scuttle and front screen, and merely designing a new longer-wheelbase nose to accommodate the new engine. At the same time it was decided that the four-cylinder engine should take up its always-planned 2-litre (actually 1,986 cc) capacity, and that the six-cylinder derivative, which was effectively a four-cylinder unit with an extra two cylinders slotted in, should be of 2,978 cc capacity. Logically, also, in view of Volvo's newly found sense concerning model numbering, the new saloon would be called a 164, where '6' in this case referred to the six-cylinder engine.

Work on the style of the new car was completed in 1964 before Jan Wilsgaard went off to North America for his one-year artistic sabbatical, the new shape being an even more elegant stretched extension of the 144's style. Because the position of this structure's gearbox and clutch could not be changed, it meant that the extra inches of the lengthy new engine would all have to reach further forward. This could not be accommodated in an unchanged shell so, to preserve the correct and acceptable weight distribution, the line of the front wheels was also moved forward to compensate. Compared with the 144S, therefore, the 164 had a 10 cm/3.9 in longer wheelbase, whereas the overall length was up by 7 cm, or less than 3 in. What *had* increased, quite markedly, was the weight—a 164 weighed an extra 130 kg/287 lb, much of which was in the cast iron engine itself.

Even so, the 'balance' of the new car was still absolutely right, not only because the new seven-bearing engine, called a B30 (compared with B20 for the two-litre 'four') was silky smooth, but because an extremely handsome front-end style had been chosen. For the 164, Volvo reverted to the rectangular shape of front grille, as one proposed for the still-born PV644 and P358 projects. Along with massive, but well proportioned, bumpers and cooling grilles at each side of the grille, and a longer bonnet sweep which many observers think actually improved the shape of the whole car, it was a handsome machine with which to face the 1970s. It can have been no more than coincidence that one of Volvo's greatest rivals, BMW, chose the same year and season in which to show their first six-cylinder cars for some years, in their case with a choice of 2.5-litre and 2.8-litre engines.

For 1969, therefore, Volvo not only kept on building two-door Amazons, but they had a full line up of 2-litre 140 Series models, and the 164 saloon as the flagship. It was no wonder that all the corporate indicators still pointed upwards, with 5,000 people now working for Volvo in Gothenburg, with American sales increasing for the 21st record month in succession, with a car assembly plant opened in Malaysia, and with corporate turnover now approaching the four billion SKr level. In 1968, a total of 170,746 Volvo cars had been built and the company was shooting for 200,000 at the beginning of the 1970s.

There is an interesting point to be quoted about the evolution of the 164, for Volvo were still very touchy indeed about the secrecy of their prototypes being preserved up until the last moment. At first, with a lot of cutting and carving around, the engine could be tested in a 144, and next in an Opel (called, internally, a 'Vopel'—what else?), before the definitive long-wheelbase body shell was ever put on the road. It was in cars like this that the new ZF-manufactured gearbox, and the power-assisted steering, were tested, and refined. Jan Wilsgaard once laughingly reminded a colleague of the attachment he had had to the still-born P358 project, and that, when the 164 was launched, complete with 358-like nose and grille, some people said to him: 'Well, I see you got the front through, at least!'

For the next six years, although many new derivatives of the cars were produced—a new engine one year, new facia the next, new grilles, tail lamps and

140s, 240s and safety

Above *The obvious car for police to use to chase fast Volvo drivers in Sweden, was an even faster Volvo!*

Below *Building 145 estate car body shells, prior to painting and final assembly.*

Above *The simple, some say plain, interior of the original 144. This particular car had the optional air conditioning and the optional automatic transmission.*

Below *Among many additional safety features tested by Volvo in the early 1970s were children's seats, forward or rearward facing, and special 'safety carry cots'.*

Above *The 1971 Volvo range included four-cylinder and six-cylinder cars, the 1800E coupé and the special raised-roof 'Express' estate car.*

Below *The Volvo Express was a limited-production machine providing even more space than normal in a 145, with the aid of a raised roof line and a built-in roof rack.*

larger bumpers to keep North American legislators happy—their basic design was never disturbed. Could it be that Volvo management was not only completely happy with the way the cars had been received, but that they were all increasingly pre-occupied with something new? It would not be until the early 1970s that this mystery was solved.

Consolidation, and improvement, of the range continued. For 1971, for instance, not only was a 2-litre fuel injection engine offered on the two-door cars (a slightly less powerful version of that already fitted to the 1800E coupé), along with wide rim wheels, bigger and better brakes and a revised interior, but the wheelbase of all the 140/160 Series cars was increased by 2 cm (or rather less than an inch). Such a change was certainly not made to improve the roadholding of the cars—the difference was indiscernible, and achieved by moving the rear wheels slightly backwards relative to the body shell—and it has never been discussed, or explained, by Volvo management.

The injection option was soon extended to the four-door and five-door versions of the car, and there were more safety-related refinements for 1972, but the 1973 models, announced in the autumn of 1972, included an entirely new and very smart facia and instrument panel; by this time all versions had the remote-control gear-change of the 1800 coupé type, and apart from its heavy steering and rather ponderous road behaviour, the 140 Series Volvo was beginning to look, and perform, like a BMW competitor, which is how many of its new customers looked on it.

The cars, and the company, had their critics—some thought both were too earnest, too safety-conscious and completely devoid of fun-taking frivolity. But this was not so much a Volvo failing, as a Swedish national characteristic. The Swedes are lovely, honest and straightforward people, who have come to terms with a Socialist way of government, and of life, who seem to enjoy having their affairs, and even their whole life-styles, arranged for them, and who make a virtue out of this experience. These attitudes, naturally enough, influenced the cars they began to build in the 1960s and 1970s—and the rest of the world seemed to go along with that.

Certainly, sales continued to climb, as the Torslanda and overseas assembly plants were expanded and made more efficient, for more than 200,000 cars were sold for the very first time in 1970, and in 1973 this record was pushed up to 252,036. A quarter of a million Volvos in a year! The company's founders, Assar Gabrielsson and Gustaf Larson, could never even have visualised this way back in the 1920s. In 1971, for instance, the two millionth Volvo car had been built, a mere six years after the first million had been completed. To do this, of course, the company had to live almost entirely on its exports—by the early 1970s four out of every five Volvos built in Sweden were being sent overseas. The decision to build the Torslanda factory near the docks was paying off handsomely, every day, and every week.

For 1974 which, if only had we known it then, was to be the last year of 140 Series production, Volvo produced the first of their 'bumper cars'. I have not just invented this nickname myself, for it was freely applied by the motoring writers when they got their first view of the 1974 models. Massive bumpers, several inches clear of otherwise unmodified bodywork, were intended to meet the new United States legislation, where well over 50,000 Volvos (as many as in Sweden) were being sold every year. This, along with the moving of the fuel tank to a less vulnerable position, the stiffening up of the doors, the standardisation of electrical seat heating

140s, 240s and safety

on many models, and the inclusion of persistent (and—let's be fair—hated by many) safety belt warning lights, was yet another move towards greater and greater passive safety and security for the customer, in which Volvo was a world leader.

Nor was the specification of the six-cylinder 164 neglected. For 1972 the car not only benefitted from development changes being introduced on the four-cylinder models, but a top-of-the-range version (the 164E) was introduced with Bosch fuel injection instead of a carburetted engine—which pushed up the peak power from 145 to no less than 175 bhp. Without doubt, this was the fastest Volvo yet sold, for in overdrive form it could reach 120 mph, at the penalty (not thought too critical at the beginning of the 1970s) of a fuel thirst of about 18 mpg.

It was not until the end of the 1960s that the last sub-derivative of the old PV444 design was at last built, this being the PV445 estate car, which by that time was looking narrow, upright and out-of-date, though it was undeniably useful for certain specialised tasks. Certainly there was a view, at Volvo, that neither the old Type 220 (Amazon-based) estate car, nor the new 145 could completely take its place, and it was for this reason that the specialised 145 express was revealed, to take over from the PV445. The Express, still on the standard 144/145 wheelbase and floorpan, was sold either as a van or as an estate car, in each case with the four passenger doors still in place. The express, however, differed from the 145 because it had a substantially raised roof line aft of the front seats, and ahead of the roof bulge there was a neatly fenced off storage area for outside loads.

Also, at the end of the 1960s, Volvo had been rationalising and expanding their affairs, for in 1969 they not only took over the Svenska Stalpressings AB company at Olofstrom, but they began planning a new and very advanced proving ground, to be built at Hallered. The Olofstrom body factory had been supplying pressings to Volvo ever since the first OV4s were built in 1927, but had never been under full financial control until now.

For 1971, Volvo offered Bosch fuel-injection as a high-power option on the 140 Series cars, which slotted neatly into the existing engine bay.

126   *The story of Volvo cars*

Above *VESC was styled at the end of the 1960s for possible production in the early 1970s. Picture this car without the enormous bumpers or the extra roll-over roof protection—would it have been more saleable than the 240/260 models which were built instead?*

Below *Truly massive front bumpers, with deformable structures, as fitted to the VESC safety prototype.*

But still there was an uncanny silence from the engineers and a complete lack of rumours regarding new models for the 1970s. Something, for sure, was on the way, for an advanced and well-equipped complex was being built in the trees behind the main administrative building. Suddenly, in 1972, Volvo unveiled their Volvo Experimental Safety Car (VESC for short)—something which was ostensibly no more than a research project; in 1982, however, I discovered that it could have been more, much more, than this.

140s, 240s and safety

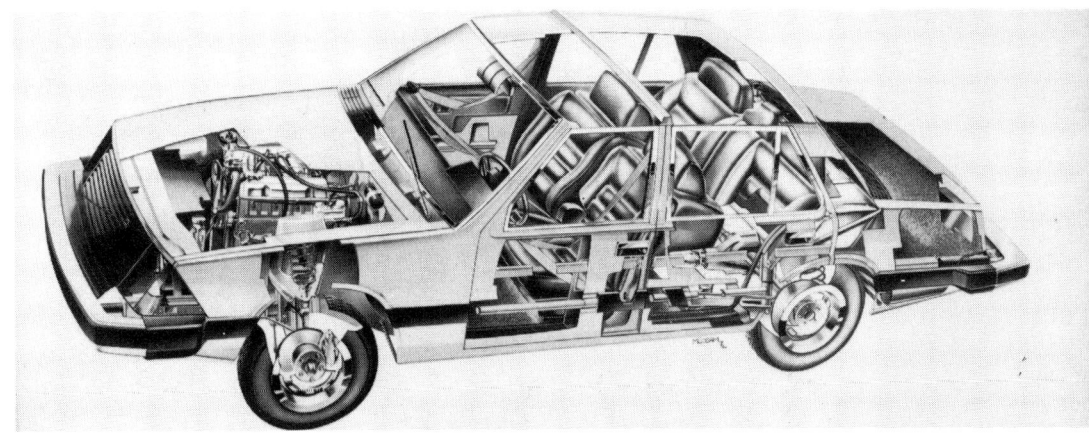

Above *Volvo's Experimental Safety Car (VESC) first shown in 1972, tried out many advanced ideas which were eventually standardised on later models. But there was more to VESC than this. In rather less specialised form, the body style might have been a production model, but it was dropped in favour of the more conservative 240 Series cars.*

When the VESC was unveiled in April 1972, only the truly prescient and deep-thinking observers saw more than a machine to meet and subsequently overcome the mass of legislation flooding out of North America. Volvo themselves said that they were building a fleet of ten of these cars (at a time when most 'safety' prototypes were built in ones, or twos at the most), that the programme had got under way in 1969, and that when the American ESV requirements were released in 1970, that 70 of the 82 requirements were equalled or exceeded by their own achievements.

Rolf Mellde's project team had managed to include air bags (instead of safety belts) for each front and rear seat occupant, energy-absorbing front and rear bumpers, anti-impact passenger door beams, pop-up head restraints on seats, anti-lock braking, automatic fuel supply cut-off, and semi-passive safety belts which only came into operation when the car's engine was started. VESC was not, it was stated, intended for series production, and most of the fleet was to be totally destroyed in various tests.

Which was all very well, and very commendable as far as it went—but the information revealed did not go very far. There was always the nagging suspicion that Volvo was not the sort of company to spend a great deal of money, not only in developing new safety features, but in evolving a completely new style of body shell, and engineering that body shell, if they were only going to build ten cars.

In 1982, when I was over in Sweden carrying out research for this book, I was privileged to look at the company's store of old, precious and abandoned project vehicles, and it was then that things became more clear. There, stored in one corner, was not only a surviving example of the VESC, but another car which looked just like VESC, without a lot of its fittings. The basic body style was exactly the same, as were the large safety bumpers, but items like the external roll-cage protection, and some interior fittings, were not present. In short, this looked much more like the prototype of a real car, than a stripped out safety car.

When I talked to Hakan Frisinger, the president of the Volvo Car Corporation, he

The story of Volvo cars

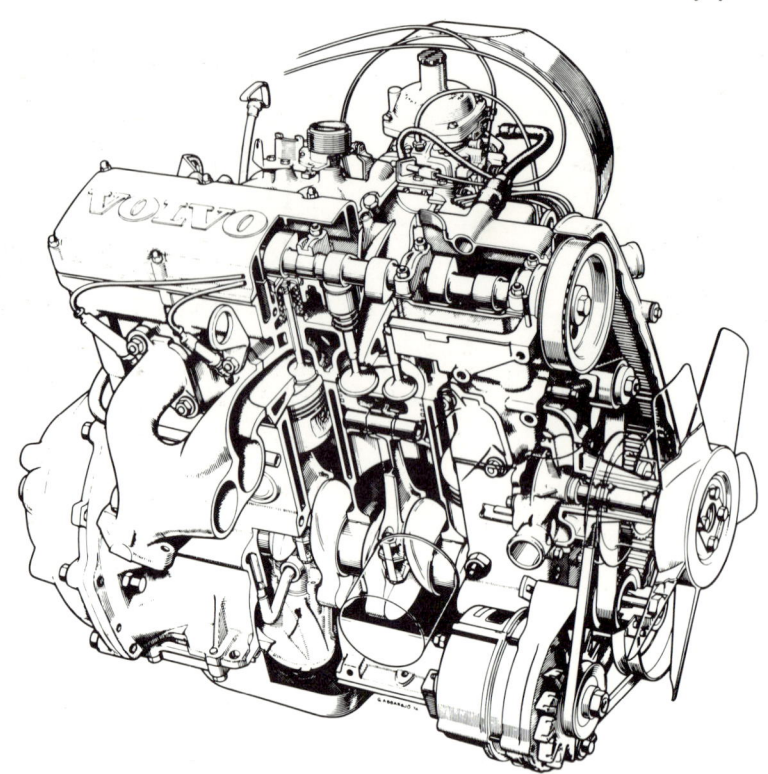

Above *For the 240 Series cars, Volvo developed the B19/B21 overhead camshaft engines, which were installed in the engine bay at an angle. Their original plan had also been to build a V-8 version of this basic design, but it was cancelled in favour of the PRV V-6 project.*

Below *Power and stability, if not for competition purposes, were both present in the two-door 242GT models.*

140s, 240s and safety

Visually, the 240 Series cars were very like the 140 Series, except that they had a more restrained version of VESC's wedge nose.

confirmed my suspicions—that, before the end of the 1960s, Volvo were thinking about a successor to the 140 Series models, and that the favoured design was that eventually to be found hidden away under all the VESC's fittings. 'The style, and the chassis, could have been very practical for production,' Mr Frisinger told me, 'but at a certain stage a decision was taken *not* to put that car into production, but to announce it instead as a VESC. It was not really a question of too much investment being needed. Really there was not enough belief among management in the car at that time. I was closely involved in that project—we didn't know if we could get satisfactory fuel consumption, and secondly there were still very big uncertainties regarding safety regulations. Just one example—we didn't know if we could meet proposed regulations regarding windscreen angles, or pass the crash test.'

I wondered if he was still happy that it had been cancelled, and he said he was. But he also admitted that perhaps the 240 Series styling which eventually appeared was not adventurous enough: 'But today we are happy that we didn't go ahead with the VESC type styling, for some of it would not have been modern today. Even today, if I had to choose between VESC and 240 styling, then I would choose 240. Definitely.'

Even though the 'production-type' VESC project was dropped at the beginning of the 1970s, work on new components for new models never faltered. In particular, Volvo found themselves looking at not one, but two, new engines. By its outward appearance and behaviour, the company may look staid and strictly conventional at times, but behind closed doors all manner of exciting projects are started up.

By 1968, when the six-cylinder version of the current Volvo engine was introduced for the Type 164 saloon, that family of engines was beginning to look old fashioned. In essence, if not in detail, it stemmed from the PV444 of the mid-1940s, and that was more than 20 years ago. In particular, the overhead valve gear and the breathing limitations placed upon the unit were behind the times, compared with BMW and Mercedes-Benz.

130 The story of Volvo cars

Above *The 264s were always distinguished with different radiator grille and headlamp treatment from the 244s.*

Below *Cars were getting more complex all the time—this was the V-6 engined 2.7-litre Volvo 264, as announced in 1974, complete with new MacPherson strut front suspension. Aft of the screen, the structure was similar to the old 140 Series cars.*

140s, 240s and safety

In the beginning, Volvo began looking at one new engine family to replace all their old ones, and after much study, decided that instead of this encompassing a 'four' and a straight 'six', it should be the combination of a 'four' and a V-8. It is always an over-simplification to say this, but in effect the V-8 could be two 'fours' at 90 degrees, on a common crankcase, using identical heads, valve gear and many moving parts like pistons and connecting rods. The fact that the 'four' would be a 2-litre unit, and the V-8 a large, heavy and powerful 4-litre did not disturb anyone, as fuel was still cheap, and large-engined competition was intensifying on all sides, and no economic planner was yet able to forecast, or even guess, the fuel price/shortage problem which suddenly appeared in 1973.

Although the new 'four'-cylinder engine did not need to use any common parts from the old design, it might help, so the new design started out on that basis. Using something like the basic dimensions of the old engine (in terms of cylinder spacings and cylinder block height), the designers decided to produce a single overhead camshaft engine, with a cogged belt drive to that cam; the V-8 engine, to follow, would be broadly similar, but naturally with increased complication.

The very first examples of each design, produced more to prove out the cam drive and the cylinder head details, looked almost prehistoric in concept, as the belts were exposed, and the cylinder heads and cover castings not at all 'styled', while the V-8 engine, with two of everything, looked to be a mechanic's nightmare. I know, because I have seen examples of each, which are still stored by Volvo, for museum use one day.

The next stage, of course, was to 'productionise' the engines and to lay down the tooling—but before then, great political events had intervened. Hakan Frisinger summarised very neatly that: 'Around 1970, we were planning a V-8, but then we cancelled that because we couldn't justify the investment.' (Money, money—the lack of it has killed off far too many exciting new-car projects in recent years.) 'Then we got into association with Renault–Peugeot, and at least one reason was because of the possibility of a V-8 engine.'

The 264GL's facia and controls, in this case with automatic transmission.

But, surely, the engine which appeared was, and is, a V-6? 'Yes, correct, but the project had been for a V-8 in the very beginning, then PRV (the V being Volvo) came to the conclusion that it should be a V-6 instead. Let's be clear—the original objective must have been to use a V-8, or there is no good reason for having that 90-degree V-angle!'

I ought to clear this up. In the beginning, Peugeot and Renault, both of France, had got together in co-operation in 1966, with the intention of producing more and more common components in years to come and helping each other in marketing strategies. At this time neither of them had a large 'flagship' on sale and the joint development of an engine to rectify this was considered. The engine proposed at first, which was to be brand new from end to end, and top to bottom, was to be a V-8. It was pure coincidence (but good engineering practice) that it was to be a single-cam-per-bank design like the new Volvo layout, though the camshafts were to be driven by chain. Naturally enough, because it was a V-8, the angle between cylinder banks, to give optimum balance, was to be 90 degrees.

Volvo got in on the act because they had already been talking with Renault about the DAF car business (discussed in a later chapter) and because, somehow, the chief executives of sizeable car corporations often talk to each other in confidence, exchange secrets, and keep abreast with what is going on in the world of motoring. . . .

It was at about this time that Gunnar Engellau, Volvo's chief since the mid-1950s, reached Volvo's standard retiring age, and passed over control to a dynamic young ex-lawyer called Pehr Gyllenhammar. This young man, only 36 years old when taking over from Engellau, who became Volvo's chairman, had originally qualified as a lawyer, and studied international law in England, before joining Scandia Insurance and directing its long term planning from 1966; by 1970 he was Scandia's managing director, and he took over as president of AB Volvo in May 1971. Incidentally, he was also Engellau's son-in-law.

The formalising of a joint engine development and manufacturing project with Peugeot and Renault, therefore, was one of the first truly big deals to which Gyllenhammer was a signatory, for I have photographic evidence which shows that he, Pierre Dreyfus of Renault and Francois Gautier of Peugeot, initialled the agreement on June 29 1971.

The new company, set up for this project, was called 'Société Franco-Suedoise des Motors PRV' and I am sure I need only point out once that PRV means Peugeot-Renault-Volvo. A brand new factory in Northern France, at Douvrin, was to be built for engine manufacture, and the new unit was to be used by each of the three companies for its own 'flagship'.

As conceived at first, the new 'co-operative' engine was to be a 90 degree V-8, of about 3.5-litres, and work progressed far enough for enormously costly transfer line machinery to be ordered. It could not have been an easy decision, therefore, for the group to decide that such an engine was too large, and that the easy way to make it smaller was literally to chop two cylinders off one end, and turn it into a V-6 instead! The definitive 'Co-op' engine became a 90 degree V-6 unit of 2,664 cc—there being no time, or money, to change the order for tooling. (The ideal vee angle for a V-6 is 60 degrees, but 90 degrees is still acceptable, as Citroën and Maserati had already proved with the high-performance unit they were using for the Citroën SM coupé, and as Renault themselves were proving with a more specialised design used in sports racing and eventually GP cars.)

Volvo certainly took delivery of V-8 engines from Douvrin (at least one is stored,

With the 265, Volvo linked their up-market engine with the estate car body style for the first time—and very successfully, too.

in full view, along with some of their historic vehicles), but never engineered a car to use this version of the unit which is, of course, several inches longer than the V-6 version. Was there a chance that a V-8 version of the engine would eventually appear, for any of the partners? Hakan Frisinger was both frank and discreet in his answer: 'I can only say that you will certainly not see a V-8 engine in a Volvo, but I *can* confirm that the capability of making V-8s still exists at Douvrin. It was the two energy crises which struck a big blow at the V-8, but even in 1970 we weren't forecasting big volumes for a V-8 Volvo, which explains why we had to cancel an investment on our own.'

The V-6 engine, as finalised, was a neat-looking unit, not only with overhead camshaft cylinder heads in light alloy, but with light-alloy cylinder blocks as well, the result being that it weighed about 340 lb, very similar indeed to the new overhead-camshaft unit, whose final capacity could either be 2-litre or 2.1-litre, and which was to be installed in a new car tilted over to one side at an angle of 10 degrees. The usual fatuous claims were made that this tilt was arranged so as to let the bonnet line above the engine sit lower, which is nonsense, of course. (It would take a tilt of something like 30 degrees, if not more, to allow the overall height of a four-cylinder engine appreciably to be lowered.) The real, and very prosaic reason for tilting the engine was to allow space for the carburettors (or fuel injection) and air cleaners to fit inside the width of the engine bay.

When Volvo management cancelled the 'production VESC' concept, they left the succession to the 140/160 Series absolutely undecided. To cut down the lengthy period which would inevitably follow if yet another new car was developed, and to cut down the investment required (the two new engines would be horrifyingly expensive, in any case), the company took the very brave decision to keep the bare

Above *At Kalmar, partly-assembled cars move around the factory on trolleys, which are guided electronically by wires buried under the concrete. The same principle has also been adopted in the newest Volvo truck factory near Gothenburg.*

Below *Even at Kalmar, body meets 'chassis' in the conventional way.*

At Kalmar, the flexible 'Group Assembly' process allows saloons and estates to be assembled even easier than in a conventional factory.

bones of the 140 Series cars, thoroughly to rework every detail which needed it, and to provide a completely new front end.

The two new cars—240 Series and 260 Series—which were launched in August 1974, therefore, were all new from the windscreen forward, but very familiar to all Volvo enthusiasts from the windscreen back, because the massively strong passenger compartment, six window styling and general construction of the old 140 Series was retained. In addition, it was immediately possible to offer estate car derivatives of the new cars, rather than have to wait, and spend yet more precious capital, on another type of body.

This 'conversion' (for this is what it really was) was not tackled so that the existing 140/160 Series cars could carry on—with the exception of one type of 164 which continued to be assembled at Kalmar for another year, all other derivatives were immediately replaced by new models. It was the first time in Volvo's post-war history that this had happened—when the Amazon had arrived on the scene, the PV444 had carried on undisturbed, while the Amazon/120 Series cars continued to be built for years after the 140 Series range had been unveiled. But not this time, at Gothenburg—the 140s and 160s had to be phased out before the new 240s and 260s could be started.

The main visual improvement was that there was a new nose, with something of a wedge style, and this was clearly developed—in philosophy, if not in detail—from the more consciously stylised front of the VESC prototypes. Because the new 'Douvrin' V-6 was such a compact engine (it was wider, but no longer, than the new Volvo overhead-cam four-cylinder engine), both types of engine could be accommodated in the same engine bay, and the same wheelbase, structure and front sheet metal could be used for both types. This was a great saving, and made life much easier for the production planners, especially those connected with body assembly jigging. The new car's wheelbase, however, was not the same as that of the old cars. Because Volvo had thoroughly re-engineered the front of the car, not least by ditching the conventional coil spring and wishbone front suspension of the 140s, in favour of a MacPherson strut layout, which could not only spread shock loads more widely in the structure, but allowed significantly more space around the engine, in the engine bay, they were also able to choose a wheelbase of 264 cm (103.9 in). This was 2 cm longer than that of the last 140s and 8 cm shorter than that of the 264 saloons.

The importance of this rationalisation cannot be stressed too highly—for not only were Volvo only faced with building a single new engine family in the future, but a single basic body shell as well. The lengthy six-cylinder engine, used only in Volvo 164 cars between 1968 and 1975, could speedily be consigned to the spare parts catalogue. There was no doubt, however, that Volvo had been very cautious in the styling of its new models, and more than one journalist suggested that the customer was actually being cheated—although new engines were being provided, the prices were being raised significantly, and in reality he was only getting 'half of a new car'. When would the rest of the new car be ready?

Jan Wilsgaard agrees that he and his styling team would have liked to make more changes (on the basis that a completely new body shell was not permissible) but his brief excluded any sheet-metal alterations around the passenger cabin, to the glass shapes, or to the rear end, though he did tell me that there was a considerable amount of discussion about the height of the boot sill, and the shape of the lid itself. The original 240/260 Series cars, therefore, kept the same tail as the 140/160 Series had had since 1966, and changes proposed before announcement would not, in fact, be made until later in the 1970s.

Now, and only now, of course, the reason for the use of large free-standing bumpers on 1974 models of 140/160 cars became clear, for they had obviously been designed with the new car's styling in mind, so that similar energy-absorbing devices could be used on the new cars, to meet the American '5 mph, no damage' legislation.

Because the new cars were loosely based on the body shell and production tooling of the obsolete models, they could go into series production at once, and were already seen on the roads before the end of 1974. Nor was there any delay in making all the derivatives available—right from the start there were two-door and four-door saloons and the five-door estate cars, all with the new four-cylinder overhead camshaft engine (which, in its initial top tune, produced 123 bhp gross), although the V-6 Type 264 was only available at first in four-door saloon style.

Within a year, however, the merits of careful product planning, and easy interchangeability, became apparent—for 1976, Volvo finally phased out the old 164, and added a two-door saloon and a five-door estate car option to the V-6 'chassis'. Within reason, therefore, a Volvo customer could sit down in the showroom and 'design' his new car, which could range from an 82 bhp two-door four-cylinder Type 242 saloon, right up to a 140 bhp four-door V-6 Type 264 saloon. There were complications, of course—at first a six-cylinder estate car had less power than the saloon equivalent, and the fuel-injected 'four' was only on offer with the four-door or five-door body shells, but product planning is like that, and sales certainly did not seem to have suffered as a consequence.

The naming of the new cars, incidentally, was just as logical as it had been for the

140s, 240s and safety

140/160 models—indeed, the method was exactly the same. Perhaps it confirms that the new models were really 'Mk 2' 140s and 160s, because they were called 240s and 260s! The only really new combination, of course, was that the 265 model appeared as a six-cylinder estate car. But then, there never had been an estate-car 'six' before 1975.

Those observers who were disappointed by the conventional appearance of the new cars clearly had not troubled to look under the surface for all the new features, particularly the safety fittings and details which were making such a name for Volvo all around the world. Presumably, too, they were not taking any notice of the proof of the long life of the cars which was also building up for the Swedish car makers, not only in Sweden and in North America, but in many other countries. If the VW Beetle was the archetypal workhorse for territories where a lack of maintenance was to be expected, the big Volvos were now *the* standard by which the anti-corrosive properties of other cars could be measured. Surveys by various government authorities proved, time and time again, that a Volvo, if properly looked after, lasted years longer than its competitors, and that anything up to 20 years could be expected without any extraordinary measures being taken. So it had *not* been sheer bravado, therefore, which induced Volvo to start providing mileage recorders reading up to 999,999 miles in the 1960s.

One reason, too, why Volvo had not produced a startling new car in 1974 was that management had embraced an entirely new social concept of working which, if successful, promised to revolutionise the mass production of cars, and other products, in years to come. The concept was known as 'Group Assembly' and, to turn theory into practice, Volvo chose to build a new factory at Kalmar, on the east coast of Sweden, a full five hours' drive from Gothenburg.

The four millionth Volvo passenger car, completed on October 12 1979 at Torslanda. Hakan Frisinger, President of the Volvo Car Corporation, salutes one of the assembly workers.

By the 1960s, several sociologists were beginning to question the accepted way of building consumer products. The 'tyranny of the assembly line', as it was often described, invariably confined a workman or woman to one place on that line, and to one particular job. For up to eight hours a day, perhaps, the same simple assembly or manufacturing job would have to be repeated—hundreds upon hundreds of grindingly boring times. There must be a better way, it was suggested—better, not because it was more profitable to the makers, or resulting in higher wages for the workforce, but because it could introduce more variety, more job satisfaction, into the task.

Volvo listened to these theories—for, at the time, they were only theories—checked them out, consulted their advisers and, at the beginning of the 1970s, decided to act—but not in Gothenburg, where any major change in working practices would cause huge disruption. Gothenburg's factories were already full up and the overseas plants were also busy. If a social experiment was to be tried, it should be in a new location. Not only would it make the costs of running such an enterprise easy to identify, but it would allow a new workforce to be taken (one without rigid ideas of the 'old' methods)—and it would allow production to be increased.

The Kalmar location was chosen because the Swedish government pointed out that a previous government-only plant in the region was due to close and that they wanted to avoid unemployment. Accordingly, and after certain financial inducements had been agreed, Volvo laid down an entirely new factory—indeed, an entirely new type of factory.

In 1973, Volvo opened a new factory at Kalmar, in eastern Sweden, where they introduced the fashionable 'Group Assembly' concept.

140s, 240s and safety

The cars in the 140/160 Series which were assembled at Kalmar would be technically identical with those assembled at Torslanda, or Ghent, or anywhere else. The major difference would be that there would be no moving assembly line, where a part-completed car passed the same station every minute or so. Instead, cars would take shape on trolleys, worked on by groups of workers. There would, indeed, be many work stations, but these would not be in a rigid line, operating to a rigid timetable—one group would finish a series of tasks before handing over the trolley to the next group. In any one group, perhaps, the person fitting steering columns one day might be found fitting foot pedals the next, and brake servos the day after that.

The personnel concept was startling enough, but visitors to Kalmar were more likely to be transfixed by the way the body shells were moved around the place. Supplied complete and ready painted from Torslanda, the shells were put on specially designed trolleys or carriers, each of which had its own on-board electric propulsion system. Guidance, however, was provided by circuits laid under the concrete floor, and computers made sure that each trolley moved precisely to its next station when the group previously involved signalled that they had finished. Space age? For sure, it was, when first used at Kalmar. Now, however, it qualifies as conventional engineering, for one lorry plant I saw during my tour of Volvo facilities in 1982 also uses the same principle—and this is for trucks of up to 44 tonnes capacity.

Planning for Kalmar began in 1971, building in 1972, and the very first car was completed early in 1974. Capacity was set for a maximum of 30,000 units a year, and at first every one of these was to be a six-cylinder 164 saloon, specifically

Assembly and testing of overhead-camshaft B19 engines.

intended for the North American market. For any other car company, the fact that Kalmar came on stream just after the first 'oil shock' of autumn 1973 would have been a disaster—but Volvo, as my appendices show, were not seriously affected.

At first, Volvo had problems at Kalmar, as Hakan Frisinger made clear: 'For some years productivity at Kalmar was low, but we have improved tremendously in the last four years. The situation in the early 1980s is that Kalmar is as efficient as any other plant we have, even Belgium.'

I wondered, therefore, if the sociologists had been wrong at first, in their propaganda about Group Assembly? 'Yes, but there were many other reasons, for none of the workers were originally *car* workers, and had no industrial backgrounds. But now, I want to emphasise, we *believe* in group assembly, and it has since been installed in all factories in different ways.'

Productivity certainly has improved. In 1981, a total of 27,100 cars were assembled at Kalmar, compared with 40,200 at Ghent, Belgium, and 10,300 at Halifax, Nova Scotia. As this book is written, Kalmar continues to expand, and has concentrated on 240 Series production in recent years; now that the 760GLE model has been introduced at Torslanda, and it is acknowledged that the 240 Series will eventually fade away, I expect Kalmar to be the last outpost of 240 Series assembly in the mid-1980s.

By the mid-1970s, however, developments in other parts of the Volvo empire were making more news than the Kalmar project. Not only had Volvo introduced new cars (the 240/260 Series) which were by no means popular with every potential customer, but they had moved into partnership with Holland's only domestic make of car, the DAF. Demand for Swedish Volvos sagged, if not actually crumpled, and DAF was an interesting, if unprofitable, venture. It was critical time for Volvo—the late 1970s was going to present an extremely bumpy ride!

Chapter 8

Expansion overseas
New factories, DAF and Renault

I have already noted the way in which Volvo set about making a lot more cars during the 1960s. Not only did they build the completely new Torslanda plant near Gothenburg, but they also commissioned new assembly plants in Canada and in Belgium, to look after special export opportunities. But even greater things were brewing for the 1970s.

At this point I ought to recall the 1960s which, as far as the European motor industry was concerned, was the decade of the mergers; it was a process which completely changed the face of the business. There were mergers in almost every country—in Germany, VW took over Audi while, in Italy, Fiat absorbed Ferrari, Autobianchi and Lancia. Citroën of France annexed Maserati, while in France Peugeot and Renault moved closer together. In Britain, Leyland took over Standard-Triumph, then Rover, while BMC joined forces with Jaguar, and eventually the British Leyland colossus was formed. Not all these financial marriages were wise, and not all were destined to prosper, but they created an uneasy atmosphere which independent firms like Volvo found it almost impossible to ignore.

In talking about Volvo's links with Peugeot and Renault, made in the early 1970s, Hakan Frisinger commented that: 'We were looking for a partner, no doubt about that. But at that time, we were searching for one partner for smaller cars, another partner for larger cars. At that time, to get stronger—merely to survive, in some cases—just about everyone in the business was looking for a partner.' However, even when the PRV/Douvrin deal was signed in 1971, Volvo never admitted that they had been looking around at other potential deals, nor that they had been approached by other companies, and turned them all down.

Even before the end of the 1960s, Volvo had become interested in a tie-up with DAF of Holland. Superficially, one would have expected the main advantage to be in merging DAF's truck-building interests with those of Volvo, for both firms were noted for their heavy commercial vehicles, and competed head-on at various levels. In fact, however, DAF always wanted to keep their trucks to themselves—it was their newest enterprise, the DAF car, which was on offer.

The Van Doorne family of Eindhoven, in Holland, had been building commerical vehicle trailers since 1928, and trucks since 1950, but surprised everyone by announcing the original DAF Daffodil car in 1958. Not only did Holland not have an indigenous motor car industry, which made the DAF very special, but the new car had a unique, and technically clever, belt-drive automatic

Above *When Volvo had only a minority share of DAF, they had little influence on the Dutch products. Here, in 1973, is a DAF 66 lined up alongside a 144GL.*

Below *Volvo completed their take-over of DAF in 1975 and saw to the re-engineering of the existing DAF 66 models, which then became Volvo 66s instead.*

Expansion overseas

As with all things Volvo, the 66s had to be safe—here is a prototype 66 being crash-tested to prove the point.

transmission. It had a 590 cc front-mounted flat-twin air-cooled engine, the transmission at the rear, rear-wheel drive and four-wheel independent suspension. Like the DAF trucks, it was to be made at Eindhoven and its price, when launched, was a mere £400.

Over the years, quality and performance improved and the original model was joined by the Michelotti-styled 44 in 1966. The big break-through, however, came in 1967, when the DAF 55 arrived, for this car, though based on the 44, used a water-cooled four-cylinder Renault engine of 1,108 cc. It was now the sort of car capable of making DAF 'respectable', and it even allowed them to take on a limited (and by the standards of its class, successful) competition programme. Even more important to DAF, in 'image' terms, was the fact that the clever Variomatic transmission was successfully used in a few Formula 3 racing cars.

However, even though DAF production had risen to about 65,000 cars a year by the end of the 1960s—about the same as Saab, but only about one-third the number achieved by Volvo—the project was not truly profitable, and the Van Doornes began to look for ways, either to divest themselves of the car-building business altogether, or to get into partnership with another car-maker. Thus it was that Volvo was approached for the first time.

Hakan Frisinger, now president of the Volvo Car Corporation, was the head of the original project team which Gunnar Engellau sent down to Holland to make a study of the DAF car manufacturing operation. The first visits were made in 1969 and the team's job was finished in 1970. It was a tightly-knit and highly secret mission, with only three Volvo people and three members of the Dutch family being involved.

At the time, Frisinger concluded that at this moment the project was not really viable for Volvo to become involved, as it had originally been undertaken to provide employment at Eindhoven when jobs were sorely needed, rather than on a strictly business basis, so he recommended that no link-up should be made.

The merger idea, however, did not disintegrate there and then; it was merely put into the background, and marked time for a while. As it happened, soon after Pehr Gyllenhammar took over as Volvo's president in 1971, he set Volvo on the expansionary path once again and followed up the signing of the engines deal with Renault and Peugeot by requesting a further look at the DAF operation. By 1972, DAF had not only pushed up their production towards the 90,000 a year mark, which *was* profitable, but they were building the cars at a new factory at Born, in Southern Holland, and they were preparing to launch the DAF 66 model, which was really a much-improved 55 with De Dion rear suspension and a modified type of Variomatic transmission. There were saloons, coupés and estate cars already on offer, and widespread rumours were to be found in the motoring press about yet another type of DAF, said to be called the '77', and to have a 1.5-litre Renault 16 engine.

There were many good reasons why Volvo should co-opeate with a company like DAF, whose cars were so much smaller and less expensive. It was summarised by the company, in a release, as follows: 'The reason behind the acquisition of DAF was to enable us to offer our dealers, in the shortest possible time and by tying up the least amount of capital, new products in the most expansive sector—small and medium size cars. This provided our sales organisation with increased strength and competitiveness which, in turn, produced a more secure basis for ensuring full employment . . . .'

Once reactivated, negotiations went ahead very quickly and smoothly—Volvo, after all, was a willing suitor, while DAF was available for sale. The initial deal was made at the end of September 1972, and involved Volvo taking a 33 per cent stake in Van Doorne's Personenautofabriek DAF BV—and the final agreement was signed at the start of 1973, talking bravely about 'joint marketing activities and coordination of product policy'.

The tie-up came at exactly the right time for Volvo to influence the future of the DAF car, for work was, indeed, going ahead on an additional, and larger, car. This, however, was not to have the rumoured Renault 16 engine, but the 1,397 cc

Expansion overseas

Renault engine which was the final possible stretch of that already being used in the 55 and 66 models.

There was time, but not much time, to bring to bear some of Volvo's expertise in terms of safety fittings, quality specification and a general Volvo 'image'—certainly on the new car, if not on the existing models. As far as the public were concerned, the first effect of Volvo influence was that the 55 disappeared at once, while the 66, in some versions, was treated to a larger, 1,289 cc engine for 1974. Finally, in the summer of 1975, the DAF name disappeared completely—the 44 and 46 models were dropped, while the DAF 66 was carefully re-engineered, given obvious Volvo features like the safety bumpers, a new facia, modified automatic transmission, and a Volvo look-alike front grille—and renamed the Volvo 66.

As Carl-Eric Haggstrom, of Volvo's marketing division, told me: 'The name of Volvo soon came to be reflected in the company and its cars. We started to sell the DAF 66 on the Volvo virtues which it already had—but DAF went for low fuel consumption and low price, while we tried to emphasise long-life expectancies and safety aspects.'

In the next few years, however, it was not the existing DAF/Volvo cars which would be so important to the new Swedish–Dutch company, but the next new model. Looked at in pure showroom marketing terms, there was a glaring and undesirable gap between the 1.3-litre, 88.5 in wheelbase DAF/Volvo 66 and the much larger 2.1-litre, 104 in wheelbase Volvo 240 Series cars. What was needed, to use classic product planning vernacular, was a 'gap-filler'.

That new car was already on its way, though it was not the rumoured '77' which had set the press a-talking some time ago. As stylist, Jan Wilsgaard, says: 'I happened to be in the group who were picking the model which was to go into production. We saw only two models, one of which had been styled by DAF themselves, and the other had been done by Trevor Fiore—that's a good name for an Englishman, isn't it? I understood that earlier, Michelotti had also proposed a style as well. In fact, we picked the DAF-inspired model, but changed it a lot

Left *Hakan Frisinger, President of the Volvo Car Corporation since its inception in 1979.*

Right *Per Gyllenhammar, President of AB Volvo through the 1970s, and now running the entire group in the 1980s.*

afterwards. We changed the bumpers, for instance, which were 'not Volvo' at first, we changed the grille, and we added Volvo philosophy inside, with things like new seats and facia styles, but we were really too late to do much.'

This time, at least, Volvo were able to give the car a complete Volvo identity, which was in any case appropriate, as they had increased their shareholding to 75 per cent of the shares from January 1975. The Volvo numbering sequence had been: 120 for the Amazon series, 140 for the cars which followed and 240 for the cars evolved from them. It therefore seemed appropriate to dub the new 'Dutch' Volvo the 340 Series and the first derivative, which was a three-door hatchback, was accordingly called the 343—model 3, four cylinder and three doors.

The new car made its public bow in February 1976 and was put on show at the Geneva International Motor Show in March. It was, at one and the same time, exactly as the press had expected, and it was disappointing. Most observers and pundits had expected the first true 'Dutch Volvo' to use a Renault engine and to have a family likeness to the 66, and they were even prepared for it to have similar suspension (MacPherson struts at the front, and a De Dion layout at the rear). Few, however, had expected the 343 to retain Variomatic belt-drive transmission or for it to have to use a 1.4-litre/70 bhp Renault engine (the final stretch of the 66's unit), for the ideal 'gap-filler' would have been a 1.5 or 1.6-litre car with 80 to 85 bhp.

The 343, therefore, got off to a rather shaky and stodgy start. The historic DAF/Volvo problem, with the Variomatic transmission, was being carried forward, and the 343 was suffering from it. The problem was that, although Variomatic was clever enough in its way, and was simple and amazingly easy to drive, this could even be a barrier to making sales. In recent years, after all, many DAFs had been

The first Dutch Volvo with significant Swedish engineering input was the 343 which was announced in 1976. It had originally been conceived as a DAF, which the press had always called the '77'. Like smaller DAFs, it had Variomatic belt-drive transmission.

bought by people taking the easy way out, and using the Variomatic as an ideal system for shopping trips, commuting and for local journeys in heavy traffic. Many such customers were female, and I hope I am not being anti-feminist by commenting that this reputation as a 'ladies' car' could sometimes rebound on DAF. If there was one thing the 343 did not need, it was an instant 'image' as a ladies' car and as a short-distance machine. In some ways, however, the 343 plugged its marketing gap ideally, for it had a wheelbase of 94.3 in, and was almost exactly half way between the 66 and the 244 in overall length and other dimensions.

If anything, Volvo had been too cautious with their first new Dutch model. Perhaps *Autocar*'s road test of February 1977 summed up the 343 ideally. After headlining it a car with 'gentle performance' (which, even in the economy-conscious late 1970s, could be defined as damning with faint praise), they summarised as follows: 'What, then, does the Volvo offer? Not performance, not economy, not looks: but the appeal of a new and interesting car with the promise of safety and long life . . ..' They also commented that it was an expensive car, as originally imported to the UK, but that was partly due, at least, to the parlous standing of the British pound, sterling, at the time.

Volvo will probably never admit it, but with the original 343 models, they rather misjudged their market. Down at this size and price level, there did not seem to be as many willing customers for what had become known within the company as 'the Volvo virtues'. Too many prospective buyers, having looked at and tried the 343, found it boring and—worse—were not happy with the level of quality and equipment provided. The immediate effect of the 343's reception in 1976 can be seen from this six-year analysis of DAF/Volvo production in Holland:

Year	*Production*	*Comment*
1974	75,000	Volvo took majority share of DAF
1975	61,500	Volvo 66 introduced
1976	74,500	Volvo 343 introduced
1977	54,500	
1978	64,700	
1979	90,500	343: New manual box, 5-door option

In other words, rather than adding to volume at the Born plant when the additional model had been put into quantity production, the volume had actually fallen. Perhaps it was not all coincidence that the value of Volvo's shares, as measured by Stockholm stock exchange quotations, dropped by more than 50 per cent between the spring of 1976 and the end of 1977.

There were two ways in which this disappointment could be tackled—one was to plug away at the improvement of product quality *and* to convince the customers that this was being done. The other was actually to begin upgrading, and improving, the 'image' of the car itself. The engineers in Holland, and in Sweden, were able to concentrate more and more on this as the Volvo 66 began to fade away, with the last of all being built in 1980. (A third way, which was resisted for some time, was that Volvo Sweden should admit that Volvo Car BV, as the Dutch business was now known, was not viable without further help, and extra finance and support should be called in.)

Right from the start, Volvo let it be known that the Dutch subsidiary would have to build more than 100,000 cars a year before it could become profitable—and this

148   *The story of Volvo cars*

Below *The rear quarter view of the 343/345 style shows that the hatchback incorporated a pronounced lip, which was very good for reducing drag—something which Ford attempted to claim as their own invention some years later!*

Below *By 1979, the 343 not only had a thoroughly modern facia style, but the option of a conventional manual gearbox.*

Expansion overseas

has never been achieved. The original hope was that the 340 Series, combined with the 66, would boost production to this level by the late 1970s; unfortunately for Volvo, the European recession (triggered off by the second oil shock of 1979) has intervened. Hakan Frisinger was on the main Volvo administrative committee during the late 1970s, with special responsibility for the cars division, and he now agrees that there were more problems with the DAF project than could ever have been expected.

Volvo, however, were not quitters, especially as this was their first major enterprise located outside Scandinavia and they were not about to admit defeat at such an early stage. Their first step was to attack the build quality, and the long-life prospects, of the 343s and, eventually, they were as successful as with any other Volvo car. Carl-Eric Haggstrom reminded me, when I talked to him in 1982, that up until about 1979 or 1980, the company had not had the advantage of possessing a pool of old customers. Each and every 343 sale in the first three years had to come by conquest from another manufacturer—which, as any salesman will tell you, is *the* most difficult pitch to make, especially in a market sector where there is so much choice and so many long-established marques: 'We will be up to 90,000 annual sales again in 1982, which is up to 1979 levels when the Volvo 66 was still being made. Now we have about 25 per cent of our sector, whereas we only have 8.5 per cent of the segment for the big Volvos. We are *winning* with the 343s and the sales figures prove it.'

Indeed they do. The first major advance came in the autumn of 1978 when Volvo were at last able to launch their manual-transmission 343. Development had begun as soon as the original 343 had met its public, and had been speedy and relatively straightforward for the simple reason that the four-speed manual gearbox chosen was that of the big-engined Volvos from Sweden!

The easy way, and the misguided way, to install the new manual gearbox in the 343 would have been to mate it to the Renault engine, up front. Volvo's solution was much more elegant, for they chose to retain the De Dion rear suspension (with single-leaf springs) of the original car and to mount the modified 240-Series gearbox in unit with the differential at the rear of the car. As they were later to boast, perfectly correctly, in adverts, this gave them a feature as advanced as that standardised on Alfa Romeo Alfettas and the Porsche 924 coupé. There was a normal change speed lever between the front seats and, although the linkage to the box itself was long, it was well-engineered and very acceptable.

While the press still thought the 343 needed more power (which was a real compliment to the car's 'chassis') there was no doubt that they liked the new derivative more than the original. Apart from the quality of the change, and the indefinable advantage to the keener driver that he was now in more total command of the car, and the power train, there was another advantage—the manual transmission 343, which was a full £200 *cheaper* than the Variomatic model, was considerably quicker as well. Evidently there had been losses in the Variomatic transmission, not incurred with the manual car, for *Autocar*'s road test 343 of December 1978 was 7 mph faster flat out (94 mph versus 87 mph), ten seconds quicker from rest to 80 mph, and significantly more economical into the bargain.

Clearly, potential 343 customers were being offered something for nothing—no, let me get this right, they were being offered something for a £200 rebate—and they quickly began to appreciate the move. By 1982, when the manual gearbox had been on offer for four years, Variomatic was only being fitted to about 15 per cent of all the 340 Series cars, thus confirming that the overall demand for small-engined automatics had always been somewhat limited.

The other improvement to the 340 Series car's appeal was that, from the autumn of 1979, it was also made available with a five-door layout—this being done without changing the overall dimensions or styling of the car, but merely by slotting in the four passenger doors for which the body style had always appeared to be waiting. The process, however, was not complete, for Volvo Car BV were holding their most exciting 340 Series developments for the beginning of the 1980s. Not content with upgrading the specification and appeal of the original cars, from the start of 1981 model-year they also announced a 2-litre version of the car, fitted with the 1,986 cc B19A single-overhead-cam Volvo engine, of the type (but not the actual capacity) fitted to the 240 Series saloons. This engine was only on offer with the manual transmission in the three-door or five-door body shells, and at least it provided the Dutch company with a car of more than 100 mph potential.

It was only, however, the beginning of that particular development sequence, for in the autumn of 1982, for the 1983 model year, Born's ultimate weapon (so far . . . there could be more), the 360GLT, was launched. The 2-litre 343/345GLS's engine had used a single SU carburettor and developed 95 bhp—good, but not startling. The 360GLT, also available as a three-door or a five-door derivative, also used the 1,986 cc engine (but with Bosch LE type fuel injection), a more sporty camshaft profile, and had up to 115 bhp (DIN) at 6,000 rpm. This gave the car a top speed of 111 mph, standing-start acceleration in the BMW 3-Series bracket, and handling to match because of fat 60-section tyres and lowered suspension. Perhaps the most significant change was that the gearbox had been changed to include five forward ratios (this not being on offer on any other Volvo at the end of

To complete the range of Renault-engined Volvos, the five-door 345 was also announced. This car can also be supplied with a 2-litre Volvo B19 engine.

Expansion overseas 151

1982—perhaps it will follow before this book is published) and that the whole aura of the car was more sporty than ever before. It was no wonder that Volvo's advertising for this car was positively exuberant: 'It goes like a BMW, it corners like a Porsche, it stops like a Volvo'—and the 'stopping' referred to the crash protection built in to every body shell!

All of which helped to put a brave face on what was still a rather difficult situation for Volvo Car BV. Volvo Sweden made it clear to the Dutch government that they were not willing to continue funding losses indefinitely in Holland and pointed out very discreetly that the factory at Born had been so placed, not because it was the ideal location for a new car-manufacturing venture, but because the Dutch government had suggested that it would be a good way of re-employing miners made redundant by the closure of pits in that part of the country. An immediate result was that the Dutch government agreed to finance future new-product development, covering 1979 to 1986, by the aid of a special grant of 155 million Dutch guilders (about 337 million SKr or about £40 million) to be paid gradually until 1982.

This, however, was only the start. The National Investment Bank of Holland had already taken up all of a share issue in Volvo Car BV during 1977, which reduced Volvo Sweden's majority holding to only 55 per cent. This holding, having been transferred to the newly-constituted Volvo Car Corporation in 1979/80, was reduced to just 30 per cent in 1981, when the Dutch state injected a further 250 million Dutch guilders (560 million SKr or £52 million).

The situation, therefore, had changed considerably. From being the majority shareholder in 1975 with 75 per cent of the capital, Volvo Sweden had become a minority holder, with 30 per cent of the shares, in 1981. The future of the Volvo Car BV Dutch business, was, however, assured. As one Volvo staff man put it to me, the Dutch concern now had a franchise to use the Volvo name, but any new models would have to be tested and controlled from Sweden and must continue to bear the usual Volvo virtues. Hakan Frisinger, while refusing to be drawn into detail, told me that there will be a major new model from Holland in the fairly near future and one may assume that it will be somewhat larger than the main-stream 343/345 cars, and somewhat smaller than the 240 Series cars—in other words, another classic 'gap-filler'.

While it would be true to say that the Dutch venture has not been a total success for Volvo Sweden, it has not been a disaster either. All the signs are that the public has now completely accepted the style, the philosophy and the character of the 340 Series and that sales will continue to rise. (In some territories, the UK in particular, the improvement of the 340 Series' market share has been quite spectacular.) In any case, I calculate that the Swedish parent company's total investment in the Dutch concern is still less than 1,000 million SKr (less than £100 million).

During the 1970s, however, Volvo were active in several other overseas ventures, all initially designed to underpin their plans for expansion. The most ambitious of these, the proposed mergers with Saab–Scania, and with the Norwegian state, both came to nothing, and the proposed expansion into North America had to be cut back after the huge oil price rises and the changes in law requiring much more stringent economy figures being achieved in the 1980s. It was Pehr Gyllenhammar, the vigorous young visionary, who set Volvo on this path, and he achieved his aims with the link-up with Beijerinvest AB during April 1981. Volvo, without any doubt, is now much the largest industrial combine in the whole of the Nordic area.

It was in 1973 that Volvo first said that they wanted to build a car assembly plant in the United States, one which would complement the small Canadian plant—and if this had transpired as planned, Volvo would have become the first non-American automotive company to make the breakthrough. This announcement, and the start of work, could not have been made at a worse time for, in the autumn, the Israelis and the Arabs took up arms against each other, after a lapse of only six years, and the long-term result was a dramatic increase in the price of oil, a sea-change in the United States government's attitude to cars and a series of punitive measures designed to make their cars smaller, slower and more economical. The same sort of shock (the 'second oil shock', as Volvo executives call it) occurred in 1979 when fighting between Israel and Egypt broke out again.

The result was that, although building work began at Chesapeake, Virginia, USA, it was never pushed through to a complete conclusion. Volvo decided to defer installation of assembly tooling in 1976 and in recent years the plant has only been used for pre-delivery inspection of cars imported, fully-assembled, from Sweden. In the meantime, the recession has gripped North America, the rush for smaller and more economical cars is on, and the market for new cars, whether domestic or imported, has slumped considerably. At the time of writing, it no longer looks likely that Volvo's vision of a United States assembly plant will be revived.

During the mid-1970s, Volvo hit troubled times, as did almost every other manufacturer in the business. There was not only the 1973/74 Suez crisis to worry about, but the difficulties of producing a new car from Holland, and the fact that there was a slump in enthusiasm for the Volvo 240/260 Series which did not look different enough from the 140s as far as some potential customers were concerned. The way in which Volvo came to terms with this problem, and successfully conquered it, is detailed in the next chapter.

It was, therefore, a very unsettling time for Volvo and Pehr Gyllenhammar went so far as to describe 1974 as 'a lost year' for Volvo—a remarkable statement when it is considered that a new range of cars and two new engines had been introduced and the Swedish company had also taken majority control of DAF in Holland! Gyllenhammar, with the agreement of his colleagues, therefore decided that one way to underpin the future of Volvo was to broaden its base, and this, it was reasoned, could best be done by merging with another large concern. Between 1977 and 1981 there were four separate corporate moves along these lines—the first two of which ended rather humiliatingly in failure *after* the public had been informed.

The first attempt, in one way logical, and in another way inexplicable, was that Volvo tried to get together with Saab-Scania, in 1977. It was logical, in that it would group the whole of the Swedish motor industry together in one conglomerate, but it was inexplicable (to the author, and several other motor industry observers) because there was a distinct lack of potential 'dovetailing' in the product lines.

Perhaps I should not over-simplify the situation but it was a fact that, in 1977, Volvo's main private car seller was a 2.1-litre saloon, while that of Saab was a 2-litre (and a larger version of that car was planned for introduction in 1978) and it was also true that Volvo and Scania were both noted for producing heavy trucks in the same price and weight ranges. Volvo built aero engines and supplied them to—Saab. Neither was it strictly true to say that either company was running for cover. Both were profitable, and both had active forward plans. But both, it was admitted, were suffering a decline of sales in North America.

An announcement about merger talks was made on May 6 1977, but negotiations

Expansion overseas 153

then dragged on, and on, into the summer, with no agreement being reached. Saab-Scania certainly seemed to lose heart after considering the implications more closely (for it was quite clear that Volvo would become the dominant partner, even though the original proposal was for a straightforward merger, with no question of an aggressive take-over being mounted by either side) and, in August, their directors decided to adjourn the discussions. Accordingly, on August 28 1977, Volvo had to announce that the deal was off. Saab were relieved, and even went so far as to issue a statement confirming that their financial status was sound, that they were making big investments in new models (the 900, though we did not know it at the time) and that they were by no means in the doldrums.

Pehr Gyllenhammar and his board were downcast, but not shattered. They were still convinced that they must face the future with a partner and, in 1978, they tried again. This time, in a move which astonished the Swedish nation, they did not propose to link up with another industrial group, but with another nation—for *this* time Volvo were proposing to join forces with the Norwegian government!

In an announcement made on May 22 1978, Volvo proposed to get together with the Norwegian state, to transfer much of its non-automotive activities to Norway and to receive 750 million SKr venture capital from Norway, in return for which that country would get a 40 per cent shareholding in the restructured company. An intriguing comment, at the time, was that 'the development of a new automotive prototype, built of light materials and utilising advanced techniques' would be launched. Who knows how far such a project had proceeded at Volvo or whether it was merely a 'Brave New Idea'—certainly that description bears no relation to the massive Type 760 of 1982—and in any case the clear inference was that it was produced to build part, if not all, of this advanced new car in Norway.

One of Volvo's unsuccessful attempts to merge with another organisation came in 1978-9 when they proposed to get together with Norwegian government interests. At the initial press conference, Per Gyllenhammar posed with Oddvaar Nordli, Prime Minister of Norway.

It was a complicated proposal in which oil exploration interests, aviation and truck changes were all involved, and at first all appeared to go well, in spite of the fact that the Swedish government must have been puzzled and taken aback, if not downright hostile. The final agreement, setting up a new Swedish-Norwegian Volvo Group, was signed on December 8 1978.

Then, quite suddenly, it all began to go wrong. Volvo's directors had scheduled an extraordinary general meeting of shareholders for January 30 1979, in the hope that they would approve the proposals. However, in the weeks leading up to this meeting, it rapidly became clear that there was considerable opposition. In a terse statement, issued just four days before that meeting was due to be held, Volvo said: 'The Board establishes that there is no possibility of accumulating the qualifying majority of 66.6 per cent needed for the general meeting to approve . . . since those who have already committed themselves to vote against the proposal do, in fact, represent approximately 40 per cent of notified shares. The agreement with Norway can therefore not be implemented.'

A great deal, apparently, had been at stake and one major worry for important shareholders was that Volvo would lose part of its sovereignty at once and stood a chance of losing its majority in the business during the 1980s, as more and more capital had to be injected. Mr Gyllenhammar, in fairness, was now beginning to look like a loser, in the same way that Lord Stokes had begun to lose credibility at British Leyland only a few years earlier. His next attempt, however, which was revealed less than a year later, was more successful; not only did it look right, but already it seems to have been of benefit to Volvo. Hakan Frisinger recalls what happened during 1979: 'We still needed to get stronger to survive. We already had close co-operation with Renault in the PRV engine project, but then they approached us to see if we were interested in them taking a share of the whole of Volvo. We said no to that—but that if they were indeed interested in Volvo cars then yes, we could discuss it. So we made a deal, and made it quickly.'

Expansion overseas

The deal, in effect, involved hiving off the whole of Volvo's car operations into an easily-identifiable separate business, giving it a new name—the Volvo Car Corporation—and for Renault to take a minority shareholding in that business. That way, it was thought, the new partnership would be at its most efficient.

This, Volvo's third set of 'marriage vows' in less than three years, was made public just before Christmas 1979 and was approved by Pehr Gyllenhammar and Renault's Bernard Vernier-Palliez at a meeting in Geneva. The basis of the agreement was that Renault would immediately invest 170 million SKr (about £20.4 million), in exchange for which they would have 10 per cent of the voting shares. Not only that, but they would increase this shareholding to 15 per cent by the end of 1981 (which has been done) and to 20 per cent by 1986.

The agreement (which, at the time, included Volvo Car BV, the ex-DAF operation in Holland) was intended 'to increase competitiveness through co-operation in research, product development and production methods' and applied *only* to cars. As Hakan Frisinger, who became President of the new Car Corporation, later told me: 'It covers the basic design of new engines, gearboxes and so on—although they make front-wheel-drive cars and we make rear-drive cars, this will not be a disadvantage. We are not talking about new common motor cars or body shells, but about common components. We will maintain our profile and they will maintain theirs, definitely with different cars. Originally we said that it would be the middle of the 1980s before there was any evidence of the work we have been doing, and that still applies.'

It takes a long time, of course, for new designs to be brought into production these days, for the investment involved, and the complication of new machinery, is so great. When I talked to Hakan Frisinger in 1982, he assured me that Volvo's strategic plans had been firmed up as far ahead as 1988—in other words, six years ahead. 'Only economic disaster will move us from that,' he said.

The last corporate move of all should also be mentioned here, even though it was

Left *The signing of an historic agreement on June 29 1971—to set up the PRV 'co-operative' to produce V-6 engines for Volvo, Renault and Peugeot. Left to right are: Pierre Dreyfus (Renault), Per Gyllenhammar and François Gautier of Peugeot.*

Right *The 264's V-6 engine, as delivered from the PRV factory at Douvrin, in France. It must be good—the testers have written 'Bonne' on the crank pulley!*

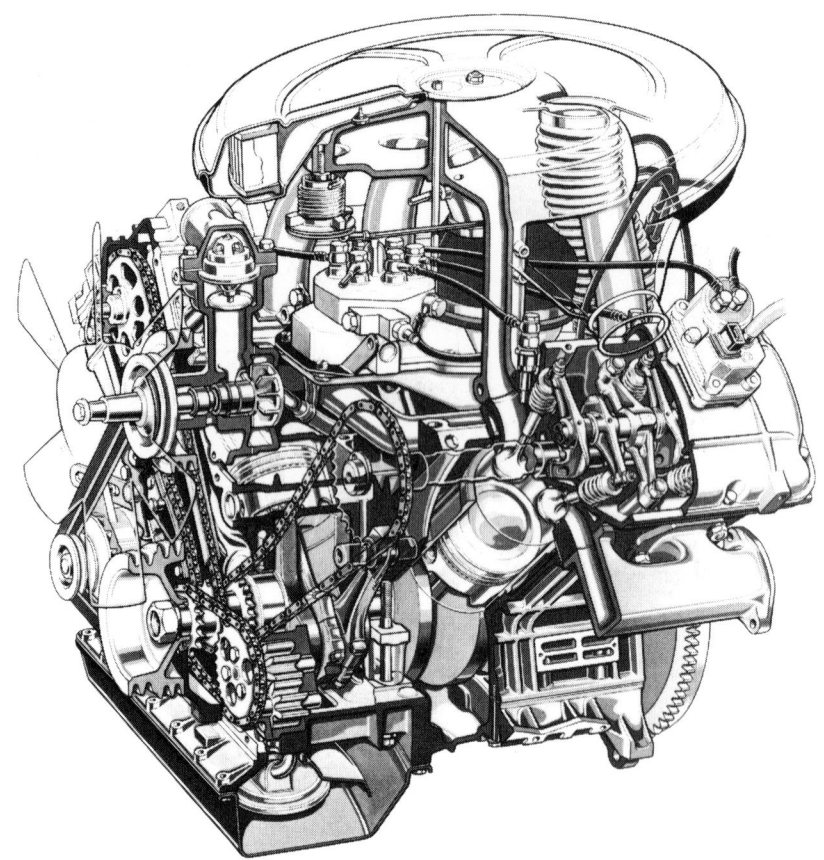

The B27E was Volvo's official name for the new 2.7-litre V-6 engine, developed in co-operation with Peugeot and Renault. The 90-degree V-angle confirms that this was originally to be a V-8 engine!

not completed until 1981, towards the end of the events covered in the next chapter. Even though he had made a successful agreement with Renault, Pehr Gyllenhammar was not content—the rest of Volvo, after all, had not been affected by the deal. Accordingly, on November 17 1980, Volvo announced that they were to join forces with a large Swedish group called Beijerinvest AB—and that this was to be a true take-over with Volvo offering a complex mixture of shares, debentures and cash, in a total deal which was going to cost about 1,250 million SKrs (about £120 million). There were no car or truck manufacturing interests involved in this deal, for Beijerinvest was a conglomerate whose principal activities included oil exploration and production, food production, and several other export/import activities.

I ought to put this deal, which was finally approved in May 1981, with nearly 97 per cent of Beijerinvest shareholders accepting the Volvo offer, into perspective. Although the cost, to Volvo, looks huge, it was more than matched by operating profits (of 1,425 million SKrs) in 1981 alone. It meant that the newly-enlarged Volvo group is now considerably larger than any other concern in Scandinavia, but

Expansion overseas

it also means that Volvo cars make up a minority of the operation. To be specific, in 1981 (the last year for which full figures were available when I was finalising this book), the AB Volvo group made sales totalling 48,017 million SKrs (£4,538 million), whereas car sales were 13,569 million SKrs (£1,283 million)—or about 28 per cent. In other words, although it was, and is, Volvo cars which made all the headlines, they now represented only about a quarter of the business.

The Volvo Car Corporation still had much of which to be proud in 1981, for not only were 210,400 240/260 Series cars built all round the world, but 79,600 'DAF' Volvos were built in Holland. The Dutch company was still not profitable, but the Car Corporation's total profits for the year were 525 million SKrs (about £50 million), or 37 per cent of AB Volvo's total earnings.

Compared with 1977 (Volvo's low point in the decade when car sales were down and the proposed deal with Saab-Scania had collapsed) and with profits at a mere 351 million SKrs, the corporate position was now transformed. In 1977, some top executives had been looking ahead with trepidation; now, only a few years later, prospects were exciting. A lot, an awful lot, had happened, and the image of the Volvo was very different. The 240/260 Series had been thoroughly reworked and an entirely new range of cars had been introduced.

Chapter 9

Volvo for the 1980s
New styles, new engines, new partners

By 1977, Volvo were in trouble, though they were still making money. Car sales were down, production in Sweden fell for the fourth year in succession, and their dealers were having to work very hard to move the latest products. To introduce the 240/260 models as much-modified 140s had been a big gamble which Volvo management had had to take—but it was looking as if they had guessed wrong. If only the new cars had been launched before the Suez crisis, everything might have been all right—and if only they had been brisker and more fashionable . . . .

Right from the start, at the end of 1974, however, Volvo were struggling. Faithful customers initially gave the latest cars a friendly, if not exactly ecstatic, reception but repeat orders began to fall away. Hakan Frisinger summed up the problem very accurately: 'In the middle of the 1970s, we lost some of our image with this car. The quality suffered—yes, really—and perhaps the car didn't look different enough from the old 140 Series. We had to get more product development implemented on the car—for our competitors were very progressive. So we started up in 1976 and 1977 with a stronger product development programme. We had had to pay for it, but we have been very successful in changing the car—we have added new engines and so on, to move the car into different markets.'

The image problem was neatly encapsulated by what the British monthly magazine *CAR* called the big Volvos at the time: 'For: Built like a tank. Against: Looks like a tank. Sum-up: Feels like a tank.' It meant that in one way Volvo had certainly achieved their long-term objective, but that in another way they were alienating many motorists because of this. The long-term objective had been to develop the safest possible car—and the problem was that many motorists objected to what this involved. One feature—the use of all day 'running lights' which meant that the car's side lamps were *always* illuminated when the car was in use—infuriated countless non-Volvo owners when it was first introduced and there are still many motorists who look on this as an aggressive, 'look-out-I'm-in-a-Volvo-and-I-want-to-be-noticed' attitude. Inside the car, too, there were the flashing lights, and the buzzers, all of which irritated motorists who did not want to be forced into wearing seat belts.

It might have been possible for a car of this type to be forgiven if it had been fast, agile and economical, but the mid-1970s Volvos were not at all like that. It was almost as if the company had opted out of the status race and were providing cars which they thought motorists *ought* to have, instead. It may not have been intended, but it was the image that came across, nonetheless.

The result, which combined indifference to the latest cars with a general decline in sales of big cars after the 1973/74 oil price rises, was a considerable decline in sales. This was the pattern which developed between 1973 and 1977:

Year	Torslanda production	Kalmar/Belgium production	Total production
1973	181,200	50,600	231,800
1974	157,200	58,700	215,900
1975	138,300	65,300	203,600
1976	138,800	67,500	206,300
1977	107,200	51,300	158,500

In formalised company language, the solution applied was to 'get more product development' into the car—which, in motoring buffs' terms, meant getting more excitement and more pzazz into the showrooms. One early way of doing this was to present something more exclusive, a car which not only looked different from the conventional saloons, but one which was really rather special. What was needed was a new type of Volvo to catch the eye of the customers—something which, in a dealer's language, might 'increase showroom traffic'. The car chosen to do this job was one conceived years earlier—the controversial 262C coupé.

It all stemmed from the death of the 1800ES sporting model in 1973. Even though the 1800s had never made much money for Volvo, they had been well-liked little cars, but Volvo had never managed to justify the development of a new model to replace them. In 1973, however, Jan Wilsgaard's styling department was encouraged to try again. 'Pehr Gyllenhammar called me up one day,' Wilsgaard recalls, 'and said that he had an idea while he had been in North America. The dealers had been asking for something to follow the P1800, but using mainly standard parts. He asked me to do some sketches, which I did, and he approved them. I could build a prototype, he said—but, guess what!—I didn't have a budget for this. Mr Gyllenhammar, however, said, "Don't worry about that, we will fix it somehow".

'I went out and bought a secondhand 164, not a 264 because we hadn't introduced the car yet [it was still 1973] and sent it down, with drawings and some components, to Sergio Goggiola in Turin. He cut the car about, and made up a lowered two-door car in a plaster mock-up. I flew down to Turin to look at it, but was so scared by the looks that I actually had to raise the roof line a bit. Then we approved the model—interior and exterior—although we knew that Volvo couldn't build it in Sweden, as it would disturb our facilities too much.'

Pehr Gyllenhammar, however, was determined to put such a car on sale—everyone at Volvo agrees that it was 'his baby', one that he enthused about (and, incidentally, one that he kept on driving, years after it went out of production), and one that he wanted to see made, even though it was an indulgence by normal commercial and profitability standards. He had given Hilsgaard authority to look for other ways of having the cars built. Wilsgaard said: 'I actually asked Goggiola "Which Italian company could help us build this car?" He recommended Bertone in Turin, for their good quality and finish. So Volvo production people came down, looked around, said OK—then turned the whole company upside down. They were good, but not good enough for Volvo—before we gave them the contract, they had to rebuild their whole painting system to suit us. That has benefitted everyone since, Fiat included, but I guess they didn't like us so much at first . . . .'

Above *When the low-roof-line two-door style was being developed, it was first applied to the straight-six as a 162C (nose just visible) but then definitely applied to the V-6 wedge-nose car in the centre of the frame.*

Below *The Bertone-built 262C coupé had a lowered roof line and only two doors, but was mechanically identical to the 264GL saloon of the period. The Bertone badge is visible on the front wing behind the wheel-arch cut-out.*

Styling of the 262C coupé which was introduced in 1977, was by Jan Wilsgaard's studio in Torslanda, but assembly was by Bertone in Italy. This style originated on a 160 Series car in the early 1970s.

Except that it was now necessary to build a second prototype, using a proper 264 body, underframe and running gear, there were virtually no changes from the style which Goggiola had evolved. Bertone had no influence on the style, which was by Wilsgaard's studio in Gothenburg, though they made suggestions regarding the interior and the wheels which were not, in fact, adopted. Volvo executives now believe that they should have authorised a completely different facia style, but this would have delayed the car's introduction and increased the investment required considerably.

The 262C, as the new car was called, made its world debut at the Geneva motor show in March 1977 where, to be frank, it had a mixed reception. Although more mature reflection usually made the new squared-up two-door body style look neat, even distinguished, it was too easy for the motoring press to dismiss it at first glance. As *Autocar* said: 'By comparison with the Mercedes coupés, the Volvo 262C seems almost calculated to shock. Up to the waistline it does not differ from the saloon . . . On top of this base is a squared-off glasshouse with a more steeply-raked screen, which looks rather small for the rest of the car, and is graced with large blind spots in the rear quarters.'

No matter. The 262C was going to be much more costly than the 264GLE four-door saloon which had the same 'chassis' and running gear and, according to the original announcements, the planned production rate was only about 800 cars a year—600 of which were earmarked for the United States, 50 for Sweden and the rest for other European countries; no right-hand-drive version was ever made. The 262C was never meant to be a mass-production car (nor could Bertone really have coped with it, if it had been) though it sold more strongly than anyone could have hoped. Bertone's contribution to the project was to manufacture some minor components, buy in a few more, but essentially to assemble the entire car from CKD kits of sub-assemblies supplied by Volvo from Sweden. Within the limitations of this project, they did a remarkable job, and in about three years (the last 262C was built in the summer of 1980, though last sales were not made until 1981) a total of 6,622 examples were built. All had PRV V-6 engines, latterly of the

2.85-litre variety, many had automatic transmission and most had full air-conditioning.

Bertone, indeed, forged a more permanent relationship with Volvo than merely building 262Cs. Not only does the Italian company have high hopes of building more such cars (when I visited Turin in 1982, and saw empty spaces at the Grugliasco factory, and asked what was being done about this, my guide smiled enigmatically and said: 'We are waiting for Volvo'), but it has also been involved in the building of two other types of special Volvos—the lengthened 245-type 'Transfer' estate cars and the 264TE executive saloons, both of which eventually settled on a wheelbase which was a whopping 73 cm (28.7 in) longer than usual.

All standard parts for these stretched Volvos were supplied from Sweden while, in Italy, Bertone cut the body panels about as appropriate and added new floor, roof and rear door pressings to complete the job. The market for such machines is strictly limited—about 280 Transfers, and 335 264TEs were built before production ceased in 1981—but they tend to go to highly prestigious customers. No fewer than 125 TEs were supplied to East Germany, for the use of Communist party bosses, while many 245 'Transfers' became hearses. Volvo, however, are now out of this market, which was too small and too specialised—such conversions are now carried out privately by coachbuilders in Sweden.

All this, of course, was merely playing with the problem. Pehr Gyllenhammar was quite unrepentant when he gave an interview to Edward Seidler of *L'Equipe*, which was syndicated widely throughout the world. When Seidler accused Volvo of making dull cars, the president retorted with: 'I am willing to admit that we have never designed cars that have a strong immediate appeal to people. Maybe we would have sold better with more appeal and flair in our cars. We don't like to

Volvo's proving grounds at Hallered, for which new facilities are always being planned.

Volvo for the 1980s

design ugly things, but our fairly utilitarian approach is certainly a good one in the long term, and we will stay with it.'

This was all very serene and unflappable on the surface. However, when this interview was taken in the autumn of 1977, the 262C had already been put on sale, and the engineers, now able to use their new proving ground at Hallered, were aiming for a complete transformation (I can think of no more appropriate word to describe their aims) in the behaviour of the cars.

The result of lengthy deliberation, which began in 1974 and involved a close and analytical study of all their competitors' products, was that a new handling package was introduced for the 1980 model year—one which killed most of the original plough-ahead under steer, firmed up the suspension rates and made the cars much more nimble to drive fast. Jeffrey Daniels, writing in the influential magazine, *Executive Car*, in the summer of 1982, made these comments: 'From 1980 onwards, therefore, however little the change was recognised at the time, the 200 Series Volvos steered and handled a great deal better. The shift in character was underlined in the following model year when the hideous USA-style bumpers were thrown away and replaced by lighter, slimmer, fittings . . . .'

But that was only a part of the rejuvenation process, all adding up to a reformation of Volvo's car-building philosophy. The most important moves were to indulge in more—and more obvious—annual improvements to the equipment and body styling while, at the same time, it was decided to expand and improve the available range of engines. Volvo, in fact, had done very little to excite the enthusiasts with their engine policy in recent years—in 1969, when the new 164 had been put on sale, the range of power from basic four-cylinder to top-of-the-line

The 264TE was handsome from any angle and it was almost impossible to see how and where the wheelbase lengthening had taken place.

Among the special products produced by Volvo in recent years have been long-wheelbase 264TE saloons and similarly stretched estate cars, both of which had three rows of seats, or only two rows if the jump seats were folded flat.

'six' was 90 bhp to 145 bhp (net); by 1976 that range had been considerably modified, but the span was now from 82 bhp to 140 bhp (DIN). Even though the 'DIN' rating was a little more stringent than the 'net' rating of the 1960s, the implications were obvious—Volvo had stood still for seven years.

First, however, the company decided that they must provide a diesel-engine option for the 240 Series to bring them into line, at least, with Mercedes-Benz and to fill a need which was apparently developing all over Europe, where the price of diesel fuel was usually so much less than that of petrol. In the early 1970s, in fact, Volvo had actually designed their own diesel engine. It was not a modified version of the existing four-cylinder petrol engine, for such conversions were not then considered normal, nor would the resulting unit have been as smooth and refined as Volvo standards made necessary. Instead, an entirely new in-line 'six' was designed and partly developed. Such a unit, of course, would have cost a great deal of money to put into quantity-production and, when the analysts added up the figures, it was reluctantly decided that the project was not viable.

Volvo then set off on a shopping trip around Europe—but since they only really wanted a six-cylinder diesel, they soon settled on a deal with VW of West Germany. The VW-Audi group was in the middle of a truly massive re-equipment and investment programme, involving not only four-cylinder, five-cylinder and six-cylinder engines, but involving petrol and diesel versions of most of them. The deal made was that Volvo would have first call on the new 2.4-litre six-cylinder VW diesel and that VW would only use four-cylinder and five-cylinder diesels in their passenger cars—in fact the records show that the new diesel 'six' in the Volvo was announced at the same time as the closely related 'five' was put on offer in the Audi 100, both cars being exhibited for the first time at the Paris Show of October 1978.

The diesel engine, in fact, produced a peak of 82 bhp, which made it the least powerful of all engines offered in the 240/260 Series cars at the time. For 1979, in fact, the first stages in the up-grading of performance began, with the smallest (1,986 cc) petrol engine being boosted to 97 bhp, and 140 bhp (2,316 cc) 244 GLT being announced, and the PRV V-6 engine being tuned up to 148 bhp. North American engine ratings, of course, were less than these because of the exhaust emission limitations; the V-6, for example, produced 127 bhp in the USA.

There was more to come. As usual, the special police cars built by Volvo (the special products division can build about 800 such cars every year) were given the most powerful engines first of all and, during 1979 and 1980, a special series was built with a 2,127 cc turbocharged engine. Sure enough, for 1981, this became a production option, the new 244 Turbo having no less than 155 bhp on tap. Such an engine, although not as smooth and silent as the PRV V-6, would have embarrassed the old-type 264s, so perhaps it was just as well that the engine size of these French-built units was enlarged to 2,849 cc, and peak powers also raised to 155 bhp (or 132 bhp for the USA) at the same time. There were still more changes for 1982 when the run-of-the-mill 2,127 cc overhead cam engine, powering most of the 240 Series cars, was enlarged to 2,315 cc, changing its type from B21 to B23, and its peak power output from 107 to 112 bhp.

A lot had been done, therefore, to rejuvenate the cars, as there had always been something new to talk about—the 262C for 1978, the new diesel and a new nose for 1979, the unheralded handling package for 1980, the turbocharged engine for 1981, and the enlarged 'middle-size' engine for 1982. Along the way, too, there had been time for the facia to be restyled and for the boot sill at last to be lowered (a change suggested by the styling department in 1972, six years before it was finally adopted), while power-assisted steering was finally standardised on the four-cylinder cars for 1982.

It was no wonder, therefore, that *CAR* found itself able to alter its opinions of the car for, by the beginning of 1982, their thumbnail sketch of the car said: 'For: Solid build, looks improved by recent mods—along with ride and handling. Against: Lots of body roll, uninspiring engine. Sum-up: Acceptable at last . . ..'

The sales statistics told their own story. After the low point experienced in 1977, this is what happened in the next four years:

Year	Torslanda production	Kalmar/Belgium production	Total production
1977	107,200	51,300	158,500
1978	123,600	56,400	180,000
1979	145,600	64,700	210,300
1980	115,700	52,400	168,100
1981	126,000	67,200	193,200

The reduction of 1980 and 1981, which had been shrugged off by 1982, was almost entirely due to a general slump in demand experienced by car makers throughout the world.

The fact was, however, that production of cars at Torslanda was still a long way below the peak years of 1972 and 1973—within ten years, Volvo's Torslanda volume had slipped by nearly one third, even though some of the shortfall was made up by deliveries of components for extra production at Kalmar, in Belgium, or in various other assembly plants throughout the world.

Volvo, though, were not at all despondent about this, as I found when I talked to the product planning chief, Dan Werbin, and his chief, Hakan Frisinger. Werbin merely pointed out that: 'We are specialists and we have the right characteristics to be viable. When the going starts to be rough, people tend to make a safe investment, and in this business that means, more and more, buying a Volvo.' Frisinger explained further: 'With the big cars and a potential of 250,000 cars a year—that means we are *big* in a special segment. We are second in Europe in that segment and we have got stronger in the last few years.' I am sure I do not need to emphasise that the market leader is Mercedes-Benz, which shows us what sort of prestige, and standing, the Volvo car now has.

Even so, by the mid-1970s, as soon as the 240/260 Series cars had been launched, Volvo began to work on another new car. Their philosophy, as usual, was to produce a large/medium car, one which would—or, at least, might—replace the existing model after a considerable period of overlap. In the event, it took a long time to produce such a car—too long, as some deep thinkers in Sweden now privately admit—but the result, badged as the 760GLE, was officially launched in February 1982.

It meant, incidentally, that for the first time since the end of the 1960s, more than 12 years earlier, two very different types of car were being manufactured side-by-side at Torslanda. Hakan Frisinger has told me that, ideally, Volvo should only be building two product lines, but that from time to time it is quite possible to build three—the three in this instance being the 343/345 cars in Holland, the 240s and the 760s in Sweden.

Volvo for the 1980s

Since 1979, Volvo have offered a six-cylinder VW diesel engine option in 240 Series cars which is rugged and simple with direct fuel injection and a single overhead-camshaft valve gear operation.

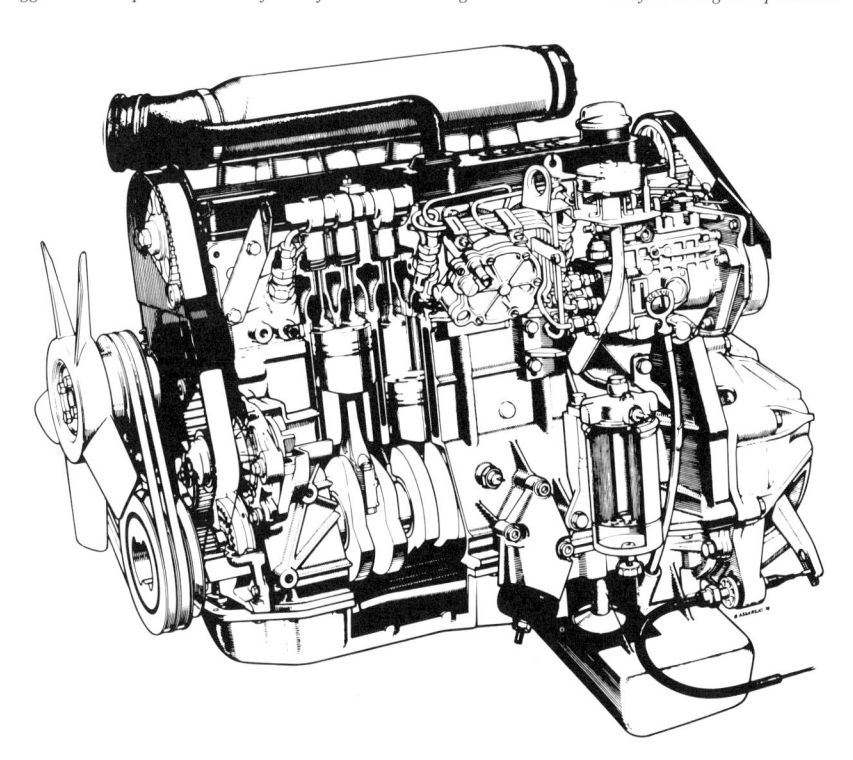

Work on the new car started in 1975, with Jan Wilsgaard's styling department starting to develop body styles, and the engineers, led by Rune Gustaffson, starting to design a new chassis, all beginning together. More than ever before, the new car was to be product planned in some detail and it had to be designed with a long production run in mind. For the mechanical engineers, the big decision to be made was about the rear suspension, and for everyone there was the vital question of the wheelbase to be settled. The philosophical problem, in a way, was that the 240/260 Series cars had not really been new models, and all the designers were setting out on a voyage of discovery which they had not completed in the 1960s-designed VESC, while many of them had not even been involved in the original 140 Series cars designed in the early 1960s.

Dan Werbin recalls that it was always the intention to make the new car very roomy, which explains why the chosen wheelbase was eventually a lengthy 277 cm, which was 12 cm, or 4.7 in, longer than that of the 240/260 Series cars. The choice of rear suspension was difficult, not least because some of Volvo's principal rivals are BMW and Mercedes-Benz, both of which have independent rear suspension, and because in North America, where many of the new cars could be expected to sell, very few full-sized (or, rather, 'Intermediate' cars in Detroit-speak) cars have sophisticated suspension of any type. Volvo knew, for instance, that their PRV partners, Peugeot and Renault, both built big cars with independent rear suspension, but they also knew that the new British Rover did not.

Rune Gustaffson described the initial work: 'The basic layout was always as you see it. At first there were many discussions, but fairly quickly we settled on a fairly long wheelbase. We developed cars, pre-760, with various rear suspension layouts—De Dion, for instance—and some years earlier we also had a trailing arm layout as well. But we didn't have much time "to play" with this car—there really isn't much "play" time left in engineering design, any more—and we settled on the special type of rear axle location you now see on the car, as having the best balance for what we wanted.'

The new car seems to have several project codes. One of the early ones was the P1155 (as one cynic at Volvo suggested: '1155—yes, five minutes to 12 o'clock, we were running out of time, and fast) and it was called P31 for a time, but in the end it

Left *A bonnet-full of engine! This is the turbocharged derivative of the overhead-camshaft four-cylinder Volvo unit, complete with intercooler ahead of the water radiator. The turbocharger itself is hidden away near the exhaust manifold.*

Right *In earlier non-intercooler form, the B21 Turbo engine passed pressurised air over the top of the camshaft cover.*

settled on the '01' project. 01? Who knows, really, whether that is significant—could this be the very first of a new type of Volvo? Does it even matter?

Jan Wilsgaard's work on the style of the new car began late in 1975 and a lot of different models were built for the project. Even earlier, of course, at the stylists' 'play period' when shapes are not necessarily being developed with a particular car in mind, there had been schemes for a new and more sharply-profiled four-door car. The brief from the product planning department, which was becoming as important part of Volvo as it was in many other car-making concerns, was that the style should take account of the need for good aerodynamics. It should have a low front and a relatively high rear, a large boot and, of course, it should be as up-to-the-minute as possible.

On this occasion, too, it was decided that outside consultants should be invited to have a go. Among others, Volvo's favourite consultant, Sergo Goggiola, was allowed to produce a model, as was Georgetto Giugiaro's Ital Design but, at the end of the day, when a face-to-face viewing of models was arranged, it was Volvo's own style which was chosen for further refinement. Wilsgaard himself, not his underlings, had locked himself away for weeks in 1975 to develop his own ideas of the way the new car should look. More than ten models were eventually produced before he was anything like satisfied, and before he was ready to show his ideas to management.

Gradually, and quite unstoppably, the new car began to take on the profile that is now becoming familiar all over the world. It was already shaping up to be a rather 'sharp-edged' car—no doubt because cars like the Cadillac Seville and other new United States products were making this shape of car very fashionable in a market most important to Volvo—and it was tending to have the upright grille, the high tail and the rather upright rear window.

Dan Werbin has no doubt as to why this happened: 'We wanted good boot access, and this meant a large boot lid, so soon we found that we had to have the rear window like that—not vertical because it was pushed back by the roof and the top rail, but because it was pushed forward ahead of the boot lid.' But it was a controversial shape, and Volvo knew it. For the very first time in their history they organised 'clinics' in North America and in Europe where their unbadged, full-size clay model was displayed alongside familiar competitors, and where members of the buying public were asked to comment on all of them.

'The first time we showed the new car,' Wilsgaard recalls, 'there were several points of criticism—the sloping bonnet, the tilt of the windscreen, the body side "belt" line was thought to be too low, the rear window thought to be too vertical, and the rear deck (boot) lid thought to be too high. The only thing we actually changed was the windscreen—we raised the line a few degrees to a more upright position. A few months later, at the next clinics, everything seemed to be liked except the rear screen position—some people still say this is too straight up, but there seem to be fewer and fewer of them.'

Early in 1977, the basic shape of the new car, in saloon car form, was settled, as the accompanying photograph shows. By August 1977 the styling department were able to show a completely detailed wooden model, which was then committed to tooling for press tools to be manufactured. So far, so good—but it was to take nearly another five years before the car could go on sale, and in those five years the face of motoring, and of modern motor cars, changed considerably.

Volvo are putting a brave face on it, as these words are written, and they may yet prove that Volvo's long-established quality/long-life/safety image is more important than mere styling, but it is a fact that very very few new models announced in the 1980s have the same type of sharp-edged styling. Ford (with the Sierra) at one end of the spectrum, the Mercedes-Benz (with the new sub-Volvo-sized 190E) at the other, have both gone for rounded styles, while the sensation of 1982, the year in which the 760GLE was announced, was certainly the ultra-smooth new Audi 100.

To complain about the new Volvo's style, however, is to miss the fact that it is significantly more aerodynamic, with a better wind-cheating shape than the old-

Sketching the way towards the 760GLE, with a sleek idealised shape in the centre, and a semi-Concept Car likeness at the top of the photograph.

Volvo for the 1980s

Above *The 760GLE, whose shape was fixed by 1977/78, is nevertheless more aerodynamically efficient than the 240/260 Series.*

Below *Volvo for the 1980s—a head-on view of the latest 760GLE model, announced in 1982.*

Left The carefully detailed facia and control layout of the 760GLE —this car having the manual gearbox plus overdrive installation.

Below Are you sitting comfortably? In the 760GLE, you should be, in chairs like these.

Bottom While the 760GLE retains a live axle, and coil-spring rear suspension, as on all other post-war Volvos, it has a new form of axle location—to a sub-frame which has its own special mounting to the body shell.

Volvo for the 1980s

type 240/260 Series. Independent figures released in 1982 show that the old car had a drag coefficient (C_d) of 0.45, whereas the new 760GLE's C_d is 0.40—in relative terms, therefore, Volvo had made an improvement of 11 per cent.

According to Rune Gustaffson, the first true running prototype was ready by February 1978, and by the time the second round of oil price increases got under way in 1979, the design and development programme had acquired a momentum of its own. Hakan Frisinger admits that it took a long time to bring the 760GLE from project to production car and I detected a *frisson* of regret about this when he assured me that progress would be a lot quicker with the next new car.

Only two 'first generation' cars were built in the engineering workshops, and these were followed by ten 'second generation' prototypes. Third generation cars, which followed in 1980, were partly tooled, and were widely used for proving rather than for experimental purposes. The company, incidentally, has its own wind-tunnel, completed in 1971, but, during the design process, checks were made in the two most noted independent tunnels—those at the British MIRA testing facility and at the Pininfarina factory in Turin.

Did the 1979 'second oil price shock' cause any major changes to be made to the concept of the 760GLE, I asked? Gustaffson said not: 'It all went ahead as planned, including the four-speed Japanese-built automatic transmission and the four-speed manual box plus British overdrive. We have already developed a five-speed gearbox for the Dutch-built Volvo, but not yet for our own big car.'

There was, of course, an enormous amount of work needed to be done to get the car ready for production, and so much more legislation to be satisfied. No fewer than 15 V-6 (PRV) engined cars had to be crashed into barriers, or otherwise destroyed, to satisfy the legislators, and at least the same number with the diesel engine. Cars were sent all over the world for endurance and environmental testing—to nearby Lapland for very cold weather, to Africa for hot and rough road testing, and to California when it is hot and humid there. Much development work on air conditioning, the fitting now so essential for marketing purposes in North America, was also carried out in the USA, with the aid of specialists.

Teams of engineers (some Swedish, some hired on contract work from the UK, Europe and the USA) were sent to try out the cars in all possible conditions. As Rune Gustaffson commented: 'Living, as we do, at the end of Europe, every time we go over to the continent it's a shock to us. You know the sort of speeds they have in Germany—every time that is a surprise!' To the Swedes, a law-abiding race who drive in a speed-limited country where the police are very active, the 100 mph-plus speeds on the German autobahns continue to be a real eye-opener.

Naturally the prototypes needed to be disguised but, as the 760s looked so 'American' in some ways, even down to their approximate bulk (for American cars were becoming smaller and more similar to the new Volvo with every year which passed), they could be badged as American cars, and no one suspected a thing. It was not until mid-1981 that the usual 'spy cameras' could capture a definitive 760GLE prototype on test, and have photographs published all over the world.

Whether it realised it or not, the public got its first sight of the new car's general layout in March 1980, when the Volvo Concept Car, a sharp-edged estate car, was put on display at the Geneva Motor Show. The VCC was entirely different from the well-known 245/265 estate cars, actually having a considerably lower nose and less rear overhang. It was not until the 760GLE was launched in 1982 that we realised that VCC was, to all intents and purposes, a rather specialised edition of the

The Volvo Concept Car was exhibited in 1980. Much of this car's style and chassis engineering was in fact intended for the 760GLE. Does that mean that an estate car version of the 760GLE will soon follow?

new production car. Jan Wilsgaard told me that VCC was conceived long after the production car's shape had been finalised: 'It was model No 12 in the sequence of cars we built—we didn't just want publicity, we also wanted to test out some ideas on the public, and get their reaction to the general shape.'

Some VCC features were to be used in the new production car—such as the four-speed 'high-overdrive' automatic transmission, the choice of engines and the new type of rear suspension which had extra axle location, via a strong sub-frame attached to the underpan, to optimise ride refinement. The special fittings included a front under-bumper spoiler which was automatically deployed when the road speed rose above 70 kph/44 mph, light-alloy body skin panels and ultra-thin glass, a new type of passive front seat safety belt, and an instrument display including cathode ray tubes, and back up from a microprocessor. VCC, however, like other Volvo exhibition cars, had a short public life and was put into retirement at the end of the year. It had achieved its object—not only of reminding people that Volvo was still very much in the 'safety car' business, but that their stylists had not been idle.

Although the new car had been 'surprised' on test in 1981 and the usual 'scoop-happy' magazines had suggested it would be launched later that year, it was not actually revealed until February of 1982. Almost every forecaster got its title wrong, by the way—some pundits reasoned that, since the 200 Series cars were in existence and the 300 Series cars were being built in Holland, then the new car would be the 400 Series. What they omitted to think out was Volvo's logical way of working things out—as far as the Swedish company was concerned (and, more importantly, I would think, the staff and computers controlling parts stocks) there already *had* been a 400 Series which was the old PV444 model of the 1940s and 1950s. They couldn't call it the 500 Series because of the PV544, nor the 600 Series because that was the name given to the DAF/Volvo 66 in certain markets in the 1970s. The next in line was the 700 Series, and that is what was chosen.

The new 760s were to be assembled at Torslanda but, as the existing cars were also to be continued unchanged, there was a considerable amount of rebuilding and reshuffling to be done in 1981. Although the 760 was different from the existing

The Volvo Concept Car of 1980, with many forthcoming 760GLE features. Wouldn't this estate car style look nice in production?

cars in many ways (except in some of the mechanical components used) it was too similar to the 264/265 models in many ways. Accordingly, in the reshuffle, all the PRV V-6 engined 264/265 Volvos were dropped, and assembly of the 244/245 models was concentrated on a single final line. At the time of writing, 760GLE assembly had not commenced at Kalmar, Ghent, or any other 'satellite' plant already building the older models.

A comparison with the obsolete 264 saloons is interesting. Although the 760GLE has a longer wheelbase, it has almost exactly the same overall length (which was one reason why assembly at Torslanda was so easily mixed with the older models). Some weight, in fact, has been saved by the use of modern computer-aided design techniques—a late-model 264GLE weighed 3,294 lb at the kerbside, whereas the 760GLE weighs in at only 3,031 lb with the same engine, transmission and back axle.

Right from the start, however, the 760GLE was available with several different engines, which makes one wonder just how long the overlap with the 240 Series cars can continue. For 1983, just a matter of months after the original announcement had been made, 760s were listed with two different diesels and two petrol engines. Both the diesels were the now-familiar straight six-cylinder VW units of 2,383 cc, the D24 having 82 bhp, exactly as fitted to the 240 D6 Diesel, while the TD24 was a turbocharged derivative, pushing out no less than 110 bhp (enough, incidentally, to endow this version of the car with a 106 mph top speed).

Naturally one of the engines was the Type B28E 2,849 cc PRV V-6, complete with fuel injection, which gave 156 bhp (132 bhp for the USA), but the real surprise was the offering of a turbocharged (Type B23ET) overhead-cam 2,315 cc four-cylinder engine, which pushed out no less than 173 bhp, and provided a top speed of 124 mph, with acceleration to 100 kph/60 mph in a mere 8.5 seconds. This engine, of course, was closely related to that already fitted to the 244 Turbo (which is a B21ET unit of 2,127 cc) and needs only 7 psi boost to produce such a high power output.

Production started up very gradually during 1982—only 2,000 cars had been built when I toured the assembly lines in September—but initial plans were to make up to 50,000 760GLEs in a full model year, more than double the rate being achieved for the 264/265 Series in 1981. It was a brave forecast for the prospects of what was already becoming a very controversial car.

Here in Britain, the motoring press received the car with interest, if not acclaim, and there were many differing comments about the styling. The British concessionaires could perhaps be accused of hyper-sensitivity, for in their advertising campaign of autumn 1982 they actually went so far as to mention this press criticism, but suggest to the readers that the customers knew more about the cars than the experts did, and that they should ignore them.

It is only the beginning of the story as far as this important range of cars is concerned, and I am sure that changes, additions and improvements will be made as the 1980s progress further. In a book which may remain in print for some time, it is perhaps unwise to speculate about the future, but I think I can guess what additional shapes we may see in due course. On the one hand, it looks certain for the saloon eventually to be joined by a five-door estate car—for Volvo were selling more than 6,000 PRV-engined 265s a year at the end of the 1970s, and the Volvo Concept Car was, after all, based on the engineering and body style of the 760GLE, but had a five-door estate car shape; it is worth noting, however, that the rear overhang of the Concept car was considerably less than that of the 760GLE production car, and I cannot believe that such a small load space will be provided on a future big estate in this series.

The question of a new sporting car, developed from the 760GLE's base, is more intriguing. Several people at Volvo, including no less important a person than Hakan Frisinger, assured me that there was a place for a coupé of some sort in Volvo's line-up, and Bertone of Turin are certainly hoping for some new Volvo

Just to show the world that they are always thinking ahead, Volvo posed three of the 1970s experimental cars together—VESC, the Concept Car, and the diesel-engined city taxi.

Volvo for the 1980s

business to keep their Grugliasco factory busy. The problem, however, is that although Volvo can design and build fine cars (like the 262C, and the earlier 1800 models) they cannot make a great deal of money from them. The time to introduce such a car is when the Volvo corporation can afford something of an indulgence, and would like an image-builder to add to their range. That day, I feel, may not be too far away.

As to the future, Pehr Gyllenhammar and Hakan Frisinger are both very confident. The factories are as busy as ever, and profitability is once again on the way up. The puzzling thing for some observers is that, although jobs are safe and wages are good, absenteeism is high. However, on sales, Volvo seem to have little to fear for, in a declining market for large cars, world-wide, their share seems to be on the increase; only Mercedes-Benz, of their competitors, is in such a happy situation.

For many years, Volvo's success has been remarkable, not least because they have had to export more than 70 per cent of the output of their Swedish factories. Having the backing of the largest Swedish company is a great help to the Car Corporation, but unless they suffer a collapse in demand before long, they should be able to finance their own operations, and new model plans, for the rest of the decade. Few of their competitors can forecast this.

Carl-Eric Haggstrom probably summed up the Volvo phenomenon very well when talking about the company's record: 'Don't forget that the US manufacturers, in recent years, have had to change so much that this has given them a blurred image with the customer. Other firms have done the same. Volvo, on the other hand, has grown in image because we stand for something that has been consistent and our credibility has increased.'

This really tells us all what we need to know. People considering buying a Volvo today know what it is like, because they know what it has *always* been like. And so they will in 1990, and even the year 2000, as well. And that, no doubt, is the secret of Volvo's long-term success.

Appendix A

Volvo cars since 1927
A technical summary

Volvo has a long and distinguished history. However, it would be very confusing to attempt to list every derivative of every type of Volvo built in the first 55 years. Instead, therefore, I have grouped the cars together into families and into major categories. But, beware! At the time of writing, Volvo are building up to 300,000 cars every year and these details are only correct as at the end of 1982.

Model series	Years produced	Engine and power	Wheelbase and chassis details	Number built	Comment
OV4/PV4 family					
OV4	1927-29	4-cyl, 1,944 cc, 28 bhp	116.1 in, separate frame, beam axle front and rear	205	Original 'Jakob' type, Tourer body style.
PV4	1927-29	4-cyl, 1,944 cc, 28 bhp	116.1 in, separate frame, beam axle front and rear	721	With fabric-covered 4-door saloon body and 4-wheel brakes.
PV650 family					
PV650 to PV659	1929-37	6-cyl, 3,010/3,266/3,670 cc, 55/65/80/84 bhp	116.1 in, separate frame, beam axle front and rear (139.8 in on PV650 Special, PV655, PV657, all sold as rolling chassis for special coachwork)	3,577	First 6-cyl Volvo—most on same chassis as OV4/PV4.
TR taxi family					
TR670 to TR679	1930-35	6-cyl, 3,010/3,266 cc, 55/65 bhp	122.0/128.0 in, separate frame, beam axle front and rear (128.0 in on TR677/678/679)	845	Special 'Taxi' Volvo, 7-seat lengthened version of PV650 Series.
TR701 to TR704	1935-37	6-cyl, 3,670 cc, 80/84 bhp	122.0 (TR701)/128.0 in (all other), separate frame, beam axle front and rear	936	Replaced TR670 Series, with latest 3.7-litre engine.
PV36/50 family					
PV36	1935-38	6-cyl, 3,670 cc, 80/84 bhp	116.1 in, separate frame, independent front, beam axle rear	501	Called 'Carioca', replaced PV650 Series, with first all-steel Volvo body shell.
PV51 to PV57	1936-45	6-cyl, 3,670 cc, 80/84 bhp or 84/86 bhp for PV53	113.4 in, separate frame, beam axle front and rear	6,905	Short-chassis, more simple version of PV36, at first with separate headlamps. Some wartime examples with 50 bhp 'producer gas' engines.

Volvo cars since 1927

Model series	Years produced	Engine and power	Wheelbase and chassis details	Number built	Comment
PV800 family					
PV800 to PV810	1938-47	6-cyl, 3,670 cc, 84/86 bhp	128.0 in, separate frame, independent front, beam axle rear	1,848	Taxi model, replaced TR taxis, with new style like PV36/PV50 cars.
PV821 to PV834	1947-58	6-cyl, 3,670 cc, 90 bhp	128.0 in, separate frame, independent front, beam axle rear	7,016	Postwar version of PV800s, with restyled nose, built-in lamps.
PV60 family					
PV60 and PV61	1946-50	6-cyl, 3,670 cc, 90 bhp	112.2 in, separate frame, independent front, beam axle rear	3,506	Designed for 1942 launch, delayed by war. Inspired by 1939 Pontiac. Replaced PV50 Series. Last 6-cyl Volvo for many years.
PV444 family					
PV444 saloons	1947-58	4-cyl, 1,414 cc (1,583 cc on PV444L) 40/44/51/ (L) 60 bhp	102.4 in, integral body/chassis, independent front, beam axle rear	196,005	All-new postwar saloon, with 2-door fastback style. First ohv Volvo engine. Full-width front style and divided screen.
PV445 estates	1953-60	4-cyl, 1,414 cc (1,583 cc on PV444L) 40/44/51/ (L) 60 bhp	102.4 in, separate chassis frame, independent front, beam axle rear	25,550	3-door estate version of PV444, at first with separate frame.
PV544 saloons	1958-65	4-cyl, 1,583/1,778 cc, 60/76 or 75/90/95 bhp	102.4 in, integral body/chassis, independent front, beam axle rear	243,995	Much revised version of PV444, with larger engines, more power, more interior space, 4-speed gearbox option, Amazon facia, one-piece screen.
P210 estates	1960-69	4-cyl, 1,583/1,778 cc, 60 and 75 bhp versions	102.4 in, integral body/chassis, independent front, beam axle rear	60,959	Reworked PV445 estate, to match changes made for PV544 saloon.
			Grand Total:	526,509 cars	
P120/Amazon family					
Type 121/122S 4-door saloons	1956-67	4-cyl, 1,583/1,778 cc, 60/75/85/90/95 bhp	102.4 in, integral body/chassis, 4-door saloon, independent front, beam axle rear	234,208	New full-width style car, to be built as saloons and estates. Same basic power train as old PV444/PV544 cars. Known as 'Amazon' only in Scandinavia.
Type 131 2-door saloons	1962-69	4-cyl, 1,583/1,778 cc, 60/75/85/90/95/100/115/118 bhp ratings	102.4 in, integral body/chassis, 2-door saloon, independent front, beam axle rear	359,819	Style as above, but with 2-door shell, same profile. Most powerful engines from 1966. 1968-69 cars with 1,986 cc engine.
Type 220 5-door estates	1962-69	4-cyl, 1,583/1,778 cc, 60/75/85/90/95/100/115/118 bhp	102.4 in, integral body/chassis, 5-door estate independent front, beam axle rear	73,197	5-door estate version of same basic design. 1968-69 models (2,897 built) with 1,986 cc engine.
			Grand Total:	667,323 cars	

Model series	Years produced	Engine and power	Wheelbase and chassis details	Number built	Comment
P1900 sports car					
P1900	1956–57	4-cyl, 1,414 cc, 70 bhp	94.5 in, separate tubular frame, independent front, beam axle rear	67	2-seat open sports car, with special frame and glass-fibre body shell, using PV444 mechanical parts.
P1800 family					
P1800/ 1800S coupés	1961–69	4-cyl, 1,778/ 1,986 cc, 100/ 108/115/118 bhp	96.5 in, integral body/ chassis, 2-door fixed head coupé. Independent front/beam axle rear	30,093	Short chassis Frua/Ghia coupé style, using mainly Amazon power train and 'chassis' components. Bodies at first by Pressed Steel Co of UK. First 6,000 cars assembled by Jensen in UK.
1800E 2-door coupés	1969–72	4-cyl, 1,986 cc, 130/135 bhp, fuel injection	96.5 in, integral body/ chassis, 2-door fixed head coupé. Independent front/ beam axle rear	9,414	As 1800S but with injection engine.
1800ES square- back 'estates'	1971–73 injection	4-cyl, 1,986 cc, 135 bhp, fuel injection	96.5 in, integral body/ chassis, 2-door fixed head coupé. Independent front/beam axle rear	8,078	Sporting estate version of 1800E, on same basic body/chassis style.
			Grand Total:	47,585 cars	
140 family					
Type 144 4-door saloons	1966–74	4-cyl, 1,778/ 1,986 cc, 85/ 90/105/110/ 135 bhp, various versions	102.4 in (103.1 in from 1970), integral body/ chassis, 4-door saloon, independent front, beam axle rear	523,808	Replaced 120/Amazon Series, same basic power train and 'chassis' com- ponents, but new six-side- window style. Volvo 'safety' image rapidly developed. 1,986 cc from 1968.
Type 142 2-door saloons	1967–74	4-cyl, 1,778/ 1,986 cc, 85/ 90/105/110/ 115/118/135 bhp, various versions	102.4 in (103.1 in from 1970), integral body/ chassis, 2-door saloon, independent front, beam axle rear	412,986	2-door version of car, four side windows, mechanically the same.
Type 145 5-door estates	1967–74	4-cyl, 1,778/ 1,986 cc, 85/ 90/105/110/ 115/118/135 bhp, various versions	102.4 in (103.1 in from 1970) integral body/ chassis, 5-door estate, independent front, beam axle rear	268,317	Estate car version of basic 4-door saloon design, with same 'chassis', nose and doors, plus huge carrying capacity.
Type 164 4-door saloons	1968–75	6-cyl, 2,978 cc, 145/175 bhp	106.3 in wheelbase (107.0 in from 1970) integral body/chassis, 5-door estate, independent front, beam axle rear	155,068	Based on 144 4-door saloon, with lengthened wheelbase, and 6-cyl version of basic 4-cyl engine design.
			Grand Total: 1,360,179 cars		
240 family					
Type 242 2-door saloons	1974 to date	4-cyl 1,986/ 2,127/2,315 cc, 82 to 140 bhp (various), carbs, injection	103.9 in, integral body/ chassis unit, 2-door saloon, independent front, beam axle rear	219,712*	Re-engineered 140 structure with MacPher- son strut front suspen- sion, wedge-nose style, many engine options.

Volvo cars since 1927

Model series	Years produced	Engine and power	Wheelbase and chassis details	Number built	Comment
Type 244 4-door saloons	1974 to date	4-cyl, 1,986/2,127/2,315 plus 2,315 cc turbocharged with 155 bhp, carbs, injection Or 6-cyl 2,383 cc Diesel, 82 bhp Or V6-cyl, 2,664/2,849 cc, 141/155 bhp	103.9 in, integral body/chassis unit, 4-door saloon, independent front, beam axle rear	804,695*	Re-engineered 140 structure with MacPherson strut front suspension, wedge-nose style, 4-door saloon style, more engine options than Type 242 and diesel engine from 1979. Diesel by VW.
Type 245 5-door estates	1974 to date	4-cyl, 1,986/2,127/2,315 plus 2,315 cc turbocharged with 155 bhp, carbs, injection Or 6-cyl 2,383 cc Diesel, 82 bhp Or V6-cyl, 2,664/2,849 cc, 141/155 bhp	103.9 in, integral body/chassis unit, 5-door estate, independent front, beam axle rear	435,108*	Re-engineered 140 structure with MacPherson strut front suspension, wedge-nose-style, 4-door saloon style, and same estate car rear as 145 estates.
Type 264 4-door saloons	1974–82	V6-cyl 2,664/2,849 cc, 125/140/148/155 bhp	103.9 in, integral body/chassis unit, 4-door saloon, independent front, beam axle rear	129,127	Re-engineered 140 structure with MacPherson strut front suspension, wedge-nose style, 4-door saloon style with new joint-venture PRV V6 engine. No diesel engine options.
Type 262 2-door saloons	1975–77	V6-cyl, 2,664/2,849 cc, 125/140/148/155 bhp	103.9 in, integral body/chassis unit, 2-door saloon, independent front, beam axle rear	3,329	264 power train, 'chassis' and nose, with 2-door saloon passenger box. Displaced by Bertone-built 262C coupé in 1977.

A mid-1970s aerial view of the Gothenburg site, with the corporate headquarters at the very top of the picture and the technical centre in the woods behind it.

Model series	Years produced	Engine and power	Wheelbase and chassis details	Number built	Comment
Type 265 5-door estates	1975 to date	V6-cyl, 2,664/2,849 cc, 125/140/148/155 bhp	103.9 in, integral body/chassis unit, 5-door estate, independent front, beam axle rear	31,880*	245-style estate body, but all 264 power train and 'chassis', with 264 nose.
Type 262C 2-door coupés	1977–81	V6-cyl, 2,664/2,849 cc, 125/140/148/155 bhp	103.9 in, special 2-door coupé body style, independent front, beam axle rear	5,622	264 power train and 'chassis', but with 2-door coupé style including lowered roof line. Built in Turin by Bertone.

760 family

Model series	Years produced	Engine and power	Wheelbase and chassis details	Number built	Comment
760GLE 4-door saloons	1982 to date	4-cyl, 2,315 cc, turbocharged, 173 bhp 6-cyl, 2,383 cc, Diesel, normal induction or turbocharged, 82/110 bhp V6-cyl, 2,849 cc, 155 bhp	109.0 in, integral body/chassis unit, 4-door saloon, independent front, beam axle rear	16,928*	New Volvo style for 1980s, first all-new body shell since 1966. Not a direct replacement for the 240/260 Series, though 264 saloons displaced. Diesel engines by VW.

Dutch-built Volvos

Model series	Years produced	Engine and power	Wheelbase and chassis details	Number built	Comment
66 2-door saloons	1975–80	4-cyl (Renault), 1,108/1,289 cc, 47/57 bhp	89.0 in, integral body/chassis unit, 2-door saloon, independent front, De Dion rear, Variomatic belt-drive transmission	77,637	Redeveloped Daf 66, following Volvo take-over. Transmission unique to Daf.
66 3-door estates	1975–78	4-cyl (Renault), 1,108/1,289 cc, 47/57 bhp	89.0 in, integral body/chassis unit, 3-door estate, independent front, De Dion rear, Variomatic belt-drive transmission	28,500	Estate version of 66 saloon, with same running gear.
343 3-door hatchbacks	1976 to date	4-cyl (Renault), 1,397 cc, 70 bhp 4-cyl (Volvo), 1,986 cc, 95 bhp	94.5 in, integral body/chassis unit, 3-door hatchback, independent front, De Dion rear. Variomatic or (from 1979) manual transmission	265,451*	New part-Volvo designed hatchback, still with Renault engine and Variomatic transmission. From 1979 with Volvo manual transmission. From 1980 with Volvo 1,986 cc engine.
345 5-door hatchbacks	1979 to date	4-cyl (Renault), 1,397 cc, 70 bhp 4-cyl (Volvo), 1,986 cc, 95 bhp	94.5 in, integral body/chassis unit, 5-door hatchback, independent front, De Dion rear. Variomatic or (from 1979) manual transmission	104,637*	As 343, but with 5-door style in same body shape.
360GLT 5-door hatchbacks	1982 to date	4-cyl (Volvo) 1,986 cc, 115 bhp	94.5 in, integral body/chassis unit, 5-door hatchback, independent front, De Dion rear. Manual (5-speed) gearbox	(Included in 345 total, above)	As 345, but with uprated Volvo engine, and 5-speed manual transmission.

*These totals are correct to the end of 1982.

Appendix B

Important company milestones
Who, what, when and where?

1924 Assar Gabrielsson and Gustaf Larson begin planning a new car.
1926 First prototype cars completed. Finance provided by SKF, and Volvo ('I roll') marque name chosen.
1927 Sales of Volvo cars, beginning with OV4, began.
1929 First six-cylinder Volvos introduced, displacing original four-cylinder cars.
1930 First Volvo 'Taxi' models sold.
1935 First 'streamlined' Volvo, the PV36 'Carioca', introduced.
1944 First public showing of PV444 prototype—first Volvo with unit-construction body/chassis, first with overhead valve engine.
1947 PV444 went on sale and Volvo's great surge forward began.
1949 Private car production overtook that of trucks and buses for the first time.
1955 First Volvo exports to the USA.
1956 New-style Amazon introduced. New P1900 glass-fibre sports car first sold. Assar Gabrielsson retired, Gunnar Engellau became Managing Director.
1958 Major revision of PV444 to become PV544.
1959 Land purchased for new Torslanda assembly plant. P1800 sports coupé prototype first exhibited.
1961 P1800 first put on sale, assembled in UK.
1963 Assembly of Volvos began in Canada—first such plant outside Sweden. P1800 assembly moved to Sweden.
1964 Torslanda assembly plant officially opened.
1965 Last PV544 saloon built—ending an 18-year run.
1966 New-style 140 Series cars introduced. One millionth Volvo car built.
1968 Introduction of Volvo 164—first six-cylinder Volvo car for many years.
1969 Work began to build new Volvo proving ground.
1971 Gunnar Engellau became Chairman and Pehr Gyllenhammer became President of AB Volvo. Start of engine co-operation project with Peugeot and Renault.
1972 Volvo took 33 per cent of DAF car division shares. Volvo Experimental Safety Car (VESC) unveiled.
1973 New Kalmar 'Group Assembly' factory opened in eastern Sweden. Last 1800ES cars built. Hallered proving ground opened for business.
1974 Volvo shareholding in DAF increased to 46 per cent. Introduction of new 240/260 Series models, replacing 140/160 Series models. New PRV V-6 engine a feature.

1975 Volvo achieved 75 per cent share in DAF car division, and name changed to Volvo Car BV, with factory in Holland. Introduction of Volvo 66, a re-engineered DAF 66. 3 millionth Volvo built.

1976 Volvo 343, partly designed and developed by DAF, introduced from Volvo Car BV.

1977 50th Anniversary of start-up of Volvo car production. Volvo 262C coupé, assembled by Bertone in Italy, put on sale. Volvo share of Car BV (Holland) reduced to 55 per cent. Short-lived proposal to merge AB Volvo with Saab-Scania.

1978 Proposals published for AB Volvo to merge with Norwegian government interests. First diesel-engined Volvo put on sale.

1979 Norwegian merger abandoned. Peak production year, so far, for Volvo cars. Establishment of Volvo Car Corporation, separate from parent company, with Renault as 10 per cent minority shareholders. 4 millionth Volvo car built.

1980 First-ever turbocharged Volvos put on sale.

1981 Volvo Group took over Beijerinvest AB, thus becoming much the largest industrial group in the entire Nordic region. Renault share in Volvo Car Corporation increased to 15 per cent. Volvo Car Corporation share in Car BV (Holland) reduced to 30 per cent after injection of Dutch state finance. 1 millionth Volvo exported to the United States.

1982 Introduction of new 760GLE 4-door saloon—the start of a new family for Volvo.

Appendix C

The rise, and rise, of Volvo car production
1927 to 1981

Year	Cars built	Comment
1927	297	Start-up of OV4 and PV production.
1928	498	
1929	577	First six-cylinder cars (PV650) and first special taxis (TR672) sold.
1930	639	
1931	693	
1932	908	
1933	631	Effects of economic Depression at their worst.
1934	609	
1935	845	Introduction of PV36 'Carioca'.
1936	913	
1937	1,815	
1938	2,132	
1939	2,834	Outbreak of war, but Sweden remained neutral.
1940	564	
1941	106	
1942	99	Volvo's all-time *lowest* output year.
1943	176	
1944	335	PV444 announced, but not yet built.
1945	416	End of Second World War.
1946	905	
1947	2,531	PV444 finally went on sale.
1948	2,988	
1949	5,362	Car production surpassed truck production for first time.
1950	7,345	
1951	11,891	
1952	10,101	
1953	17,111	
1954	27,666	
1955	32,471	First exports to USA.
1956	36,766	Amazon/P120 Series announced.
1957	48,490	
1958	63,204	
1959	79,186	P1800 coupé shown as prototype.

Year	Cars built	Comment
1960	84,326	
1961	78,527	
1962	94,570	
1963	106,775	
1964	118,464	New Torslanda factory officially opened.
1965	133,239	Last of PV444 family of saloons (actually PV544) built.
1966	136,490	New 140 Series range introduced. 1 millionth Volvo car built.
1967	148,742	
1968	170,746	
1969	181,668	
1970	204,991	Last Amazon car built.
1971	214,438	2 millionth Volvo car built.
1972	233,965	
1973	252,036	New Kalmar 'group assembly' plant opened.
1974	234,189	New 240/260 Series replaced 140/160 models.
1975	287,000*	Volvo took majority of DAF shares—and new Volvo 66 introduced. 3 millionth Volvo built.
1976	296,800*	Volvo 343 introduced, in Holland.
1977	225,700*	50th anniversary of Volvo.
1978	260,300*	
1979	320,000	Record production year for Volvo. 4 millionth Volvo car built.
1980	268,600*	
1981	289,500*	
1982	318,600*	New Type 760 Series saloon introduced.

*From 1975, annual production was quoted by Volvo to nearest 100 vehicles. The 5 millionth Volvo was due to be built in the winter of 1982/83, as this book was being finalised.

Appendix D

Prototypes and specials—not for sale

Ever since they started making cars in the 1920s, Volvo have seemed to take a cautious, even ponderous, attitude to their new-model policies. Since the Second World War, after all, only five basically different types of saloon car have been on offer—five cars in nearly 40 years, or four-and-a-half if you subscribe to the view that the 240s were really no more than up-dated 140s, eight years later. But this doesn't mean that Volvo's design engineers, and the other planners, have mostly been sitting idly around, reading the motoring magazines, and convincing themselves that better and more sensational cars *could* have been designed if only management had let them get on with it.

Far from it—the truth is that Volvo, like all other car companies, has produced any number of new designs, prototypes and specials—some of which were really only whims, and some of which might so easily have been put on sale. Some of the one-offs investigated new mechanical ideas and some were probes into more advanced styling. Some, indeed, combined a new 'chassis' and mechanical components with a new shape. There are still a few projects about which Volvo managers are still reticent, but most of the major experiments have now been revealed. This Appendix, I hope, will provide much up-to-date information about the significant 'might-have-beens'.

Happily for historians like myself, Volvo do not normally destroy a prototype after a project has been cancelled. The outdated machine is often kept in store, sometimes in running order, perhaps for display in future years, or perhaps (I suspect) because the stylists and engineers sometimes cannot bear to see so much hard and careful work go entirely to waste. To be allowed to look around Volvo's archive collection of cars, is like being permitted into a real Aladdin's Cave of motoring archaeology. In one hangar, on the perimeter of a private airfield not far from Torslanda, there are enough prototypes, and 'show' cars, to keep a Volvo enthusiast busy, and incredulous, for days. Some are 50 years old, and some were built in the 1970s; some are sporting and some had a business tycoon in mind. Volvo's planners were nothing, if not broad-minded—could one really consider a diesel-engined city-car project and a V-8 powered limousine in the same context? Not every prototype is there, I'm sure. Other more recent 'follies', no doubt, are also in store, but it may be years before these machines are revealed for posterity.

Because there have been many such cars, and because few are inter-related, one to the other, I ought to survey them separately. The story, therefore, really starts in the 1930s, at a time when Volvo was still so small that Gustaf Larson himself can have had little time to play around with his dreams for the future:

Venus-Bilo

Until the early 1930s it would be true to suggest that Volvos were really not styled at all for, like most cars of the period, they were staid-looking, upright and shaped more with an eye to production convenience and low cost, rather than style. By 1933, however, a few independent stylists had begun to show cars looking more like aeroplanes, with flowing lines and what was optimistically called 'streamlining'. The fact that much of the smooth shaping was concentrated on the tail, and a relatively bluff nose was left to fend for itself, was not considered ludicrous at the time. The real push towards full-width styling came with the North American Chrysler Airflow of 1934, but before then Volvo had already commissioned an independent Swedish consultant, Gustaf Ericsson, to build a special body on one of their existing PV653 six-cylinder chassis.

The new car, whose style was originally developed with one-tenth scale models, was a very controversial shape indeed, for it combined a slab-sided four-door cabin and a sweeping tail in which a horizontal spare wheel partly protruded for use as a 'bumper', with a drooping nose in which the headlamps were only partly recessed, and in which the much-modified radiator grille was considerably 'undershot'. In many ways this car pre-dated the Bristol by more than a decade, for there were recesses in each front wing, behind the front wheels, but ahead of the front doors for stowage of the spare wheel, tools and luggage.

The car, soon nick-named 'Venus-Bilo' by Volvo's own house magazine, was unveiled in November 1933, but was never seriously considered for series production as it was not acceptable to the ultra-conservative Swedish motorist. Nevertheless, it certainly had some influence on Volvo and on the style of the PV36 'Carioca' model which *did* go into production. PV36 was launched in 1935 and preparatory work on its body style, which not only showed traces of the Venus-Bilo shape, but of the Chrysler Airflow, could not have begun until mid-1934. As far as is known, this car has not survived.

'Venus-Bilo', a 1933 prototype built as a private venture when so-called 'streamlined' shapes were becoming fashionable. I now understand that the name was given to this car many years afterwards.

Prototypes and specials—not for sale

Philip

The long-running PV444 saloon was launched in 1944 and actually went on sale in 1947, but the next new-shape Volvo to be launched was the Amazon of 1956. In the 12 years which had intervened, however, Volvo's designers had not been idle, for several projects were started up, developed to the prototype stage, then cancelled.

The first studies for a Volvo, different and larger than the PV444, were made in 1949. Assar Gabrielsson had always had a soft spot for the larger six-cylinder Volvos, and even in the different economic conditions of the late 1940s he was tempted to produce a successor to the PV60, which was the car designed before and during the Second World War, but not finally put on sale until 1946. Like several other later projects, this car was given a code name derived from the Scandinavian calendar habit, which associates a different name with each day of the year. (Volvo are not alone in this, for Saab have adopted the same approach in the life of their cars.) One design study, formalised on November 14 1949, was therefore called 'Emil', and was really an enlarged PV444, while another, dating from December 1, was called 'Oscar'.

Neither of these projects, which leaned heavily on the latest trends from Detroit, progressed beyond the paper stage, and it was not until May 2 1950 ('Filip'—or 'Philip'—day in Sweden) that a more promising specification was drawn up. This car was to be quite a lot larger and heavier than the PV444 and was to be new in all major respects. Its wheelbase was to be 290 cm (114.2 in), which compares with 260 cm for the existing PV444, and 285 cm for the obsolete PV60 model.

As I have already mentioned in an earlier chapter, Philip was the very first car to be styled by Jan Wilsgaard after joining Volvo, direct from Art college, in June 1950. Since he was only 20 years old at the time, and had no previous experience, it was only reasonable that his first efforts should be highly derivative of another car.

At the time, the American company, Kaiser, had just launched their new range of two-door and four-door models (in February 1950), with styles by Howard 'Dutch' Darrin, and they had already become a talking point throughout the motor industries of the world, for they were much more shapely than the equivalent Fords

One attempt to beautify the PV544 came in the 1950s and was called PV454—not only the nose, but the line of the side windows, was significantly changed. Only the one car was built in 1953.

Above *PV644 was a final thought on the modernisation of the long-running PV544 shape, with something like a 164 grille grafted on to the 444/544 cabin, with a new tail. It was not liked.*

Below *Not very special, perhaps, but an interesting derivative of the PV444 fastback layout, was this convertible by Karosserifabrik.*

or Chevrolets. (It was Darrin's sports car style for Kaiser, incidentally, which influenced Assar Gabrielsson so much when he made his North American tour later in the decade, prior to having the P1900 designed—truly, in motor industry terms, this is a 'small world'.) Accordingly, Wilsgaard had little hesitation in shaping Philip along the same lines.

But before this work could begin, Philip's 'chassis' had to be designed by a team led by Edward Lindberg. Like the PV444, he gave the new car a unit construction body/chassis unit, a four-door style was to be standard, and the entire front section—bonnet and front wings—was arranged to swing up and forward, hinged just behind the front bumper.

The exterior style, by Wilsgaard, was superficially like that of the Kaiser (which had a slightly longer wheelbase, incidentally) but with softer details, more glass area and no fussy front or rear quarter windows. The rear window was completely wrap-around, and the entire tail treatment was more satisfactory. Like the Kaiser, there

Prototypes and specials—not for sale 191

Philip's nose looking 'all of a piece' which indeed it was, as the entire nose/bonnet/front wings assembly hinge forward for access to the engine and front suspension.

were rear wheel-arch 'spats' and—as a gesture to North America—white-wall tyres were chosen. The interior style was designed by Wilsaard's only colleague in the department, Rustan Lange, and a feature was the use of full bench seats at front and rear.

The heart and soul of Philip was its new V-8 engine (the old side-valve 'six' used in the PV60 was now very old, and had run out of development some time ago). Coded B8B, it was quite clearly derived from North American engines in several ways, though it seems to have been an all-Volvo unit. Volvo themselves claim that it had no common parts with the existing PV444 unit, though the cylinder stroke of 80 mm *was* the same, and the 84.1 mm bore would almost be duplicated by that of the B18 unit which followed at the end of the 1950s! It had a cast iron cylinder block and heads, wedge-type combustion chambers and overhead valves, and a swept volume of 3,559 cc. With a compression ratio of 6.8:1 it developed up to 120 bhp at 4,300 rpm, nearly three times the output of the PV444's 1.4-litre unit.

To match the engine there was also a special three-speed Volvo-designed automatic gearbox which relied heavily on a Chrysler system and engineers who had worked on them in Detroit. Surely it would have been cheaper and easier for Volvo to buy in transmissions for America? The rest of the chassis was relatively conventional, but different in detail from the PV444. Independent front suspension was by coil springs, wishbones and an anti-roll bar, while a new and heavy-duty back axle was sprung on coils, and located by radius arms with a similar inward-leaning geometry to those of the PV444. It was a massive and fast car, which took two years to build. The engine alone weighed 494 lb, while the complete car weighed nearly 3,500 lb, though it had a 100 mph top speed potential.

In fact, Philip's career was over almost before it had begun, for it was never pushed further than the completion of a single prototype. By 1952, when this car was running, times had changed, not only at Volvo, but out in the wide world. Any ideas that Assar Gabrielsson had held about a replacement for the PV60 were

'Philip' was the first Volvo shape ever produced by Jan Wilsgaard, and was completed in 1952. It had an experimental V-8 engine, and looked very much like the 1951 model Kaiser. One car was built and it still exists.

never realised (one reason, no doubt, being that the PV444 was already extending itself, and its production process, into every corner of the Lundby plant). Philip was developed far enough to be reliable, then used as executive transport at a Volvo subsidiary, then, several years later, returned to Gothenburg to join the company's collection of historic vehicles, where it still survives.

The engine was never destined for private car use (and is not at all related to the still-born V-8 project of the late 1960s) but it was eventually re-developed for use in light trucks and boats. Eventually it was put into production at the Skovde factory and used in the LV420 commercial vehicle but, by the early 1960s, had finally and irrevocably been phased out.

I looked closely at Philip when I visited Volvo in 1982 and found it difficult to relate this big, voluptuous model with the ascetic PV444 or the sturdily practical Amazon which followed. I am sure that Mr Gabrielsson was right to reject the design once he had seen it, for I cannot believe that it would have sold well for a number of years. Like many other American-style cars of the period, it was really far too 'fashionable' for that.

PV179

Unlike Philip, PV179 was a very serious project indeed for it represented a determined attempt to produce a car to succeed the PV444 and take over from it. The PV179 project, which originated in 1952 (five years after the PV444 went on sale) might have been ready for production in 1954 or 1955 and it could so easily have been a commercial success.

Work on the PV 179 (a pure Volvo project number, with no mystical significance) began as soon as the Philip design had been abandoned, with engineering by Tor Berthelius and styling by Jan Wilsgaard. Because it was always intended to be a replacement for the PV444, it used the same wheelbase, the same basic power train

Prototypes and specials—not for sale

PV179, styled by Jan Wilsgaard, was designed in 1952, after 'Philip' had been found too large and too costly to put into production. Most of the 'chassis' was later used under the Amazon, but this style was later abandoned. Swedish journalists nicknamed it 'Margaret Rose' to prolong a British 'royal' connection with Philip, even though the original inspiration was one of Sweden's own 'name days'.

(engine, gearbox and axle) and was a two-door fastback shape. It did, however, have many different suspension components, and in this context I should point out that the underside of the car was very much like the one which eventually went on sale in 1956 as the Amazon; the new coil spring front suspension and the parallel twin-trailing-arm location of the back axle were almost identical.

Mechanically, therefore, the PV179 should be familiar to Volvo enthusiasts. The Wilsgaard styled body, however, is not. In some ways there were minor similarities to the PV444—the window shapes and their angles, for instance—but the actual sheet metal was all new. The PV179 (styled in 1952, remember) had a smooth full-width style with a vertical front grille and recessed headlamps, with a flowing fastback and embryo fins at the end of the rear wings. To relieve the monotony of the side panels, there was a faint but pleasing feature crease originating over the front wheel arches and curling down just ahead of the rear wheels. On the single prototype, white-wall tyres once again gave a clue to Assar Gabrielsson's future intentions for Volvo expansion.

It was a neat and apparently cost-effective car, well-liked by Assar Gabrielsson and his consultant, Mas-Olle, and at one time Volvo's founder seemed to be determined to get it into production as soon as possible. But that major influence on Gabrielsson, Helmer Petterson, who had been one of the originators of the PV444 during the war years, did not like the car (why not—perhaps because he had not been consulted at the project stage?) and made his views most forcefully clear; his view was that the PV179 car was too large and too heavy for the PV444 engine to give it acceptable performance, and that the existing PV444 should be face-lifted instead. That he had an ulterior motive is proved by the fact that *his* next project was to evolve the PV454 of 1953, already mentioned in an earlier chapter.

In due course, Gabrielsson cancelled the car—the style, not the chassis—for much of the engineering content went into the successful development of the Amazon range, and this helps to explain why the Amazon could be prepared so speedily. Although Volvo never gave the car a name, once pictures of the cancelled project had been released to the Swedish press, they started calling it 'Margaret Rose'—which continued the rather tenuous British Royal Family connection to follow Philip (Prince Philip, HRH the Duke of Edinburgh), and the Elizabeth cars (see below).

The single PV179 prototype was written off in an accident, when being driven by Volvo engineer, Raymond Eknor, after it had been rolled. It was never repaired.

Elizabeth I and Elizabeth II

These two cars were not true Volvo prototypes, as both used standard PV444/PV445 underbodies, suspensions and running gear. One of them, however, was used by Volvo to study styles which later led to the Amazon car, and therefore had a place here. The original car came about because a Monaco-based Swedish entrepreneur, Gosta Wennberg, was considering the possibility of marketing PV444s with special coachwork. In 1952, therefore, he bought one of the new PV445 Duett rolling chassis (which was the commercial vehicle/estate car derivative of the PV444, with a box-section separate chassis instead of a unit-construction shell) and commissioned Vignale of Turin to produce a special four-seater two-door body style. This prototype, completed in 1953, was 'contemporary Italian' with traces of Alfa Romeo 1900 and Fiat 1400/1900 in its lines and it certainly looked much more stylish than the standard PV444.

Wennberg sent the car to Gothenburg for Volvo to inspect and they were duly impressed. However, a study of the interior 'package' dimensions showed that the layout had been rather restricted by the separate chassis frame of the PV445. Accordingly, Volvo themselves commissioned Vignale to produce a second car and supplied a complete unit-construction PV444 underbody for that purpose.

The Swedish press had already seen the first car by this time, for Wennberg was looking for all the publicity he could attract, and as they already knew about Jan Wilsgaard's Philip they decided to confer a British Royal Family connection by calling the Vignale car Elizabeth. (The fact that this car was already one out of sequence was not revealed to them then, for the PV179 project was still highly secret at the time.)

Vignale's second effort, though clearly based on their first, was an even more graceful style, and showed fewer standard-Italian features. The grille in particular, could no longer be compared with that of an Alfa Romeo, and the lines were slightly more crisp. This car, when finished early in 1954, was instantly dubbed 'Elizabeth II'. However, Wennberg's dream of selling a limited number of the cars (200 cars at 20,000 SKr each—considerably higher than the price of a standard PV444—was once mentioned) came to nothing.

Historically, however, Elizabeth I was important because Jan Wilsgaard based his 1953 '55' study on it in 1953, and it was the very successful Amazon which evolved from the '55'. The '55' mock-up, in fact, has similar lines to Elizabeth I, right down to the Alfa-style 'horsecollar' grille, but the sweep of the wing crown line, particularly towards the rear, was already beginning to look rather like that of the Amazon. The Elizabeths may have survived—but Volvo do not have them in their collection.

Prototypes and specials—not *for sale*

Above *'Elizabeth'—another name provided by the Swedish press—was what this prototype, privately sponsored by a Monaco-resident Swede, was called. It was built in 1953, and styled by Vignale, eventually assessed by Volvo, but never progressed.*

Below *This was the '55' clay model, styled by Jan Wilsgaard in 1953—the original Amazon evolved from it.*

P358

To my mind, the P358 was one of Jan Wilsgaard's finest still-born efforts. It says much for its lines (created in 1958/59) that when I first saw the pictures of the car I was convinced that it represented an update of the late-1960s Type 1964 saloon!

P358 was a 'flagship', or prestige-builder, in every way and I really cannot take seriously the suggestions that it might have been a taxi as well; it was far too grand for that. The fact was, however, that Gunnar Engellau had seen Volvo's initial reception in North America, had never forgotten the way that American cars had always seemed to be popular in Scandinavia and decided to look at ways of building a truly large Volvo car.

P358 was a large (112 in wheelbase) four-door saloon style proposed by the Volvo styling studio in 1958, and would have used 'Philip's' V-8 engine and a choice of either four-window or six-window styling. It was a very fine concept but it never progressed beyond the mock-up stage.

In terms of chronology, I ought to mention that the last of the 800 Series Volvo taxi-cabs, which had their heritage firmly rooted in the 1930s, were built in 1958, that Volvo's styling studio had just completed its work on the Amazon range of saloons and estates, had converted the PV444 into the PV544, and had entrusted the development of the new 1.8-litre engined sports coupé to the Ghia/Frua/Helmer Petterson combine. Their decks were therefore cleared for a look at a new type of car.

Prototypes and specials—not for sale

Volvo tried to update the PV544 into PV644, in 1959/60, with the squared-up nose, different side windows and a longer tail. Only the one running prototype was built. The rear view of the PV644 project shows the more upright rear window, the more roomy boot and the sail panels at each side of the rear quarters.

Perhaps, this time, the code number, P358, can be given a meaning, for it was decided to base its design around the Volvo V-8 engine originally laid down for Philip and now being used in a truck. The engine's capacity was 3.5-litres, therefore 3.58, or 358, made an ideal number for the project. The new car was to be based on a 285 cm wheelbase (112.2 in) which was slightly less than had been proposed for Philip, and it was to have wide tracks (145 cm/57.1 in) as before. The V-8 engine, now a production item, could be rated at 140 bhp for automobile use, though even at this stage (ten years before such an engine ever saw the light of day, and before its four-cylinder 'base' unit was developed) there was talk of an alternative B27 straight-six cylinder engine also being offered.

With the P358 style, Jan Wilsgaard did not have to be influenced, or inspired, by any other car. The result was a massive but graceful shape, with a straight-through wing line and crisp sharp-edged contours which would not have disappointed any of the Italian styling houses, so dominant at the time. The nose included a proud near-square grille featuring the diagonal Volvo motif. The two headlamps, at the front corners, were supplemented by extra long-range driving lamps below and inboard of them. The side was laid out so that there could be three side windows or two. The rear quarters could be blanked off if required so that there could be more privacy in the rear seat of this car—as it was thought likely that it could be a tycoon's machine, this was a very desirable feature.

By any standards, P358 was a handsome style and it would undoubtedly have remained in fashion through the 1960s. It never proceeded beyond the mock-up stage, however, for at the beginning of the 1960s there were two major problems. One, a perennial one at Volvo in the 1950s and 1960s, was that there seemed to be no place in the factories where such a car could be built in what were likely to be limited quantities—and the other was the way in which the United States market changed.

It was, I remind you, the period during which Ford launched the Edsel, a bigger, faster and completely vulgar version of the type of car P358 really was—and Ford lost tens of millions of dollars in its failure. Jan Wilsgaard now recalls what happened: 'The compacts came then, and that scared them.' 'Them', we may assume, were Gunnar Engellau and his North American dealer chain.

The original Glasspar style for the Volvo P1900 sports car of 1954 with a hard top and smoothly rounded tail.

Prototypes and specials—not *for sale*

Jan Wilsgaard at his desk—the sketch is of P172, the proposed successor to the P1800 coupé.

P172 and P183

These were two sporting projects which I have already mentioned in Chapter 5 but I ought to repeat their significance here. P172 was invented by Jan Wilsgaard during his 'sabbatical' stay in California in 1964/65 and was to be a bigger, more roomy and much faster sporting coupé to replace the 1800S sporting cars by the end of the 1960s. It was to use most of the 'chassis' and running gear of the 164 saloon, due for announcement in 1968, which is to say that it was to use the new and rather heavy in-line ohv six-cylinder 3-litre engine with conventional coil spring independent front suspension and a live rear axle.

As with the 1800S, it was only to have been built as a fixed-head coupé, but it would have had much more generous 2+2 accommodation. Comparison shots with the 1800S (reproduced elsewhere in this book) show that it would have been a little wider, and even a little higher, with remarkably sleek lines and completely smooth side panels. The boot, to keep the North Americans happy, would have been enormous and at about $6,000 it would have been good value for money in that continent. (The 1800S cost rather more than $4,000 when P172 was being developed.) It was cancelled because the investment required in new body shell tooling would have been too high and, yet again, because it would have required too much space at the new Torslanda factory. In addition, the Volvo dealers in North America were not convinced that it was 'right' for that continent where the bulk of sales would have had to be made.

As far as I can gather, no complete prototype of P172 was ever built, though its influence certainly lingered on into the 1970s. Any stylist looking at P172 would surely agree that traces of it remained when the two-door Type 262C came along in 1977. P183, of course, was the alternative style of 'square-back' derivative of the 1800E coupé, dubbed 'Rocket' by Jan Wilsgaard, and this car *was* not only built, but has been retained by Volvo. When I tentatively asked if the prototype was for sale, I got a very dusty answer....

There were two distinctly different 'Rocket' window shapes in this emphatically different square-back layout for an 1800ES model. This particular car, only a clay mock-up at this stage, had a rounded rear quarter window while this side of the same clay mock-up featured a louvred, longer layout. The rounded style was the shape actually built up for assessment.

Prototypes and specials—not for sale

Above *In 1966, Jan Wilsgaard's staff found time to prepare this smooth fastback hard-top style on the basis of the 1800S coupé body shell.*

Below *On the desk are two aerodynamic shapes, plus an early study of the possible form of the 760 Series (a full-size prototype was actually built of this car). Behind is the 'Rocket' prototype of the late 1960s, as constructed to Wilsgaard's designs by Frua. That car is still held in store by Volvo.*

When the original 145 estate car was being styled, it had unique rear door frames, and a more upright tail panel which still featured the very large glass area, and would have provided an enormous stowage space, even bigger than it actually became on the production car.

'Modern follies'

By the end of the 1960s, Volvo were becoming much more highly 'institutionalised' and formal in their future product policy. This, and the onset of more, and yet more, legislative requirements to be solved before existing cars could be sent overseas (and particularly to North America), meant that there was less time for the engineers to play around and create 'might-have-beens'. However, on the basis of standard products, there was still time for the stylists to develop several new cars which did not get into production, but which have mostly been preserved for posterity.

I have already noted how the Bertone-built 262C coupé took shape and that the very first car of this type to be built was actually a 162C. This, therefore, had the now-familiar 262C coupé cabin and tail but this was on the slightly-longer Type

Prototypes and specials—not for sale

164 underpan, with the straight-six engine and the 164-style nose. According to Volvo's own records, that car was built in 1974, just before the last of the series production 144/164 cars were built.

In 1976 and 1977, two closely related cars were built as one-offs and were very logically coded P243 and P263 respectively. If you look for just one moment at the logical way in which the 240/260 Series cars are given numbers, these cars must, of course, be three-door hatchbacks—and that, indeed, is what they were. Both cars had similar body styles, the 243 having the B21 four-cylinder engine, and the 263 having the PRV Douvrin V-6 2.7-litre engine. Forward of the windscreens, and in their doors and side panels, these hatchback prototypes shared panels with the two-door saloons or the 262C coupé, as appropriate, but there was quite a lot of difference around the cabins, the roof and, of course, around the tail.

These cars were eminently practical and, philosophically, were descendants of the last of the 1800ES square-backs, but we can guess that the usual two factors—investment and complication for the factory—made sure that they were shelved. Both cars are still in store.

Before the definitive long-wheelbase 264TE was produced (and, in at least one case, while production was in progress) other versions on that theme were investigated. At least two different prototypes were built in Styling, one with an 8 cm longer wheelbase than standard, the other with 15 cm extra inserted in the floor, but both were converted to have two, rather than three, side windows and the rear doors were lengthened in each case. Like the 262C coupés, these cars were given wider 'modesty' steel panels at the rear quarters which would allow more privacy for the back-seat occupants.

Other, more recent, projects are no doubt still hidden away at Torslanda, especially some of those connected with the 760GLE, which is still such a new design. One of the early styling 'feelers' towards the 760 shape, probably built in the early 1970s, has been allowed out and it is a rather more simple shape than that eventually adopted for production in 1982.

One of several prototypes built on the basis of the 240 Series cars in the 1970s was the Type 243 hatchback, which used the same floor pan, running gear, screen and doors as the 242DL. Would it have been a success?

Above *By the beginning of 1977, the now familiar Type 760GLE style was beginning to emerge. This is a see-through full-size model, not a running prototype, and was built of clay.*

Above *The final wooden model of the 760GLE, in August 1977, in the form which would be approved for production. It took nearly five more years to get it into the showrooms.*

Below *Two intriguing shapes—nearest the camera is the Concept Car, shown here in 1976, but destined to go on display in 1980. There is a lot of 760GLE in this car. Is this what the production estate car will look like? Behind the estate is a very early, squared-up idea of what a 760GLE should look like. It still exists, in the Volvo company's secret store.*

Prototypes and specials—not for sale

Electric car, city taxi and gas-turbine project

In recent years, Volvo have shown three different vehicles, not even intended for sale, but really to prove not only that they have the technological capability in almost every sphere, but that they also understand the way in which the world of motoring may be changing, and that Volvo can accommodate that change if necessary.

The electric car dates from 1976, and was built more for Volvo to learn, than for them to test the market in such machines. It was an upright, and very basically styled machine, using conventional lead-acid batteries for power storage, and it was even shorter than the ubiquitous BL Mini.

The city taxi, however, was a much more serious, and considerably larger, machine. If not as lofty as a Range-Rover, it certainly has the bulk of that car, with touches of 760 styling in its lines (and therefore remarkably advanced for 1976, when it was announced) and for obvious reasons there was a large sliding rear passenger door on the right side of the car (which is the kerb-side of the car in almost every country in the world, Britain and the 'Empire' nations being the obvious exceptions).

It had a six-cylinder diesel engine and front-wheel-drive, both of which were Volvo novelties at the time. Front-wheel-drive has remained an experimental project, but now we know not only that Volvo are taking six-cylinder diesels from VW for their production cars, but that they had developed similar units of their own before entering such a co-operative deal.

Perhaps the most intriguing prototype of all, only briefly shown in 1981, and still undergoing active development, is the gas-turbine engine car. This is currently a one-off machine based on a normal Type 264 saloon and has a KTT (Kronogard Turbine Transmission) engine mounted where the V-6 piston engine would normally be.

When I saw the car, it looked to me to be merely a 'just for fun' experiment. Volvo Car Corporation president, Hakan Frisinger, has other ideas: 'Such cars will

The experimental 'city taxi' of 1976 which was powered by a six-cylinder VW diesel engine, soon to be offered in the 240 Series cars.

In 1981 Volvo exhibited a gas turbine-engined 264, but this is still an advanced research project, not likely to be ready for sale until the 1990s, if ever. The engine was developed by United Turbine AB, a subsidiary of the Volvo group, at Malmo in the south of Sweden.

not be economical, or cheap enough to build, at least during the 1980s. Certainly it cannot be built before 1995. But the parent company (AB Volvo, not the Car Corporation) still likes to see advanced projects going on. It is still very far away, but in the 1990s . . . .'

Work on the project actually began way back in 1974 through an AB Volvo subsidiary, United Turbine AB of Malmo, and the word 'Kronogard' comes because it was the professor of that name who has led the team ever since. The car shown in 1981 had not then run on the road, but was expected to do so by 1983.

The performance of the turbine-engined prototype was expected to be similar to that of a conventional Type 264, for the engine itself weighs only 397 lb and the peak power output (at 70,000 turbine rpm!) is about 140 bhp. Professor Kronogard sees the turbine's most significant benefit in being able to run on a whole variety of fuels—for the only basic requirement is that this should be capable of being vaporised. Petrol, diesel, paraffin, alcholol-based brews, LPG and other types can all be used.

But there is still a very long way to go before the obvious advantages of simplicity, potential fuel-economy saving and very 'clean' exhaust gases can be made to outweigh the usual turbine drawbacks of great expense and the enormous tooling-up capital required to put an entirely new type of prime-mover into production. One thing, however, seems certain—that if the gas-turbine has a future, then Volvo's United Turbine will be one of the first concerns to realise it.

There must be other 'follies' or 'might-have-beens' which I have not mentioned in this Appendix—either because I have not been allowed to do so, or because they are still considered too secret to be put out to grass at the moment. But I think we have seen that, although to most of the world, Volvo and their cars have usually had a rather conventional reputation and been solid and reliable, their thinkers—engineers, stylists and product planners—have usually been anything but that. And don't forget that the 'follies' of yesterday often influence the production cars of tomorrow.

Appendix E

Trucks, buses, tractors, aero and marine engines
The other faces of Volvo

Even though the most famous Volvo products have usually been the private cars, these have often represented only a minor part of the company's business. In the early 1980s, for instance, the cars generate less than one-third of the group's financial turnover, and even in the 1930s and 1940s there were more trucks and buses being built.

Even before the first Volvo car had been sold, the company's founders were planning to develop a light truck from the OV4 car chassis, and detail design work began early in 1927. The first sales of *Lastvagnarna* (which is Swedish for trucks) were made in 1928 and right away they began to outsell the private cars.

In 1930, for instance, a total of 1,256 trucks (chassis or complete machines) were built, which compared with 639 cars, while, in 1939, there were 4,171 trucks compared with 2,834 cars. In the meantime, Volvo had also started to build bus chassis as well, the first in 1932, and, by 1939, production of these exceeded 500 a year. It is worth remembering, too, that the rugged but technically unexciting side-valve six-cylinder unit, used in all Volvo's 1930s cars, was also invaluable to the truck division, and was used up until the end of the 1940s.

It was during the Second World War, however, that Volvo's interests widened even further, for they took a part-interest in an aeroplane engine manufacturing business (with Saab, their near-neighbours at Trollhattan, as principal customers), expanded their interests in military vehicle building (tractor units, special trucks and many derivatives), designed their first agricultural tractor (the T41, for medium to large farms) and made more and more marine engines at the Pentaverken at Skovde.

Once the PV444 car had been put into production, however, it soon overtook the trucks and buses; since 1949, in numbers if not in terms of value, private car production has always been way ahead. But the trucks were getting bigger and more complex, while the buses were getting to be more versatile—and with the return of prosperity to the free world, overseas trade increased and exports began to grow.

For many years, all Volvo cars, trucks, buses and tractors were built at the original Lundby factory but—as I have already made clear in earlier chapters—the site rapidly became overcrowded. A new private car assembly plant was built at Torslanda and officially inaugurated in 1964, though the last cars were not built at Lundby until the end of the 1960s.

In the meantime, the trucks got diesel engines, longer and heavier-capacity chassis and a great deal of derivatives. Turbocharged diesel engines were on offer from

Above *How about this under the bonnet of a 760GLE? Actually it is a turbo-jet engine for the Saab Viggen fighter 'plane. Built by Volvo, of course, but Saab don't like to admit that.*

Below *In the beginning, Volvo built more trucks than private cars, as this posed shot, outside the old Lundby factory, confirms.*

Trucks, buses, tractors, aero and marine engines

Above *Volvo invented the 'Bendibus' layout. This is an early example, in Zurich, Switzerland. Some countries, notably the UK, do not allow such machines to operate, as yet.*

Below *A 1971 BB57 bus, hard at work in Bolivia. By Bolivian standards, there is a lot of space left inside that bus!*

At the beginning of the 1980s, Volvo took over the White Truck corporation of North America. Rejuvenation of that concern is already under way.

1954, and the last of the petrol-engined machines were built in the early 1960s (these were the V-8 engines originally developed for the 'Philip' prototype car of the early 1950s). A massive new assembly hall for bus and truck assembly had arrived at Lundby in 1953 which raised production potential to 15,000 commercial chassis a year.

But the commercial vehicles, like the cars, soon began to run out of space. In the early 1960s a new tractor-assembly factory was opened at Eskilstuna, a tracked-vehicle plant opened at Bolinder-Munktell in 1963, assembly of trucks from kits at Alsemberg in Belgium began in the same year . . . the activity was incessant. These days it is difficult to get around the environs of industrial Sweden without finding some evidence of Volvo industry.

Truck and bus investment intensified in the 1970s and a few very simple statistics bear this out. In 1971, the car side of the business accounted for 59 per cent of the 6,100 million SKr turnover—ten years later the turnover had increased to 48,000 million SKr, and the car division's contribution had slipped to a mere 28 per cent. Much of that increase had come from the inclusion of 'energy' interests, but the truck and bus share had almost caught up with that of the private cars. Truly, in the

Trucks, buses, tractors, aero and marine engines 211

If you have to knock down part of the original Lundby factory, what better truck to cart away the spoil than an N-model (normal control) Volvo truck?

last decade or so, Volvo has become a very different company, for the group, in total, had 220 work sites by 1981, in Sweden alone, with another 100 in 30 other countries. In 1981, too, the truck division expanded when the troubled White Truck Corporation of North America was bought up.

So—what is AB Volvo today? It makes private cars, trucks of many shapes and sizes, buses to suit all markets, urban and long-distance, Western or Third World, tractors and earth movers, marine engines and small boats, massive turbojet aero-engines for the Swedish Air Force (under licence from Pratt & Whitney of North America) . . . but that is only motor vehicles and related products. Especially since the acquisition of the Beijerinvest group in 1981, Volvo is also involved in the harvesting and exploration of oil, the production of food (one company, called Abba, but nothing to do with the world-famous Swedish pop group!) and many other related activities.

And that, mark you, was the situation in 1982. But Volvo's president, Pehr Gyllenhammar, is still young by many business standards, still apparently ambitious and highly likely to take AB Volvo off on other enterprises in the coming years. Will it all be very different in the year 2000?

Above *The F86 Series was one of the longer-running, and most popular, of all Volvo truck designs. This was the later version, with revised cab styling.*

Below *It takes all sorts and sizes—the 1982 range of trucks produced by Volvo.*

Trucks, buses, tractors, aero and marine engines

Above *The LV101/LV102 bus of 1951 had front style similarities to the post-war Volvo taxis.*

Below *Volvo make double-decker buses too. The complication here is that the chassis are built at Irvine, in Scotland, the body parts at Falkirk, also in Scotland, and these examples are at work in Indonesia!*

Index

Note In order to keep this index to a manageable length, not every competing model of car which appears in the text is mentioned, nor all the non-private-car Volvo products. (Illustration caption references are printed in **bold** type.)

A
Abrahamsson, Einar, 23
Acropolis rally, 96, 100, 101, **101**
Adriatic rally, 98
Albinsson, 37
Andersson, Gunnar, 52, 93-105, **94, 96, 97, 98, 101**
Andersson, T.G., 82
Audi Quattro, 105
Autocar, 62, 65, 84, 112, 116, 147, 149, 161
Autosport, 99, 100

B
Beijerinvest AB, 151, 156, 211
Berthelius, Tor, 49, 192
Bertone, 92, 159, **160, 161**, 161, 162, 177
Bird, John, **97**
Bohringer, Eugen, 100, 102
Borgert, Gunnar, 28
Browning, Peter, 86

C
Callbo, 98
Car, 158, 166
Car Classics, 15
Carlberg, Erik, 15, 17, 23
Carlsson, Erik, 100, 101
Cars of the 1930s, 25
Chrysler Airflow, 29, 30, 188
Citroën SM coupé, 132
Coggiola, Sergio, 89, **90**, 159, 161, 169
Consten, Bernard, 96, 98

D
DAF, and Dutch company, 102, 104, 132, 140, 141-157, **142**
DAF 66, **142**, 144, 145
DAF 77, 144, 145, **146**
Daniels, Jeffrey, 163
Darrin, Howard 'Dutch', 189, 190
Dreyfus, Pierre, 132, **154**
Dutch government finance, 151

E
East African Safari rally, **95**, **98**, 100
Eknor, Raymond, 72, 73, 74, 82, 194
Engellau, Gunnar, 35, 36, 50, 51, 59, 60, 61, 62, **63**, 64, 68, 77, 80, 82, 89, 96, **107**, 110, 119, 132, 143, 195, 198
L'Equipe, 162
Ericsson, Gustaf, 188
European Rally Championship, 93, **97**, 98, 99, 100, 101
European Rallycross Championship, 104
Executive Car, 163

F
Finnish 1000 Lakes rally, 98, 99, 100, 101, 102
Fiore, Trevor, 145
Ford Escort RS1700T, 105
Freyschuss, 15
Frisinger, Hakan, **7**, 127, 128, 131, 133, **137**, 140, 141, **144**, 149, 151, 154, 155, 158, 166, 173, 177, 205
Frua, 77, 83, 89, 196, **201**

G
Gabrielsson, Assar, 10, **11**, 12, 13, 14, 15, **16**, 17, 18, 21, 23, 30, 33, 35, 39, 41, 42, 43, 47, 48, 50, 51, 54, 55, 56, 59, 60, 65, 70, 71, 72, 74, 96, 124, 189, 190, 191, 192, 193, 194
Galco AB, 11, 14
Gatsonides, Maurice, 98
Gautier, François, 132, **154**
Gendebien, Olivier, 100
German rally, 96
Ghia, 77, 196
Giugiaro, Giorgetto, 169
Glasspar company, 71, 72, **198**
Gott, John, 99, 100
Grondal, 93
Gustaf Adolf, King, 65, 66
Gustaffson, Rune, 70, 92, 168, 173
Gyllenhammar, Pehr, **88, 107**, 132, 144, **145**, 151, 152, **153**, 153, **154**, 154, 155, 156, 159, 162, 177, 211

H
Haggstrom, Carl-Eric, 145, 149, 177

Index

Hammond, Vic, 108
Harper, Peter, 96, 98

I
Ingier, 98
Ital Design, 169

J
Jensen Motors, 82, 83, 84, 86, 87
Jern, Eric, 41, 42, 45
Johansson, Hilmer, 20
Jowett Javelin, 38

K
Karosserifabrik, **190**
Karmann, 80
Kolwes, G, 96
Korff, Baron von, 100
Kreidler, 58
Kronogard, Professor, 206
KTT turbine engine, 205, 206
Kurt, Erling, 64

L
Lancia rally, 105
Lange, Rustan, 54, 191
Lanstadt, Hans, 11
Larson, Gustaf, 10, **11**, 11, 12, 13, 14, 15, **16**, 17, 18, 23, 24, 25, 28, 30, 31, 32, 36, 38, 39, 41, 42, 43, 50, 51, 54, 55, 65, 66, 70, 93, 124, 188
Levy, Wolfgang, 98
Lidmalm, Tor, 110
Lindberg, Edward, 32, 42, 190
Lindblom, Carl, 32, 36, 37, 38, 39, 42, 47
Ludvigsen, Karl, 15, 50

M
Mas-Olle, Helmer, 15, 20, 56, 110, 193
Mellde, Rolf, 127
Michelotti, Giovanni, 145
Midnight Sun (Swedish) rally, 93, 96, 98, 99, 100, 101
Mikkola, Hannu, 102
Mille Miglia, 99
MIRA, 173
Mitchell, Nancy, 98
Molander, Great, 98
Monte Carlo or Bust, 93
Moss, Pat, 98, 99
Motala Werkstad, 73
Motor, 48, 49, 60, 84

N
National Investment Bank of Holland, 151
Niger, Jerry, 71
Norcros Group, 83
Nordiska Kullafabriken, 18
Nordli, Oddvaar, **153**
Norwegian government merger project, 153, **153**, 154

O
Ogle Design, 89
Ornberg, Ivan, 23, 28, 30, 32, 39
Osterberg, Silvia, 100

P
Palm, Torsten, **98**
Pentaverken, 15, 20, 24, 41, 73, 207
Petersen, Olaf, 15, 18, 25, 48, 73
Petterson, Helmer, 39, 41, 42, 43, 44, 45, 49, 50, 51, 54, 57, 74, 77, 80, 82, 193, 196
Petterson, Pelle, 77
Peugeot company co-operation, 131, 132, 141, 144, **154, 156**, 168
Pininfarina, 173
Polish rally, 101
Pomeroy, Laurence, 60, 61
Poppe, Peter, 11
Pressed Steel Co, 82, 83, 86, 87
PRV project and engine, 131, 132, 133, 135, 141, **154**, 154, **155, 156**, 161, 165, 168, 173, 175, 176, 203

Q
Quistgaard, Eric, 72

R
RAC rally, 93, **95**, 100, 101
Reiss, 96
Renault company co-operation, 131, 132, 141-157, **154, 156**, 168
Renault 5 Turbo, 105
Roos, Axel, 42
Rosqvist, Ewy, 98, 99, 100, 102
Ross, Klaus, **97**, 100
Rydell, Anders, 55

S
Saab 99 'Gudmund', 15

Saab-Scania merger proposal, 152, 153, 157
Sagvall, Karl, 15
Scania-Vabis, 10, 12, 13
Schanche, Martin, 104
Schjolin, Olle, 32, 36, 37, 38, 39, 42
Sedgwick, Michael, 25
Segre, Luigi, 77
Seidler, Edouard, 162
Shell 4000 rally, **97**, 100
Singer, Charles, 51
Singh, Joginder, 93, **95**, 100, **101**, 101
SKF Co, 10, 11, 14, 15, 17, 18, **19**, 20, 23, 27, 30, 31, **55**
Skogh, Carl-Magnus, 100, **101**, 101
Soderstrom, Bengt, **98**
Soisbault, Annie, 98
Stokes, Lord, 154
Svenska Flygmotor, 35, 36

T
Thulin, 10, 12, 13
Tidaholm, 12
Trana, Tom, 52, 93, **95, 96**, 100, **101**, 101
Tritt, Bill, 71, 72
Tulip rally, 96, 100

U
United Turbine AB, 206, **206**

V
Van Damm, Shiela, 98
Van Doornes family, 143, 144
Vernier-Palliez, Bernard, 155
Viberg, Sven, 38
Vignale, 194, **195**
Viking rally, 93, 98, 99
Villoresi, Luigi, 96
VW company co-operation, 165, **167**, 175, 205, **206**
Volvo car types:
 Prototypes:
  City taxi, **176, 205**, 205
  Concept car (VCC), **170**, 173, 174, **174, 175, 176**, 176, **204**
  Electric car, 205
  Elizabeth I, 194, **195**
  Elizabeth II, 194
  Emil, 189
  Gas turbine car, 205, **206**, 206

3000GTZ, **90**
Mazuo ZT92, 116
Margaret Rose, **193**, 194
01 project, 169
Oscar, 189
P31, 168
P172, **87, 88**, 89, 199, **199**
P183, 89, 199
P243, 203, **203**
P263, 203
P358, 52, 106, 119, 120, 195-198, **196**
P1155, 168
Philip, 50, 53, 54, 64, 189-192, **191, 192, 193**, 194, **196**, 197, 210
55 project, 51, 53, 54, 55, 194, **195**
65 project, 51, 54
PV40, 36, 38
PV179, 50, 51, 53, 54, 56, 110, 192-194, **193**
PV454, 50, 51, 54, 55, **189**, 193
PV644, 52, 106, 120, **190, 197**
Venus Bilo, 30, **188**, 188
VESC, **126**, 126-129, **127, 129**, 133, 135, 168, **176**
Production cars, pre-1944:
Jakob, 15
OV4, **12, 16, 17, 19**, 20, 21, 23, 66, 125, 207
PV4, **19**, 20, 21, 22, 27, 45, 93
PV36 'Carioca', 26, 28, 29, 30, 31, 188
PV51, **27**, 31, 32, 33, 36
PV52, 31, 32, 36
PV53, **28**, 32, 34, 36, 38
PV54, 32, 36
PV55, 32, 36
PV56, 32, 33, 34, 36, 38
PV60, **31**, 32, 33, 36, 45, 49, 54, 189, 191
PV650, **24**, 24, 25
PV651, 25, 27, 28
PV652, 27, 28
PV653, 27, 28, 30, 188
PV654, **26**, 27, 28
PV658, 28, 29, 30

PV659, 28, 29, 30
PV832, 23
TR701, 29
TR801, **29**, 29, 32, 196
TR802, 29
Production cars, post-1944:
P1800 coupé and derivatives: 52, 58, 63, 64, 65, 69, 70, **74-85**, 77, **90**, 92, 100, **123**, 124, 159, 177, 196, 199, **199, 200, 201**, 203
P1900, 50, **71, 72**, 70-74, 80, 190, **198**
PV444, 33, 34, 35-52, **36-46**, 53, 54, 56, 57, 58, 61, 62, 65, 70, 71, 72, 73, 74, 93, **94**, 96, 98, 106, 110, 112, 116, 125, 129, 135, 174, 189, 190, **190**, 191, 192, 193, 194, 196, 207
PV544, **46**, 49, 50, 51, 52, 62, 64, 66, 69, 86, **94, 95, 98**, 98, 100, 101, 102, 106, 111, 116, 174, **189, 190**, 196, **197**
120/Amazon Series, 50, 51, 52, 53-69, **54, 56-62, 64, 67-69**, 74, 80, 83, 86, 87, **97**, 100, 101, 102, 106, **109**, 110, 111, 112, **113**, 116, 117, 125, 135, 146, 189, 192, **193**, 194, **195**, 196
140 Series, 68, 87, **97, 98**, 102, 104, 106-129, **107-113, 115, 116, 117, 118, 119, 121, 122, 123, 125, 126, 129, 130**, 133, 135, 136, 137, 139, **142**, 146, 158, 168, 187, **202**, 203
160 Series, 49, 52, 89, 110, **114, 116, 117**, 119-129, 133, 135, 136, 137, 139, 159, 163, **190**, 195, 199, 203
240 Series, 44, **109**, 110, **119, 128, 129**, 129-140, **130**, 146, 147, 150, 151,

152, 157, 158, 162, 163, 165, 166, **167**, 168, **171**, 173, 175, 176, 187, **203**, 203, **205**
260 Series, 44, **119, 126**, 129-140, **130, 131, 133**, 152, **155**, 157, 158, 159, **160**, 161, 162, **163, 164**, 165, 166, 168, **171**, 173, 175, 176, 203, 205, 206
262C coupé, 92, 159-163, **160, 161**, 165, 177, 199, 202, 203
760GLE Series, 41, 140, 153, 158-177, **170-171, 172, 174**, 175, **201**, 203, **204**, 205
Dutch-built Volvos:
66 Series, **142, 143**, 145, 146, 147, 149, 174
340 Series, 102, **102**, 103, **103**, 104, **104**, 105, 145-157, **146, 148, 150**, 166, 174

W
Walfriddson, Per-Inge, **102**, 104, **104**
Walter, Hans, 99
Wennberg, Gosta, 54, 194
Westerberg, Henry, 14, 17, 30, 37
Werbin, Dan, 166, 168, 169
White & Poppe, 11
White Truck Corporation, **210**, 211
Wilsgaard, Jan, 50, 51, 52, 53, 54, 55, 56, **56**, 59, **59**, 63, 65, 71, 72, 80, **85, 88**, 89, 108, 110, 112, **113**, 117, 120, 136, 145, 159, 161, **161**, 168, 169, 170, 174, 189, 190, 191, 192, **192**, 193, **193**, 194, 195, **195**, 198, 199, **199, 201**
Wingquist, Sven, 10

Z
Zachrison, Ake, 72
Zagato, **90**

At Kalmar, the flexible 'Group Assembly' process allows saloons and estates to be assembled even easier than in a conventional factory.